Congress and United
States Foreign Policy

Congress and United States Foreign Policy

Controlling the Use of Force in the Nuclear Age

Edited By

MICHAEL BARNHART

State University of New York Press

Published by
State University of New York Press, Albany

© 1987   State University of New York

For information, address State University of New York
Press, State University Plaza, Albany, N.Y., 12246

Library of Congress Cataloging in Publication Data

Congress and United States foreign policy.

"The studies in this volume were written for the
Jacob K. Javits Collection Inaugural Conference,
held in October 1985, at the State University of
New York at Stony Brook"—Pref.
    Includes index.
    1. War and emergency powers—United States—
Congresses.   2. Nuclear arms control—United States—
Congresses.   3. Legislative power—United States—
Congresses.   4. Executive power—United States—
Congresses.   I. Barnhart, Michael A., 1951–
II. Jacob K. Javits Collection Inaugural Conference
(1985: State University of New York at Stony Brook)
KF5060.A75C66 1987   342.73′412   86-23057
ISBN 0-88706-465-5   347.302412
ISBN 0-88706-466-3 (pbk.)

To the memory of
Senator Jacob K. Javits

Contents

Preface

While a wide range of scholars have examined the U.S. Congress, its role in American foreign policy has been studied by a relatively small number, nearly all political scientists. While these works, such as those by Crabb and Holt, Dahl, Destler, Frank and Weisband, Platt, Rourke, Wilcox, and Sofaer (a legal scholar), among others, have made important contributions,[1] relatively few participants on the inside—such as Jack Sullivan, a contributor—or historians on the outside have directed their attention and brought their perspectives to Congress and foreign policy. The over-thousand page *Guide to American Foreign Relations since 1700*, for example, lists exactly fourteen titles under its "Congressional Role" section, and several of these are some studies mentioned above.

This is not to assert that the role of Congress has been altogether ignored. Excellent studies exist on this theme in such wide-ranging areas as territorial expansion in the nineteenth century, debates over acquiring Cuba and the Philippines, the defeat of the Treaty of Versailles, the isolationist legislation of the 1930's, the decision to recognize Israel, and the rising dissent over involvement in Vietnam. But a sustained, focused analysis by historians and policy makers and analysts of the role of Congress in controlling the use of force has not yet appeared.

This study approaches the question in three parts. The first, with an introduction written by Ann-Marie Scheidt, who has mined the Javits collection deeply, directly explores congressional efforts to control the ability of the Executive to use force. It centers on the keystone of these efforts, the 1973 War Powers Act, and includes a study of how that act came into existence by Senator Javits. The second part examines the influence Congress has wielded over nuclear arms control, through both Strategic Arms Limitations Treaties, SALT I and II. The third ranges more widely, casting light on how Congress has operated to channel American military assistance, covert actions, and open warfare over the past forty years. Each part begins with an historical overview, so that the oft-repeated fault of assuming that the world was created in 1945—and that all issues considered before that time have no bearing on today's world—might be avoided.

Michael A. Barnhart
Stony Brook, New York

NOTES

1. Cecil V. Crabb, Jr. and Pat M. Holt, *Invitation to Struggle: Congress, the President and Foreign Policy* (Washington: Congressional Quarterly Press, 1980); Robert A. Dahl, *Congress and Foreign Policy* (New York: W. W. Norton & Company, 1964); I. M. Destler, *Presidents, Bureaucrats, and Foreign Policy* (Princeton: Princeton University Press, 1972); Thomas N. Frank and Edward Weisband, *Foreign Policy by Congress* (New York: Oxford University Press, 1979); Alan Platt, *The U.S. Senate and Strategic Arms Policy* (Boulder: Westview Press, 1978); John Rourke, *Congress and the Presidency in U.S. Foreign Policymaking: A Study of Interaction and Influence, 1945–1982* (Boulder: Westview Press, 1983); Francis O. Wilcox, *Congress, The Executive and Foreign Policy* (New York: Harper & Row, 1971); Abraham D. Sofaer, *War, Foreign Affairs and Constitutional Power: The Origins* (Cambridge, Mass.: Ballinger Publishing Co., 1976).

Acknowledgements

The studies in this volume were written for The Jacob K. Javits Collection Inaugural Conference held in October 1985 at the State University of New York at Stony Brook. It was held to commemorate the opening of Senator Javits' papers, a collection of 1.8 million items. Senator Javits donated the collection to SUNY-Stony Brook in 1981.

The first debt, therefore, is to Senator Javits. His career's accomplishments and his interest in foreign affairs are responsible for this book's theme and substance.

The State of New York deserves next mention. It provided the funds necessary for this book's studies. More broadly, without its support the State University of New York and especially SUNY-Stony Brook would not exist to engage in any academic activity. Nor would people such as Evert Volkersz, head of Special Collections at the Frank Melville, Jr. Memorial Library, and his staff been able to house the Javits papers. John B. Smith, director and dean of Libraries, and Egon Neuberger, dean of Social and Behavioral Sciences, provided frequent support and suggestions from planning to publication. Mary Rogers, a graduate student in the History Department, was most helpful in preparing the manuscript for publication. William Eastman, director of SUNY Press, was as accommodating in arranging for publication as anyone could hope for. Ann Forkin and Ann Brody at Stony Brook were indispensable as well.

PART ONE

Congress and the War Power

Introduction

ANN-MARIE SCHEIDT

One of the tenets of the historical profession is that an understanding of the past is necessary for the comprehension of the present. Professor William Gibbons dedicates his paper to this principle by setting out to show how the war power in the United States Constitution—an eighteenth century document—is the product of still earlier experience with war dating to, even beyond, the Magna Carta, itself the product of dispute over an executive's use of the war power. In turn, that dispute arose from dissatisfaction with taxation for military purposes. Later English Parliaments' increased revenue power, Gibbons contends, led directly to increased war power. Indeed, Gibbons argues that our Constitution is vague on the executive-legislative boundaries on war making precisely because the Founding Fathers had such a clear notion of what those boundaries were as a result of past experience. Although Gibbons does not attempt it, a survey of the rhetoric of the American Revolution reveals frequent references to the power to make war.

If the demarcation between the power of Congress and the president over the war power seemed clear enough in the 1780's, it had blurred considerably by the close of World War II.

Cold War specialist Duane Tananbaum provides a summary of congressional efforts between 1945 and 1969 to influence major decisions that committed American might, deployed troops, or otherwise exposed the nation at least potentially to the risk of war. He finds that despite the ascendancy of the executive branch in foreign affairs during the postwar period, there were significant instances of congressional self-assertion, including the Senate's participation in rewriting the North Atlantic Treaty, the creation of the area resolution during the Eisenhower administration as a mechanism for congressional involvement in major force commitments abroad, and the development of new kinds of legislative initiatives in the altered circumstances of the 1960s.

The Constitution is ambiguous in allocating the war power. The president is commander in chief of the armed forces, but Congress declares war. Tananbaum's congressional self-assertion in the late 1940s and 1950s reflected a spirit of cooperation with the executive branch and an acceptance of executive initiative in this area of shared power. Thus proponents of congressional authority like Senator Bricker warmly welcomed President Eisenhower's overtures to Congress in requesting the area resolutions on Formosa and the Middle East, and these resolutions were approved by overwhelming majorities as appropriate embodiments of the partnership between the president and Congress on foreign policy. The Senate's revisions of the North Atlantic Treaty, which sought to preserve the congressional role in decisions on military action under the treaty, did not attempt to draw a line between executive and legislative areas of authority. In instances where Congress took positive action, it remained content to achieve the significant but symbolic impact of 'sense of the chamber' resolutions lacking statutory force. Congress' most ambitious and most persistent initiative, the Bricker Amendment, was defeated.

Professor Tananbaum points out that Congress turned to new measures in the late 1960s to influence decision making on the use of force abroad. The differences between these measures and those of the earlier period indicate the adversarial tone that entered into Congress' relationship with the president during these years. A 1969 amendment proposed by Senators Cooper and Church to the defense appropriations bill introduced for the first time the element of compulsion, seeking unilaterally to prevent the widening of the Vietnam War by denying funds to deploy combat troops in Laos and Thailand. The Cooper–Church Amendment became the model for a whole series of congressional initiatives to use the power of the purse to terminate the American involvement in Indochina. The effort to address the decision making process subsequently came together with the effort to compel presidential compliance in the War Powers Resolution, where Congress used its legislative authority in an endeavor to map the constitutional 'twilight zone' of the war power.

Specialists in the postwar period occasionally have an opportunity that is denied to their colleagues who study earlier eras: the opportunity to hear the story of an important event from one of its principal participants. The late Senator Jacob Javits' contribution to these proceedings provides a rare reflection upon the issues relating to a historic legislative enactment from the point of view of its prime mover. Senator Javits' voice is an important one for students of the origins and development of war powers legislation because of his central role in its adoption. His papers, now fully catalogued and open to scholars, constitute what may be the largest single source of unpublished material on the topic.

Senator Javits notes that the War Powers Resolution was born out of the deep frustration of the antiwar constituency in Congress at its inability to bring the troops home from Vietnam. The antiwar forces experienced many failures in their search for an effective means to legislate an end to the war. As Senator Javits indicates, they pursued two major approaches. They sought to withdraw congressional authorization—and here I believe Senator Javits had in mind not the Cooper-Church Amendment, but the 1970 repeal of the Tonkin Gulf Resolution, whose proponents, including Senator Javits, argued that this act removed the last vestige of congressional sanction for the hostilities in Indochina. Because the president held that his constitutional power as commander in chief conferred an independent authority to continue waging the war, congressional doves turned to the appropriations power, which, they contended in a fashion Gibbons' parliamentarians would find familiar, the Constitution allocated unambiguously to Congress. In votes on the draft extension and on a succession of appropriation and authorization bills, they attempted to cut off funds to support military action in specified geographic areas, through Cooper-Church and its successors, and in all of Indochina, through the Hatfield-McGovern Amendment and other efforts to set a date for final withdrawal.

The War Powers Resolution contrasts with these measures, however, in several important ways. The earlier versions excluded Indochina, by means of an exemption for hostilities under way at the time of adoption, and the resolution was not passed in final form until after American troops had been withdrawn. Moreover, as Senator Javits' remarks suggest, the resolution's supporters were a diverse combination that included not only the Senate's bipartisan antiwar constituency, but also such figures as conservative Republican Robert A. Taft, Jr., and Armed Services Committee Chairman John Stennis, a staunch supporter of the president's conduct of the Indochina war. The conservative Stennis coauthored the resolution with liberals Javits and Eagleton and persuaded many of his Southern Democrat colleagues to support it. Senator Taft was joined by Minority Leader Hugh Scott, Whip Robert Griffin, and a number of other Republicans voting against the president on the bill. Although the Senate might well have adopted the War Powers Resolution without the support of every one of these varied elements, it is unlikely that the antiwar forces alone could have mustered a majority large enough to overcome a presidential veto.

A war powers movement is inconceivable without the prolonged agony of Vietnam, but the determination of antiwar senators to enlarge their stock of legislative tools does not by itself provide a sufficient explanation for the passage of the War Powers Resolution. It is particularly to be regretted that the brevity of Senator Javits' comments does not permit him to do more than suggest the powerful influence of the constitutional issues raised by the war's opponents upon political personalities and constituencies otherwise unsympathetic to the political objectives of the antiwar program. Some contemporaries asserted that the War Powers Resolution offered an attractive opportunity to cast an 'antiwar' vote without appearing to endanger the troops in the field, as the advocates of the 'pursestrings' strategy were accused of doing, but the searching examination of constitutional principles that lay behind the War Powers Resolution went well beyond the requirements of political expediency. Fundamental issues raised on such earlier occasions as the "Great Debate" of

1951 were reexamined, in some cases by the same people, not necessarily espousing the same views.

Materials in the Javits Collection illuminate all of these complexities, probing constitutional intent over the war power issue. They emphasize the political distance consciously maintained between advocates of the war powers bill and the Senate antiwar coalition as those advocates sought to broaden their base of support. There is surprisingly little direct mention in Collection materials of another major factor in the passage of the War Powers Resolution: the domestic political implications of the Watergate case. Only one statement in Senator Javits' remarks, his ambiguous allusion to the worsening of "the situation surrounding President Nixon," can be interpreted to refer to it. Contemporary observers, however, doubted whether Congress could have overcome the President's veto—the only one of nine to be overridden in more than a year—if the President had not been significantly weakened by the widening scandal.

The debate over the War Powers Resolution had three major phases. The first took place in the Senate, and its most interesting parts occurred during the drafting of the joint bill introduced in December of 1971 by Senators Javits, Stennis and Eagleton, each of whom had earlier submitted his own bill, after hearings that consumed much of the year. (Contrary to Senator Javits' recollection, there was no vote until the following year.) The bill manifested the Senate's view that war making should be a joint legislative-executive decision and that Congress should be in a position to forbid the executive to continue hostilities it did not support. The joint bill was approved in virtually the same form by lopsided majorities in both 1972 and 1973. The Javits Collection provides invaluable insight into the drafting of the joint bill and the development of the unusual coalition that brought about its "veto-proof" passage in the Senate.

Senator Javits points out that the House took a less assertive position on the role of Congress in war powers. It initially approved a bill demanding only that the President consult with Congress and submit reports on certain kinds of foreign troop commitments. The two chambers were so far apart that the House-Senate conference on the bill in 1972 met only once. In a context of increasing internal pressure for a stronger bill, the House developed a new formulation in 1973, incorporating elements of the approach favored by the Senate. An extensive series of markup sessions in Congressman Zablocki's National Security Subcommittee of the House Foreign Affairs Committee resulted in the introduction of a new committee bill in May.

The crucial debate in the House-Senate conference of 1973 established the bill's final form as it was enacted into law. The conference grappled at length with a heavy agenda of substantive issues resulting from the major differences that still remained between the Senate and House approaches, meeting from early August, just before the summer recess, to early October.

The Javits Collection is an essential resource on this long negotiation, containing many of the successive versions of the bill that were written as the conferees, usually represented by a few senior staff members, struggled toward a compromise. In a recent series of personal interviews, the oral recollections of the participants, including staff members, provided important additional insights into the entire transaction. As Senator Javits suggests, the decisive compromise concerned the definition of presidential power. A section of the Senate Foreign Relations Committee report had called this definition "the heart and core of the bill," essential to exert sufficient congressional control over the presidency. The House negotiators adamantly refused to accept the definition, which they saw as an unrealistic effort to prejudge events. As the acknowledged expert on the Senate team, Senator Javits agreed to a House proposal to remove this definition section to a preamble without statutory effect, believing this bargain to be the price of, as he says, "getting such a law upon the books." That decision subsequently cost him the support of one of his coauthors, Senator Eagleton, who voted against the conference report saying that the legislative "baby" he had helped to father had been "kidnapped" in the conference. Senator Javits reveals in his remarks that an important consideration in his acceptance of the House proposal was the acquiescence of Senator Stennis, who had indicated in the earlier floor debate that he felt the precise content of the bill would be less important than its creation of what Senator Javits calls a "methodology" for congressional action, and Javits expressed surprise at the vehemence of Eagleton's reaction. Senator Javits may also have been influenced by a practical political sense of the relative numbers of votes his coauthors commanded.

John Sullivan, one of the leading congressional staff members involved in the development of war powers legislation and its subsequent exercise, demonstrates in his assessment of the War Powers Resolution extensive knowledge of both the uses of the Resolution in times of international crisis and the legislative history of the years following the resolution's enactment. His paper develops a number of ideas that he originally presented in a special study for the House Foreign Affairs Committee, *The War Powers Resolution*, published in 1982 as a committee print. Dr. Sullivan draws on this abundant material to argue that, in addition to playing an important symbolic role as an expression of congressional assertiveness against the military powers of the president, the War Powers Resolution has provided an effective means to deter escalating presidential adventurism in foreign affairs, even on occasions when it has not been formally invoked. He makes a persuasive case that the requirement under the resolution that the president get positive congressional support for troop commitments abroad can exercise a significant restraining influence when a military response is being considered as a foreign policy option. In emphasizing this informal impact of the resolution, Dr. Sullivan echoes the view of some contemporaries that the fundamental significance of the War Powers Resolution was political rather than statutory, in that its mere existence provides an essential lever for Congress in its political interaction with the president in the context of contemporary warfare. Other scholars will wish to test this interpretation by examining the dozen or so incidents that have occurred since 1973 in which the War Powers Resolution was or might have been invoked. Although the 1975 Vietnam evacuation, the 1978 Zaire airlift and the rules of engagement governing the conduct of U.S. military advisers in El Salvador all appear to support Sullivan's de facto restraint thesis, other events, as Sullivan admits, reflect other influences on decision making. These include the Mayaguez rescue of 1975, the Iranian hostage rescue attempt of 1980, the Grenada invasion of 1984, and—after Sullivan completed his study—the actions against Libya in early 1986.

Like Senator Javits, Sullivan emphasizes the voluntary operation of the legislation, as a tool that Congress must have, in the Senator's phrase, the "guts" to use. In this connection, Sullivan's assessment of the invocation of the War Powers Resolution in Lebanon in 1983 deserves careful consideration. He stresses the exemplary execution of the policy making process that was established by the resolution. Writing on the same subject in the Fall, 1985, issue of *Foreign Affairs*, Senator Javits questioned whether the substance of the policy decision that emerged from the process—the authorization of an "inordinately long" 18-month deployment of U.S. Marines (longer than the time periods discussed when the resolution was debated)—truly signified meaningful congressional participation in policy making. Other scholars will wish to weigh both process and results as they evaluate the long-term significance of the War Powers Resolution.

1

The Origins of the War Power Provision of the Constitution

WILLIAM CONRAD GIBBONS

In recent years, there have been numerous assertions of the right of the president of the United States to send U.S. armed forces into combat, including major conflicts such as the Korean War and the Vietnam War, without any approval or authorization by Congress. This alleged presidential prerogative is said to be based on the constitutional powers of the president and on implied presidential power derived from national sovereignty.

Congress, on the other hand, has passed the War Powers Resolution and various other measures to assert what it claims to be its constitutional role. The resolution was vetoed by President Richard M. Nixon, who called it "unconstitutional and dangerous to the best interests of our Nation."[1] He did not explain why he thought it was unconstitutional.

Constitutional objections to the resolution also have been raised by every subsequent president.[2] Moreover, each president has taken the position that a president has the authority to use the armed forces without authorization by Congress, and in each report to Congress on the use of troops since the passage of the resolution the president has said that, "consistent with" the resolution, he was making the report because he wanted to keep Congress informed, but that the action was being taken "pursuant to the President's authority with respect to the conduct of foreign relations and as Commander in Chief of the United States Armed Forces."[3]

As the debate continues over the War Powers Resolution and the respective powers of the president and Congress under the Constitution, it may be beneficial to approach the subject from a different perspective. Rather than arguing constitutionality, based on the Constitution, or implied powers, based on national sovereignty, or precedent, based on practice since the Constitution, it may be possible to gain a better understanding of constitutional intent by studying the origins of the war power provision of the Constitution.[4]

THE WAR POWER PROVISION OF THE CONSTITUTION

As approved by the constitutional convention and ratified by the states, the war power provision of the Constitution, Article I, Section 8, clauses 10–15, is as follows:

> The Congress shall have power . . .
> To define and punish piracies and felonies committed on the high seas, and offenses against the law of nations.
> To declare war, grant letters of marque and reprisal, and make rules concerning captures on land and water.
> To raise and support armies, but no appropriation of money to that use shall be for a longer term than two years.
> To provide and maintain a navy.
> To make rules for the government and regulation of the land and naval forces.
> To provide for calling forth the militia to execute the laws of the Union, suppress insurrections, and repel invasions.
> To provide for organizing, arming, and disciplining the militia, and for governing such part of them as may be employed in the service of the United States, reserving to the States respectively, the appointment of the officers, and the authority of training the militia according to the disciplines prescribed by Congress. . . .

Related to this is the commander in chief provision, Article II, Section 2, the purpose of which was to provide civilian command of the armed forces, action in an emergency, and unified action in time of war:

> The President shall be Commander in Chief of the Army and Navy of the United States, and of the Militia of the several States, when called into the actual Service of the United States. . . .

Although delegates to the federal constitutional convention and to the state ratifying conventions assumed that the president was implicitly empowered to defend the country if circumstances prevented Congress from meeting and making such a decision, this was viewed as an exigent power of command derived from the war power allocated to the legislature rather than a power of war allocated separately to the Executive. His was the power of command, not of war.[5]

The exclusive allocation of the war power to the legislature is a distinguishing feature of the U.S. Constitution. No other country in the world gives the legislature such power and authority. In this sense, the war power provision of the Constitution was and is unique, even after two hundred years. For delegates to the federal and state conventions, however, it apparently was not unique at all. Rather, they considered legislative control of the power of war to be an essential element of the kind of republican government they were seeking to establish; a government based on controlling the use of power, thereby protecting and advancing liberty and freedom while providing for the necessary strength and vigor for government to promote human progress and defend its citizens against threats to liberty from home and abroad. From their own knowledge and experience, they knew that the power of war was the broadest and most dangerous of all of the powers of government, and that the war power had to be carefully controlled in order to prevent its abuse by one ruler or a small group of rulers. Fearing any concentration of power, they were not willing to entrust the war power to the president or the Senate alone, and they were particularly unwilling to entrust it to the Senate and the president together, even though they conceived of the Senate as the President's privy council in foreign affairs. Because the power of war could have such far-reaching public effects, they were more inclined to entrust it exclusively to the House of Representatives, but the house alone would not be the proper repository either, reflecting, as it would, the vagaries of public opinion.[6] The safest course was to allocate the power to Congress as a whole. George Mason of Virginia probably spoke for most of the delegates when he supported this position, saying that he was "against giving the power of war to the Executive because not safely to be trusted with it; or to the Senate, because not so constructed as to be entitled to it."[7]

In making the decision to allocate the war power to Congress, delegates to the constitutional convention were, in a sense, merely reaffirming the earlier assumption of such power by the Continental Congress in 1774, followed in 1781 by Article 9 of the Articles of Confederation giving Congress the "sole and exclusive right and power of determining on peace and war," except for an invasion of a state, or when a state "shall have received certain advice of a resolution being formed by some nation of Indians to invade such state," and when, in either case, "the danger is so imminent as not to admit of a delay until the United States in Congress assembled can be consulted. . . ." Unlike the Articles of Confederation, however, it was expected that the proposed new Constitution would provide for a chief executive. Thus, the constitutional convention was faced with deciding what powers in the new government were "executive," and which powers allocated to Congress by the Articles of Confederation should be allocated to the executive in the Constitution.

From the beginning of the convention there was apparently little disagreement that the war power was a legislative power and should continue to be allocated to the Congress. On June 1, 1787, a week after proceedings began, the delegates discussed the proposed chief executive.[8] Charles Pinckney of South Carolina said he was for a "vigorous executive, but was afraid the executive powers of the existing Congress might extend to peace and war etc.; which would render the executive a monarchy of the worst kind, to wit, an elective one." John Rutledge, Pinckney's colleague from South Carolina, said "he was not for giving him [the executive] the power of war and peace."

James Wilson of Pennsylvania, an influential figure, and a powerful advocat. of a strong executive, said that he "did not consider the prerogatives of the British monarch as a proper guide in defining the executive powers. Some of these prerogatives were of a legislative nature; among others, that of war and peace etc."[9] According to notes of the convention kept by Rufus King of Massachusetts, James Madison of Virginia agreed with Wilson's definition of war and peace as legislative powers.[10]

Alexander Hamilton of New York, who wanted the president elected for life, (depending on good behavior), also proposed that the Senate, also elected for life, should "exclusively possess the power of declaring war," and that the role of the president should be to have the "direction of war when commenced."[11]

The convention acted on the war power provision on August 17, based on a draft of the Constitution reported on August 6 by the Committee of Detail in which the specific powers of Congress were enumerated for the first time.[12] The Virginia Plan was well as the New Jersey Plan had provided that the legislature should be empowered with the "Legislative Rights" of the Articles of Confederation, and this had already been agreed to without debate.[13] One of the legislative rights in the Articles was the right or power of war, and in its new draft the Committee of Detail provided that the legislature should continue to exercise that power. After a brief debate, this was approved following the substitution of "declare war" for "make war," the wording which had been recommended by the Committee of Detail. This amendment was moved by Madison and Elbridge Gerry of Massachusetts for the purpose, according to Madison's notes, of "leaving to the Executive the power to repel sudden attacks."[14]

The substitution of "declare" for "make" in no way changed the basic attitude of the delegates that the war power should remain a legislative power. The two words apparently were considered to be synonymous and seem to have been used interchangeably. Prior to any mention of the terms "declare war" or "declaration of war," and four days before the motion was made to change "make" to "declare," for example, Edmund Randolph of Virginia spoke of allocating the "declaration of war" to the House of Representatives.[15] Nor did the change from "make" to "declare" alter or limit the plenary, exclusive power of Congress over all wars, declared or undeclared, including those sudden attacks to which the Executive might already have responded.[16] If the delegates could have known how much controversy would subsequently arise over what the change in wording meant, however, and if they could have foreseen the way in which it was later interpreted as limiting rather than confirming the power of Congress over war, they surely would have explained their intent or used other words. For them, it was a mere change of language, not of purpose or direction.

There was some concern about the ability of Congress to exercise the war power. Charles Pickney, whose aristocratic proclivities led him to place primary importance on the role of the president and the Senate, was, according to Madison's notes, "opposed to vesting this power ["to make war"] in the legislature. Its proceedings were too slow. It would meet but once a year." Pinckney, however, had previously expressed his opposition to allocating the power of "peace and war" to the president,[17] and although he questioned whether the legislature as a whole should be allocated the war power, he apparently believed that the best alternative was to allocate the power of making war to the Senate. "The Senate would be the best depository, being more acquainted with foreign affairs, and most capable of proper resolution." The House, he said, "would be too numerous for such deliberations."

After Pinckney spoke, Pierce Butler, also of South Carolina, took the position that the power to "make war" should be allocated to the president, saying, according to Madison's notes: "The objections against the legislature lie, in a great degree, against the Senate. He was for vesting the power in the President, who will have all the requisite qualities, and will not make war but when the Nation will support it."

Both Pinckney and Butler, however, were assuming, as the convention had agreed up to that point in its proceedings, that the president would be elected by Congress for one seven-year term, and this doubtless had some bearing on Butler's comment that the president would only make war when the nation would support it. Only on September 6, three weeks after the change from "make" to "declare," and only about a week before it adjourned, did the convention vote to have the president chosen by electors from the states for a term of four years without any restriction on the number of terms.

Butler's comment about allocating the war powers to the president should also be considered in the light of the concern about presidential powers which he expressed on September 7, when the convention acted on the provision for the president to make treaties with the "advice" and the "consent" of two-thirds of the Senate, after the decision on September 6 not to have the president elected by Congress. Madison moved that treaties of peace could be made by two-thirds of the Senate without the concurrence of the president. The motion, which lost, was supported by Butler. According to Madison's notes, Butler, who cited several examples of leaders who had prolonged wars for their own purposes, "was strenuous for the motion, as a necessary security against ambitious and corrupt Presidents."[18]

Having acted on the war power provision on August 17, the convention voted on the election of the president, and then approved without debate or a separate vote the provision to make the president the commander in chief.[19]

In another important action implementing the war power of Congress, the convention approved the power of Congress to appropriate funds for the operation of the government, but because of its fear of "standing armies" it limited appropriations for the Army and the Navy to two years.[20]

Delegates to the state ratifying conventions accepted the war power provision of the Constitution as well as the commander in chief provision with very little debate or dissent. They, too, seemed to take for granted that the war power should be allocated to Congress.[21]

THE SEARCH FOR SOURCES: EARLY DEVELOPMENTS IN ENGLAND

Although it is clear that delegates to the federal constitutional convention as well as delegates to state ratifying conventions stood foursquare behind legislative control of war, little is known about the sources of that idea. Where and how did it originate? What had caused it to become such an established principle among American political leaders? Why, after the difficulties encountered during the Revolutionary War, when Congress' direction of the war seemed to leave a great deal to be desired, was the war power still deemed to be a legislative power or right?

While familiar with classical antiquity, where the assembly in Athens and the senate in the Roman republic were responsible for approving decisions to go to war, delegates to the constitutional convention naturally looked primarily to the British experience for the wisdom they were seeking, and it is thus to the evolution of political ideas and institutions in England that the search leads for sources of the concept of legislative control of war.

In Anglo-Saxon England around the sixth and seventh centuries A.D. there were the beginnings of what became the common law, and of political relationships and institutions that evolved into the English system of parliamentary government, and it is in this early period that the concept and the practice of legislative control of war, rudimentary though they were, first made their appearance in England. Based on germanic tribal customs of the Angles and the Saxons, a governing council—the witan, an Anglo-Saxon word meaning the wise—was established for each kingdom and eventually for all of the kingdoms. The witan, which consisted of men of wealth and power representing the freemen of the kingdom, chose the king and served as his council in ruling the kingdom. Continuing the tribal custom, one of the primary roles of the witan was to advise the king on matters of war and peace and to approve the military levies for local militia and supplies needed to augment the forces available to the king through his personal armed retinue. There are also indications that the witan exercised some control over the length of service of the king's retinue, known as the *fyrd*, for one thing, by establishing the custom of a two-month term of service.[22]

After the Norman conquest in 1066, the Anglo-Saxon tradition was joined with feudal ideas of counsel and consent, as well as with Roman law principles of rights and representation under which individuals, groups or communities had certain established legal rights, and could defend those rights or interests through representation, with chosen representatives having the full legal power and authority—*plena potestas*—to act for those they represented.

It was a maxim of Roman law, which appeared in the Justinian Code in the sixth century A.D., that, *quod omnes tangit ab omnibus approbetur—* what touches all must be approved by all.[23] In Roman law, this did not signify public representation or approval; rather it expressed the procedural consent given to the king by his court or council. This maxim gradually took on a new meaning in England as the king's council, or *curia regis*, which replaced the witan, began to perform more representative functions and to acquire the identity and role of a parliament, followed by the increasing involvement of knights of the shire and representatives of towns and counties and their eventual emergence as the House of Commons.[24]

Based on the ideal of a king's responsibility to protect his subjects and to rule lawfully and with justice, the principle that those affected had a right to participate through their representatives in consenting to major decisions, especially those involving war and taxes (which usually were directly connected with the making of war), gradually became established in England and on the continent.[25] The political system introduced by the Normans was more feudalistic and thus more autocratic than that of the Anglo-Saxons, however, and this resulted in greater centralization of military power in the hands of the king. Rather than for military service to be performed as necessary for the defense of the county, with local governing bodies involved in making decisions about providing local militia, the Norman feudal army was directly responsible to and under the control of the king, who, by a system of knight's fees, required all of his tenant land holders to supply men for the army. Moreover, decisions about war and peace became a matter of royal prerogative, with the king claiming the right to make war or peace without the advice or assent of a council.

The dependence of the king on others for supplying military forces or money to wage war led gradually to greater influence by the barons over war and peace. Thus, soon after the Norman conquest there were meetings between the king and great councils of barons concerning various foreign expeditions in which he wished to engage, as well as when invasion appeared to be threatened.

Conflict between King John (1199–1216) and the barons increased after the king, desiring to recover his lost lands in France, especially Normandy, imposed higher taxes, especially the tax known as scutage,[26] as well as requirements for military service.[27] By 1214, there was serious baronial opposition to King John, in part because of a heavy scutage to pay for an expedition to France, where the king was accompanied mostly by mercenaries because of the refusal of many of the barons to join the expedition. When he returned later in the year, having been forced to agree to a truce which further humiliated England, a number of the barons demanded reforms, and this, following military occupation of London by baronial forces, led to the meeting between the barons and King John at Runnymede in June 1215 at which the king capitulated to the demands of the barons contained in the Magna Carta.

THE MAGNA CARTA AND THE IDEA OF ASSENT

The Magna Carta, which is considered to be the first English legal statute, was a written compact stating traditional English rights and the responsibility of the king to govern accordingly.[28] Because it was a petition from the king's subjects, rather than being handed down by the king, and because it provided for enforcement through the council of barons, it had broad implications for future parliamentary development and for the role of parliament in the making of war.[29]

The enforcement provision is particularly significant in understanding the importance of the Magna Carta in the development of representative government. And what a remarkable provision it was! After stipulating that the king would call a meeting of the council for "the common counsel of the kingdom" in assessing new taxes, including scutage, to occur at a fixed time and place and on the basis of a written explanation of the reasons for the summons, the Charter provided for the barons to select twenty-five of their number to serve as a group to compel the king's compliance if the king or any of his officers or staff violated the agreement. If four of the twenty-five were notified of such a breach, they were to ask the king for amends. If he did not comply within forty days, the four barons would report to the twenty-five, "and those twenty-five barons together with the community of the whole land shall distrain and distress us [the king] in every way they can, namely, by seizing castles, lands, possessions, and in such other ways as they can, saving our person and the persons of our queen and our children, until in their opinion, amends have been made, and when amends have been made, they shall obey us as they did before."

It is little wonder that King John soon repudiated the Magna Carta and appealed to the Pope, who declared it null and void and said he would excommunicate those barons who attempted to hold the king to his commitment. The barons reacted by asking Louis of France to dethrone John. For a number of reasons, this move did not succeed, but within a year John was dead, as was the Pope, and in November 1216 the Charter was reissued after the papal legate and the advisers to nine year old Henry III (1216–1272) relented and accepted it. In 1225 it was reissued in its final and definitive form, and thereafter it was repeatedly reaffirmed, by Edward I on three occasions, and at least 30 times by other kings.

The contribution of the Magna Carta to the development of the idea of parliamentary control of war was important even if somewhat indirect. Although the powers of taxing and of making war and peace were still considered royal prerogatives, and the role of the barons was viewed as helping the king to govern the country and to fight its wars, the Magna Carta reiterated the principle that the king should rule with justice, and that major decisions affecting the welfare of the king's subjects should be made with the assent of the barons (magnates) or lords of the realm. These provisions were implemented by specific provisions on injustices caused by the actions of the king in preparing for or engaging in war, especially those involving taxes and military service.[30]

The issue of taxation was addressed directly: "No scutage or aid for financing war shall be imposed in our kingdom unless by common counsel of our kingdom. . . ." However, the power to tax was still considered a royal prerogative. By common law the king had to have the "common counsel" of the kingdom for imposing taxes, but those responsible for consulting with the king did not have the right to refuse consent, especially if the king took the position that the security of the country was at stake and therefore that the need for taxes was a "necessity."[31] Nevertheless, the principle of consultation on matters of taxation and war would never be stricken from English, and later American, practice.

PARLIAMENT'S CONTROL OF WAR EMERGES

Although advisers to Henry III, acting on his behalf, had accepted the Magna Carta, and the king had consulted with the council about expeditions to France in 1224 and 1229, his relations with the barons were adversely affected by a number of developments, including the failure of the 1229 expedition, and his requests for aid for similar expeditions in 1242, 1252–54, and 1255–58 were denied.[32] By 1258 he was forced to accede to a new agreement, the Provisions of Oxford, under which he accepted a greater role in the government by the council, what had become known by then as "parliament." A permanent body of 15 barons, like that of the Magna Carta, was created to oversee "matters affecting the king and the realm."[33] As a result, 1258 is said to represent the inception of organized parliaments in England as distinct from afforced meetings of the king's council.[34]

During the next several years there were eleven sessions of parliament, but the king's reluctance to accept the new arrangement, together with continued baronial resistance, led to armed battles in 1264 and 1265 between the king and baronial forces. The king prevailed and denounced the Provisions of Oxford. He continued, however, to convene parliament, which met sixteen times between 1265 and Henry's death in 1272. During this period he also met separately on one occasion with representatives of the towns (boroughs), a sign of the emerging role of the commonality or 'commons'.

Under the reign of Henry III's son, Edward I (1272–1307), the practice of including popular representatives increased, primarily as a way of getting broader support for taxes, and by the middle of the fourteenth century there were regular meetings of popular representatives. Once again, war and taxes were primary factors in bringing about these changes.[35]

In 1295, repeated tax assessments by Edward I to support various military ventures during the last half of the thirteen century led to increasing opposition from those affected: nobles, clergy, knights of the shire, and burgesses. All of these estates were called to an urgent meeting of parliament to approve new military aid for the continuing war against France, as well as campaigns against an imminent threat from Scotland and a rebellion in Wales. The writ of summons was noteworthy. Not only did it explicitly contain, apparently for the first time, the maxim, *quod omnes tangit ab omnibus approbetur*; it also invoked the concept of *plena potestas* for knights representing the shires, who were to attend with full power to approve what was agreed to as common counsel for the realm.[36]

In 1297, Edward, who was still fighting in France, as well as using his forces to pacify Scotland which he had conquered the year before, called a parliament of both barons and popular representatives to approve further financial aid. He made a strong plea for national necessity. There was again strong resistance from many of the barons, however, and the king was forced to accede to a new set of demands, the Confirmation of Charters, which expressed parliament's conception of the common law rights of subjects to be protected against onerous war taxes and special levies which had been initiated to support war making.[37] The document confirmed that such aids would not become custom, and that the king would not assess aids or related social taxes without the "common assent" of the realm and to further its "common profit."[38] At the same time, the king had the right to tax, and his subjects were obligated to support him for the good of the kingdom. By broadening representation and by arguing national necessity he was able, therefore, to strengthen his position and to circumscribe the role of parliament:[39]

> For a national war the king could identify his own ambitions and interests with those of the realm; he could mobilize the resources of the realm on an unheard-of scale; he could enlarge the territorial bounds of his rule and penetrate deeper into the political life of his people. In financial terms direct taxation at least doubled and indirect taxation could quadruple the King's normal peacetime income. . . . War finance on this scale transformed royal ambitions and authority. Although bound to use taxation for the common defense, the King could deploy it as he thought best. Assured of taxation and of the control of national finance exercised through the Exchequer, the King could exploit the opportunities offered by the development of credit to secure the utmost flexibility in financial planning. . . . Thus was kingship given a new dimension—its resources and authority becoming truly national.

PARLIAMENT'S GROWING POWER OVER REVENUE
STRENGTHENS ITS ROLE IN CONTROLLING WAR

Fourteen years after the Confirmation of Charters, Edward's son, Edward II (1307–1327) was forced to accede to another set of demands by the barons, known as the New Ordinances of 1311.[40] For the first time, parliament—which was still the king's baronial council meeting as parliament—

was also made explicitly responsible for assenting to decisions to go to war or for the king to leave the country:[41]

> Because the king ought not to undertake the act of war against anyone, or go out of his kingdom without the common assent of his baronage for the many perils that could happen to him and his kingdom, we ordain that hereafter the king shall not go out of his kingdom or undertake against anyone the act of war without the common assent of his baronage, and that in parliament, and if he does otherwise and for such undertaking has his feudal service summoned, the summons shall be as null. And if it happens that the king undertakes the act of war against anyone or goes out of the land with the assent of his baronage and needs to appoint a guardian in his kingdom, then he shall appoint him with the common assent of his baronage, and that in parliament.

Evidence of the role of parliament in assenting to war during this period is provided by the *Modus tenendi parliamentum* believed to have been written in about 1321. It stated that parliament had the duty to arbitrate in controversies relating to war and peace, and further stated that questions of war came first on parliament's calendar of standing orders of procedure. Moreover, taxes or aids for military purposes had to be in writing; could be provided only for actual war; and had to be approved by both barons and popular representatives.[42]

Although parliament continued to consist of the barons of the king's council and to operate primarily as a court during the reign of Edward II, as well as under Edward III (1327–1377), by the time of Edward II it was meeting almost every year, and by 1327 popular representatives from the shires and boroughs were being included in every meeting.[43] By the early 1330s, the knights from the shires were meeting together with the burgesses, and this assembly was beginning to be considered as a separate institution and to be called the Commons. (The king still had his baronial council, of course, but a distinction was developing between the council in parliament and the council out of parliament, and from this there later evolved the House of Lords and the Privy Council.) During this time, the right of the knights and burgesses to petition the king for remedy of grievances or the granting of privileges had also begun to be recognized, and it soon became accepted practice to make approval of taxes contingent on action by the king on petitions.

Edward III, who reigned during the first forty years of the Hundred Years' War with France (which was fought intermittently between 1337 and 1453), was even more dependent on parliament for supporting his foreign policy than earlier kings had been, and this led to an even stronger role for parliament; a development which in turn affected the royal prerogative. "[T]he pattern of the reign was concession. He needed money and soldiers and was prepared in return for them to relax royal control . . . he was pliant at home in order to permit adventure abroad."[44]

The link between taxation for war and parliament's rising power became all the stronger as the fourteenth century progressed. As England renewed its war with France in 1336, Edward III consulted actively with parliament in order to secure its support, principally its financial assistance. Parliament responded by providing generous aid, and it discussed and may even have taken action to approve the decision to go to war.[45]

Beginning in the 1350s, as the Hundred Years' War with France turned in England's favor, Edward III's relationship with his subjects and with the Commons improved, and the Commons became more closely allied with the king and the lords in ruling England: ". . . increasingly identified with the aims and assumptions of royal government, they [the Commons] began to adopt the proprietary attitude to parliament of the king and the Lords, to see themselves as rulers as well as ruled."[46] This change in the attitude of the Commons toward its role was part of the broader changes occurring around the time of the fourteenth century as a result of the decline of feudalism and the advent of the nation-state. The disappearance of feudalism, and the need for larger and more professional forces also led to the development of a national army based on indentured contracts by which the king could pay men to serve in the military, rather than having to depend upon the feudal land tenure system.[47]

Parliamentary involvement in foreign affairs and the making of war also continued to grow. By the 1370s, as the Hundred Years' War kept England in a perpetual state of military activity, parliament normally opened its sessions with a presentation on foreign affairs and a request for aid by the king's ministers, and requests by the king for parliamentary advice on foreign affairs and war were becoming commonplace. By 1400, writs of the king summoning parliament regularly referred to the need "to treat by advice of our council on the state and defence of our realm."[48] During the Lancastrian period (1377–1461) the initiative for legislation was beginning to shift to the Commons, and by the middle of the fifteenth century, most statutes, including tax laws, were originating in the Commons.[49] The Commons was assuming more of a role in foreign affairs and war, but it was reticent to take positions on matters which had traditionally been considered the province of the king and his lords and loathe to commit itself in advance to policies which would require increased taxation. Thus, in 1348 the response of Commons to the king on the war with France, a statement in which the Commons acknowledged its *right* to assent, could be interpreted both as an expression of limited competence and/or as an avoidance of commitment:[50]

> Most redoubtable lord, as to your war and the array for it . . .
> we are so ignorant and foolish that we neither know (how to), nor
> can, give advice about it; wherefore we pray . . . to excuse us and

that it please you, by the counsel of the lords and wise men of your council to ordain . . . what seems necessary to you for the honour and profit of the Realm. And whatever is finally ordained by the assent and accord of you and the above mentioned lords, we gladly assent to and hold firm and established.

A similar response was given in 1383, when the speaker of the Commons told the first of the Lancastrian kings, Richard II (1377–1399), that a proposed military campaign in France or any similar act of war was a matter for the lords rather than the Commons. The speaker said that he would "advise" a less expensive campaign, but that this was "advice" and not "consent." Richard II replied that he saw little difference between the two words.

Besides controlling the king's war power through taxation, parliament sought increased control over the terms of military service. Early in Edward III's reign parliament enacted statutes to limit tenurial obligation, to require the king to pay for service outside the county (shire) from which a soldier came, and to prevent, except in the case of a national "necessity," any soldier from being sent outside his county.[52] In 1351, it passed legislation decreeing that no one should be compelled to perform military service except by action of parliament. In the years following, these statutes, although frequently violated, were reaffirmed.[53]

With the accession of Edward IV (1461–1483), the first of three kings of the House of York, the monarchy was strengthened again, and the role of parliament became more limited. Although parliament had gained firm control over taxes, and although continued war against France during a period when war was becoming more expensive compelled Edward IV to rely heavily on taxes, Edward began extorting money from wealthier citizens through "benevolences." This new method, which parliament subsequently prohibited on several occasions, but which was used on and off by kings for about the next 150 years, was described in 1475 by an Italian diplomat in a letter from London:[54]

You must have heard that some time ago this most serene king [Edward IV] constantly said that he wanted to cross to the continent to conquer France. Especially for the last four months he has been very ardent in the matter, and has discovered an excellent device for raising money. He has plucked the feathers from the magpies without making them cry out. This autumn the king went about the country from town to town, and he made a note of how much each man from that town could pay. He sent for them all one by one and told them how he wished to cross to France to conquer it, with other words that ensnared their minds. Finally he worked to such a conclusion that there is nobody whatsoever who has not contributed money to

the value of L40 sterling and more. Everyone seemed to give willingly. I have many times seen our neighbours here who were called
before the king; when they went they looked as if they were going
to the gallows; when they returned they were elated, saying that they
had talked with the king; and because he had spoken to them so
many kind words, they did not regret the money they had paid. From
what some have told me, the king adopted this method. Whenever
any person appeared before him, he gave him a very great welcome
as though he had always known him. After some conversation he
asked him what he could pay of his own free will towards this
expedition. If the man made an honest offer, the king had his clerk
ready, who noted the name and the sum. If, the king thought otherwise, he said: "Such a man, who is poorer than you, has paid so
much; you who are richer can easily pay more" and by such means
he brought him with fair words up to the mark; and in this way it
is agreed that he has extracted a very large quantity of money.

PARLIAMENT TRIUMPANT

In the seventeenth century, parliamentary supremacy was achieved in
England, and with it, the right of the Commons to consent to war. Although
the king formally retained the royal prerogative of war and peace, by the
eighteenth century it was clear that Commons, which had gained control over
the military purse strings, the size of the army, and the conditions of military
service, was also the arbiter of whether, when, and how war should be waged.

After a long period of strong Tudor monarchs, the first of the Stuart
kings, James I (1602–1625), son of Henry VIII's sister Margaret and grandson
of Henry VII, took the throne at a time of peace and prosperity but amid
signs of unrest. Parliament had grown stronger and was becoming more
assertive, partly as a result of greater interest in parliament by the rising
merchant class, and greater competition for the growing number of seats in
the Commons.[55] The religious issue was also becoming very intense, with
the Puritans attacking dogmas and practices of the Church of England, and
the religious establishment resisting change. James, as well as his son Charles I
(1625–1649), were intent on maintaining the strength and rights of the crown
and on limiting the role and power of parliament, especially the Commons.
On one occasion James was said to have remarked:[56] "I am surprised that my
ancestors should ever have permitted such an institution [parliament] to come
into existence. I am a stranger and found it here when I arrived so that I am
obliged to put up with what I cannot get rid of."

Early in his reign, James incurred the opposition of the Commons when
he insisted on invalidating an election in favor of his own candidate, a member
of the privy council, despite the precedent established under Queen Elizabeth
that the Commons would be the judge of its own elections (another English

precedent included in the U.S. Constitution). James also insisted that the courts were agents of the king, leading to his dismissal of Sir Edward Coke, Chief Justice of the King's Bench, who had insisted that the courts of common law were independent of the king and of parliament except for the right of review by the king acting with the House of Lords as the country's highest court of law.

James, like his predecessors, was dependent on parliament, however, for money and forces with which to wage war, as well as on the political support of parliament, especially the Commons, for going to war, and this dependency led him to search for ways of circumventing parliament while at the same time forcing him to entreat for its help.

In 1621, after dissolving an uncooperative parliament in 1614, the occasion for his remark noted above, and after governing without parliament for seven years, during which he had used benevolences as one way of raising money, James I called another parliament. Relations with Spain were a major issue. In 1620, the Spanish, with whom the English had arranged an alliance in 1604, had invaded a small Protestant state in Germany, the Palatinate, governed by James' son-in-law, and James was presented with the problem of maintaining his Spanish alliance while satisfying powerful English Protestant elements which wanted England to come to the aid of the Palatinate. In his opening speech to the parliament in early 1621, James defended the alliance with Spain, but also expressed his commitment to the Palatinate and asked for immediate funds for its defense. His intentions and plans seemed rather vague, however, and parliament adjourned in mid-1621 without approving any funds.

In the fall of 1621, parliament was convened again when it appeared that financial aid to the Palatinate was urgent. A major debate on foreign policy ensued, during which it was proposed, apparently at the private urging of Lord Buckingham, one of the king's favorites in the privy council, that Commons petition the king to declare war on Spain, a move probably designed to bring pressure on Spain to withdraw from the Palatinate. This resulted in a petition from Commons which, after declaiming about the evils of "the Popish religion," urged James I "speedily and effectually to take the sword into your hands" and to aid the protestants in Europe.[57] In the petition, Commons also said they would give the king a subsidy for the Palatinate provided he approved other bills which they had passed. James I called their action an infringement of the royal prerogative. Commons then sent him a less demanding petition, but he met with a delegation of its members and told them that he was an "old and experienced king, needing no such lessons," and that the House of Commons was not competent to advise him on foreign affairs. He chided them for their claim to freedom of debate, saying, "We cannot allow of the style, calling it your 'ancient and undoubted right and inheritance,' but could rather have wished that you had said that your privileges were derived from the grace and permission of our ancestors and us."[58]

The Commons replied with a Protestation in which they asserted their right to complete freedom of debate, including matters of foreign affairs and war.[59] On December 30, 1621, the king met with the privy council and some members of parliament, and, denouncing the action of the Commons, he tore from their official journal the page containing the Protestation, and announced that parliament was dissolved.[60]

In 1624, after failing to improve relations with Spain, James I called parliament again. Faced with a divided privy council, he asked parliament for advice on whether to continue negotiating with Spain, and, if not, what steps he should take after breaking diplomatic relations. He did not want their advice; he wanted support for breaking with Spain, and financial and political support for military aid to the Palatinate and was counting on their anti-Catholic, anti-Spanish sentiment. The Commons, however, preferred a naval war against Spanish shipping. They also wanted the king to break relations with Spain, and said that they would approve a new subsidy if the king would agree to do so, as well as agreeing to let parliament oversee the expenditure of the new funds. The king agreed to parliamentary oversight, but argued that before taking the advice of parliament on relations with Spain he should be granted the full subsidy. He also denounced parliament's attempt to precipitate a war with Spain, saying that even if he agreed to accept their advice he retained full power of war and peace. Parliament responded by granting him the subsidy, but conditioned it on several things, including breaking relations with Spain.[61] In their resolutions they stated that in the war "which is likely to ensue . . . we your loyal and loving subjects will never fail in a parliamentary way to assist your Majesty in so royal a design. . . ." As explained by the sagacious Sir Edward Coke (who, after being dismissed as Chief Justice of the King's Bench for trying to enforce the common law against the king, had become a member of Commons and a leader of opposition to the king), the resolution was worded in such a way, however, as to avoid committing parliament to "future possibilities."[62] The king, reiterating his power over foreign affairs, accepted the money and ignored the advice.

In early 1625, James I died and was succeeded by his son Charles I, who had a similar view of his role and that of parliament. A few days after acceding, he called parliament, and his first request, without any explanation of its intended use or the use made of previous grants, was for a subsidy for military measures against Spain and in support of the Protestants. Meeting with resistance, he dissolved parliament.

In 1626, after an English invasion of the coast of Spain resulted in a fiasco in which English troops captured a quantity of wine and got drunk as a body, Charles again called parliament and asked for a subsidy. Parliament, intent on impeaching Lord Buckingham, began an inquiry, and the king responded by imprisoning the two principal leaders of Commons. When the Commons refused to continue, he released the leaders, but ordered Commons to act immediately on the subsidy. They refused, and he dissolved parliament again. This left Charles without the funds he needed, and he resorted to various harsh measures to obtain relief directly from the public, including making forced loans from citizens and quartering troops among the populace.

In 1628, Charles called another parliament, and without explaining its intended use he once more demanded money. Parliament reacted vigorously with the Petition of Right of 1628, the constitutional significance of which is said to have been second only to the Magna Carta, listing the various grievances against the king's methods of collecting money and administering justice, and demanding that the king respect the common law and the statutes prohibiting the collection of money without approval of parliament, enforced billeting of soldiers, imprisonment without just cause, and the use of martial law.[63] Charles, needing money, did not deny the petition, and parliament approved the subsidy.

In 1629, another parliament was called, and after it, too, resisted his demands, the king ordered the speaker to adjourn Commons. The motion was put and was defeated. When the speaker tried to leave the chair, which would have signified adjournment, he was held down by several members, and when Black Rod, the king's messenger, came to the door to take the mace, which also would have signified adjournment, the doors were locked and he was prevented from entering. Charles thereupon dissolved parliament and arrested nine of the members of Commons.

It was against this background of increasing conflict between the king and parliament that the English civil war occurred in the 1640s. In 1640, after eleven years without parliament, Charles needed money for war and again called parliament into session. After only three weeks, during which it demanded consideration of accumulated grievances, parliament was dissolved. A few months later, after Charles had failed in a military campaign against Scotland, the Scots invaded England and Charles was forced to call another parliament. This, the famous Long Parliament, impeached one of the king's principal ministers, the earl of Strafford, of high treason and had him executed. Then it passed the Triennial Act which provided that parliament would meet at least every three years and could not be dissolved without its own consent. Other acts were passed to limit the king's powers, including prohibiting special war taxes which Charles had imposed. Charles, facing a militant parliament and an angry country, was forced to agree.

In the fall of 1641, parliament met for a second session, and the conflict with the king increased. A revolt had occurred in Ireland, and parliament, concerned about raising forces which the king might use against parliament itself, at first proposed that it should approve the king's ministers, and when this was rejected it passed an act giving itself the power to appoint commanders of the militia. The king refused to agree, whereupon parliament declared the act to be law notwithstanding the king's disapproval.

In August 1642, the English civil war began when forces loyal to the king clashed with the New Model Army of parliament led by Lord Fairfax and Oliver Cromwell, both members of parliament. Between then and 1649, when Charles I was executed, a number of proposals were made for reforming the government.

A basic goal of the civil war was legislative control of the war power, including the making of war and peace, the raising of money and forces for war, and the conditions of military service. This was a major theme in the political tracts of the time written by those who favored limitations on the power of the king and a stronger role for parliament. One of the most flamboyant of these, as well as one of the most knowledgeable, was William Prynne (1600–1669), a lawyer, Puritan, and political activist who had been imprisoned for life and had his ears cut off and the initials "S. D." (seditious libeler) branded on his cheeks for writings in the 1630s critical of the religious establishment and practices of the Church of England.[64] In 1640, Prynne was released from prison by parliament, and in 1643 he wrote a series of tracts under the general title, "The Soveraigne Power of Parliament and Kingdomes."[65] Prynne, who was known as an antiquarian, eventually becoming the keeper of England's official historical records, and who copiously documented his writings by references to classical as well as English history, believed that parliament should have full control over the war power. After citing a number of examples from English history of conflicts between the king and parliament, in which parliament had insisted on its right to consent to the making of war, Prynne argued that as a result of these and other precedents, "It is evident that the principal right of concluding, denouncing [proclaiming] war or peace, resides in the Parliament, and that the King without its previous advice and consent ought not to proclaim any open war, since the subjects' estates and persons must support, wage it, and receive most disadvantage by it."[66] "For thus it will come to pass besides," Prynne said, "that things very well thought on and deliberated by many have for the most part better success, than those things which are rashly begun by someone; that the Subjects, who not unwillingly bring their estates and lives into danger, will less fear the loss of both, will fight more valiantly, and will put forth all their strength in prosecuting and ending the combat of war, even for this reason, that themselves have been the advisers of the war."[67]

From its general power of war, Prynne said, parliament had full authority over all of the aspects of preparing for and waging war, and after listing these he concluded:

> In one word, wars have been ended, leagues, truces made, confirmed, and punishments for breach of them, provisions for preservation of them enacted by the Parliament, as infinite precedents in the Parliament rolls and printed acts demonstrate. So that our Parliaments in all former ages, even in the regions of our most martial Kings, have had the sovereign power of ordering, settling, determining both the beginning, progress, and conclusion of our wars, and the chief ordering of all things which concern the managing of

them by sea and land; being indeed the great Council of War, elected by the Kingdom, to direct our Kings; who were and are in truth but the Kingdom's chief Lord Generals, (as the Roman Emperors and all Kings of old were their Senates, States and People's General, to manage their wars and fight their battles) the sovereign power of making and directing war or peace being not in the Emperors or Kings themselves, but in their Senates, States and Parliaments. . . .

Prynne's views, while highly political and polemical, illustrated the attitudes of the more militant advocates of parliamentary sovereignty who were in control of parliament when these tracts were published in 1643—and who deeply influenced the American Founding Fathers. Although the involvement of parliament in such matters had already given it considerable influence, those who were struggling to assert its right to represent the public in all areas of national policy wanted more explicit recognition that the sovereign should get parliament's consent before going to war, and that parliament, rather than the king, should have control over the armed forces. One indication of this was the provision in the Propositions of Newcastle in 1646, which parliament offered to the king as a basis for peace, "That by Act of Parliament the concluding of war or peace with foreign Princes and States, be with advise [*sic*] and consent of both Parliaments [Commons and Lords], or in the intervals of Parliament, by their commissioners."[68]

This same position was taken by leaders of the army which parliament had created to fight the king's forces. Their document, "The Heads of the Proposals," which was submitted to the king for his approval in August 1647, provided, among other things, that parliament should meet regularly, and that a council of state should be established for a seven-year term as a privy council to the king, with "power as the King's Privy Council, for and in all foreign negotiations; provided that the making of war or peace with any other kingdom or state shall not be without the advice and consent of parliament."[69]

On October 18, 1647, with the failure of both parliament and the council of the army to secure the king's assent to reform proposals, a group of more militant officers and men representing five cavalry regiments, who were disparagingly called "Levellers" because of their belief in political equality, issued a pamphlet, "The Case of The Army Truly Stated," urging their senior officers to take action.[70] "All power," they said, "is originally and essentially in the whole body of the people of this Nation, and . . . their free choice or consent by their Representors is the only original or foundation of all just government. . . . This power of commons in Parliament, is the thing against which the king hath contended, and the people have defended with their lives, and therefore ought now to be demanded as the price of their blood."

On October 28, leaders among this group in the army drew up their own proposal, "An Agreement of the People," based on these concepts of popular sovereignty. It provided that supreme power should be vested in a parliament consisting of the House of Commons. There was no mention of a king. It also provided that parliament's power would include making war and peace and "treaties with foreign states":[71]

> That the power of this, and all future Representatives of this Nation, is inferior only to theirs who choose them, and doth extend without the consent or concurrence of any other person or persons, to the erecting and abolishing of offices and courts, to the appointing, removing, and calling to account magistrates and offices of all degrees, to the making war and peace, to the treating with foreign States, and, generally to whatsoever is not expressly or impliedly reserved by the represented to themselves. . . .

Faced with strong pressure from the Levellers in the army and their supporters outside, especially in London, Oliver Cromwell and his senior offices called a meeting at Putney in late October 1647 to discuss the situation. The Levellers presented their draft of the agreement. Remarkably enough, there was a stenographer present and the debate was recorded.[72] During the debate, Cromwell took the position that the agreement involved "very great alterations of the very government of the kingdom," and that what was needed was a plan that "the spirits and temper of the people of this Nation are prepared to receive and to go along with." The agreement, he said, should be considered by the parliament.

Rejected at first,[73] the agreement was adopted in essence in 1649 by the Rump Parliament, which consisted of only ninety members out of an original 504, after the two-fifths who supported the king had left in 1642 and Presbyterian members had been excluded in Pride's Purge in 1648. The Rump Parliament voted to abolish the monarchy and the House of Lords and declared England to be a "Commonwealth or Free State." Executive functions were vested in a Council of state with forty members, including thirty-one members of parliament (then consisting only of the House of Commons), which was to elect its own president. The council was to direct the armed forces under the supervision of parliament, and the approval of parliament was required for major decisions of state, including war and peace.

In 1653, the Commonwealth fell when Cromwell dispersed the Rump Parliament. He then called a meeting of representatives whose members were selected by the army from among men "fearing God and of approved fidelity and honesty." He avoided calling it a parliament, but when the group assembled it called itself by that name. With only 140 members it became known as the Nominated or Little Parliament. This system also failed, and Cromwell then became Lord Protector under a constitution, the Instrument of Government, prepared by his officers.

Under the Instrument of Government the Lord Protector was to ". . . direct in all things concerning the keeping and holding of a good correspondency with foreign kings, princes and states; and also, with the consent of the major part of the Council, have the power of war and peace."[74] Parliament, however, "in case of a future war with any foreign state," was to be "forthwith summoned for their advice concerning the same." Also, in the event that "necessities of the State shall require it," the Lord Protector, "with the advice of the major part of the Council," was to summon a meeting of parliament to consider the situation, and any such parliament could not be dissolved before three months without its consent. The Instrument of Government also provided that parliament would control the financing of war, but gave the Lord Protector power to raise such funds if necessary in the absence of parliament, subject to its subsequent approval.

Even though Cromwell had purged members who might be opposed, the first parliament called under the protectorate in September 1654 insisted on greater control over the armed services and the war power. A new constitution was proposed by some members which, if it had passed, would have required Cromwell to secure the consent of parliament before using the armed forces, or the advice and consent of the council if parliament was not in session. It also provided in some detail for parliamentary supervision, together with that of the council, of foreign affairs:[75]

> That the power of making war is only in the Lord Protector and the Parliament.
>
> The sitting of the Parliament, no peace can be concluded, but by consent of Parliament; and in the interval of Parliament the power of making peace shall be in the Lord Protector and the Council, with such reservations and limitations as the Parliament shall approve.
>
> That the said Lord Protector, by the advice and consent of the major part of the Council, shall direct in all things concerning the keeping and holding of a good correspondence with foreign kings, princes, and states.

The new constitution was debated late in 1654, but in January 1655 parliament was dissolved by Cromwell before any action could be taken on the proposal.

Cromwell was succeeded briefly by his son, Richard, who was less effective, and the army resumed power. The old Rump Parliament was reconvened, but by this time discontent was widespread and, after a series of events, Charles II (1660–1685), son of the executed Charles I, was called to the throne and the monarchy was restored.

During the reign of Charles II and his son, James II (1685–1688), the struggle between parliament and the king continued, with war and taxes again among the chief issues in dispute. In the Glorious Revolution of 1688, James was forced to flee to France, and William III and Mary (1689–1702) were called to the throne by parliament.[76] William agreed to certain terms stipulated by parliament, based on traditional principles of the common law, and these were enacted by parliament in 1689 as a Bill of Rights. One of its provisions was, "That the raising or keeping a standing army within the kingdom in time of peace unless it be with consent of parliament is against law."[77] The 1689 Mutiny Act reiterated parliament's control over the army by requiring annual reapproval by parliament of the existence of the army as well as its size. And in the Act of Settlement of 1701, parliament gained even greater control over war and peace through a provision requiring its consent for waging war for territories not under control of the crown.

By the early eighteenth century, England, with its trinity of King, Lords, and Commons, had firmly established its "balanced constitution" of monarchy, nobility and democracy, and there began a long period of relative stability in English politics.[78] While the conduct of foreign affairs and the making of war and peace continued to be considered royal prerogatives, and the advent of a cabinet system shifted the locus of conflict from one of parliament versus the king to one of the opposition party versus the party which controlled the cabinet and acted for the monarch, the House of Commons exercised considerable control over major foreign policy commitments and decisions on war and peace.

NOVUS ORDO SECLORUM

The American Revolution took place in this setting. Its leaders, faced with having to establish a government, drew on their collective knowledge and experience for the political and legal ideas and principles to devise not just a new order, but, as they conceived it, a new order for the ages.[79] From classical antiquity and from English history, from philosophical and legal treatises, and from political pamphlets, speeches and sermons of the day, they developed the concepts for a constitution designed to protect and promote the political rights which their English forebears had fought to establish. Foremost among these rights was that of legislative control of the power to prepare for and to make war. They never doubted or questioned the fundamental importance of this right, grounded, as it was, in the common law, but neither did they leave much of an explanation of their decision to allocate the war power to Congress. They probably did not feel the need to explain it. They doubtless assumed that future generations of Americans would know the history of political ideas and institutions, and would understand.

NOTES

1. Veto message, 25 October 1973, House Document 93–171 (Washington, D.C.: Government Printing Office, 1973), 1.

2. See John H. Sullivan, *The War Powers Resolution*, A Special Study of the Committee on Foreign Affairs, House of Representatives (Washington, D.C.: Government Printing Office, 1982).

3. For a compilation of such statements see *The War Powers Resolution, Relevant Documents, Correspondence, Reports* issued as a Committee Print by the Foreign Affairs Committee, House of Representatives (Washington, D.C.: Government Printing Office, 1983).

4. Very little has been published on the origins of the war power provision of the Constitution. There is one relevant article by Francis L. Coolidge, Jr. and Joel David Sharrow, "The War-Making Powers: The Intentions of the Framers in the Light of Parliamentary History," *Boston University Law Review*, Special Issue (1970), 5–18. See also Abraham D. Sofaer, *War, Foreign Affairs, and Constitutional Power: The Origins* (Cambridge, Mass.: Ballinger Publishing Co., 1976), 6–15; W. Taylor Reveley III, *War Powers of the President and Congress* (Charlottesville: University Press of Virginia, 1981), 53–55; Edward Keynes, *Undeclared War: Twilight Zone of Constitutional Power* (University Park, Pa.: Pennsylvania State University Press, 1984), 11–16, 22–25; Charles A. Lofgren, "War-Making Under the Constitution," *Yale Law Journal* 81 (March 1972): 673–702 at 697–699.

5. As Senator Jacob Javits concluded, "There can be no doubt that the constitutional intention was to endow the president with all the powers that ultimately adhere to a military commander but, at the same time, to withhold from him the ultimate authority on the gravest political decision of whether to 'declare war'." Jacob K. Javits, "War Powers Reconsidered," *Foreign Affairs* 64 (Fall 1985): 130–140, at 132. Sofaer reached the same conclusion in his meticulous critical study (p. 3). The commander in chief provision, he said, is ". . . consistent on its face with the notion of the President as agent of the legislature. It reads most readily as a grant to manage military engagements and other objectives authorized by Congress." Louis Henkin agrees: "There is little evidence that the Framers intended more than to establish in the President civilian command of the forces for wars declared by Congress (or when the United States was attacked). . . ." Henkin, *Foreign Affairs and the Constitution* (Mineola, N.Y.: Foundation Press, Inc., 1972), 50.

6. Edmund Randolph of Virginia favored allocating the power to declare war, as well as the power of "origination of the means of war," to the House of Representatives. *The Records of the Federal Convention of 1787*, 4 vols., rev. ed. Max Farrand (New Haven: Yale University Press, rev. ed., 1937), II: 279.

7. Ibid., 319. The argument was also made that " 'make' war might be understood to conduct it which was an Executive function. . . ." For George Mason, "make" was preferable to "declare" because of the connotation that if Congress were to "make" war it would be in charge of fighting war, and thus would have full control over the power of the "sword" as well as the power of the "purse." He believed, as did most of the delegates, that the purse and the sword "ought never to get into the same hands whether Legislative or Executive," and that although Congress should make the decision to go to war, the president should hold and should use the sword when so authorized. Mason was fearful of a single executive, however, and favored a council to help to control the Executive, as well as to protect the Executive against legislative usurpation. Ibid., I: 139–140.

8. Ibid., 65.

9. Ibid., 64–65. In the Pennsylvania ratifying convention in November 1787, Wilson explained to the delegates, "This system will not hurry us into war; it is calculated to guard against it. It will not be in the power of a single man, or a single body of men, to involve us in such distress; for the important power of declaring war is vested in the legislature at large: this declaration must be made with the concurrence of the House of Representatives: from this circumstance we may draw a certain conclusion that nothing but our national interest can draw us into a war." Jonathan Eliot, *The Debates of the Several State Conventions on the Adoption of the Federal Constitution*, 5 vols. (Philadelphia: J. B. Lippincott Co., 1836), vol. II: 528.

10. Farrand, I: 70.

11. Ibid., III: 622, 624.

12. The following language (Farrand, II: 181–182) was reported on August 6 by the Committee of Detail, and can be compared with the final language of the Constitution given above:

"The Legislature of the United States shall have the power . . .

"To make rules concerning capture on land and water;

"To declare the law and punishment of piracies and felonies committed on the high seas, and the punishment of counterfeiting the coin of the United States, and of offenses against the law of nations;

"To subdue a rebellion in any State, on the application of its legislature;

"To make war;

"To raise armies;

"To build and equip fleets;

"To call forth the aid of the militia, in order to execute the laws of the Union, enforce treaties, suppress insurrections, and repel invasions. . . ."

13. Ibid., 16–17.

14. Ibid., 318. There was never a final separate vote on the war power provision, nor was there a separate vote on the whole of Article I, Section 8. The vote on the change from "make" to "declare," according to Madison's notes, was seven to two, and became eight to one after Connecticut changed its vote following remarks that "'make' war might be understood to 'conduct' it which was an Executive function."

15. Ibid., 279.

16. As Louis Henkin has noted (p. 80): "There have been suggestions that the power of Congress to declare war was intended to be only a formal power to declare formal wars, and that wars can be fought by the President on his own authority if they are not 'declared.' That view is without foundation: the Constitution gave Congress the power to decide the ultimate question, whether the nation shall or shall not go to war." Other authorities agree. According to Sofaer (p. 32), "Nothing in the change signifies an intent to allow the President a general authority to 'make' war in the absence of a declaration; indeed, granting the exceptional power suggests that the general power over war was left in the legislative branch." See also Reveley, pp. 81–85.

At another point, however, Henkin suggests (p. 52) a very broad interpretation of the commander in chief provision: "The President has power not merely to take measures to meet the invasion, but to wage in full the war imposed upon the United States. In our day of instant war, all assume that the President would have the power to retaliate against a nuclear attack, if only on the theory that retaliation was a form of defense and might prevent or deter a second strike; *probably, he has authority also to anticipate by a preemptive strike an attack he believes imminent.*" (emphasis added)

17. See his comment on 1 June cited in fn. 8 above.

18. Farrand, II: 541.

19. There was a brief debate (ibid., 405) on the provision for the president to appoint persons, including the military, to office. As reported from the Committee on Detail on August 6, the provision read: "He shall commission all the officers of the United States; and shall appoint officers in all cases not otherwise provided for by this Constitution." Roger Sherman of Connecticut objected to the last part of this provision, saying that it would be a mistake to allow the President to appoint general officers in the Army in time of peace: "Herein lay the corruption in G. Britain. If the Executive can model the army, he may set up an absolute Government; taking advantage of the close of a war and an army commanded by his creatures." After some consideration, it was agreed to reword the provision, and to require the advice and consent of the Senate for all presidential appointments, including all general military officers. See Art. II, Sec. 2 of the Constitution.

20. Ibid., 509.

21. For comments in the state conventions, many of which pertained to standing armies and the militia, see Eliot, II: 97–98, 136–137, 195, 278–279, 282–283, 348–349, 473, 528; III: 58–60, 91, 172, 201–202, 206, 232–233, 393–394, 410–411, 611; IV: 107–108, 114–115, 262–265. There is a good chapter in Reveley on the ratification debates. He concludes (pp. 102, 104): "The declaration of war clause . . . posed no problems for even those state delegates most allergic to the new Constitution. . . . As in Philadelphia, the inattention to this clause must have stemmed from the unanimous expectation that it left the President no independent war-making authority. . . . Evidence is compelling that the Ratifiers, like the Framers, understood the President as commander in chief to be simply 'first general and admiral,' a man whose 'energy' could save the country during military crisis but who had authority neither to commit America to war nor to govern any but the strategic and tactical aspects of its conflicts, once begun." See also Sofaer (pp. 38–60), who reaches similar conclusions.

22. See Michael Powicke, *Military Obligation in Medieval England* (Oxford: Clarendon Press, 1962), 225. See also F. Liebermann, *The National Assembly in the Anglo-Saxon Period* (Halle A. S., Germany: Max Niemeyer, 1913), 60–61.

23. Justinian, Code V, Tit. 59, 5, cap. 3. See Gaines Post, *Studies in Medieval Legal Thought: Public Law and the State, 1100–1322* (Princeton: Princeton University Press, 1964), 165–166.

24. On these points see G. O. Sayles, *The King's Parliament of England* (New York: W. W. Norton & Co., Inc., 1974), and H. G. Richardson and G. O. Sayles, *Parliaments and Great Councils in Medieval England* (London: Stevens and Sons Ltd., 1961).

25. For parallel developments were occurring on the continent, where various rulers were being forced, largely because of the impact of royal wars, to submit to baronial approval of decisions affecting war and peace, see J. C. Holt, *Magna Carta* (Cambridge: The University Press, 1965), pp. 64–65.

26. Scutage, from the Latin word *scrutum*, meaning a shield, was a tax levied on vassals, whose feudal land tenure (knight's fee) was at the pleasure of the king, to pay for hiring mercenaries in lieu of the performance of military service by the vassals themselves.

27. On this point, see H. G. Richardson and G. O. Sayles, *The Governance of Mediaeval England from the Conquest to Magna Carta* (Edinburgh: The University Press, 1963), 76 ff.; and Sayles, *Law and Legislation; from Æthelberht to Magna Carta* (Edinburgh: The University Press, 1967), 136–137.

28. See Richardson and Sayles, *The Governance of Mediaeval England*, ch. 19. For the text of the Magna Carta see *English Historical Documents, 1189–1327*. ed. Harry Rothwell, vol. III of a multivolume series (New York: Oxford University Press, 1975), 316–324.

29. On this point see J. C. Holt, "The Making of the Magna Carta (Charlottesville: The University Press of Virginia, 1965), 55, and Sayles, *Law and Legislation*, 153.

30. On these points see Powicke, op cit., 227, and Holt, *Magna Carta*, 64–65, and 132–134 and 218–219.

In what is generally considered to have been an earlier version of the Magna Carta, the "Unknown Charter," thought to have been written in the spring of 1215, it was provided that overseas military service should be limited to Normandy and Brittany. This was not in the Magna Carta itself, but the issue of the terms of military service, which had been one of the principal complaints of those opposed to John's policies, was raised in another form. For the text of the "Unknown Charter" see *English Historical Documents, 1189–1327*, 310–311.

31. "The representatives of the lower clergy, the shires, the boroughs, the merchant classes may expostulate, dispute the amount, seek exceptions, earmark grants for the purpose put forward: the king may agree to some of the conditions and, as is the way in politics, then find it impossible to keep them and jettison them. All this made little difference in the final result. The England of the Middle Ages could no more than the England of 1940 have withstood the argument that the safety of the state was at risk, that there was a threat of invasion, that war was inevitable and justifiable." Sayles, *The King's Parliament of England*, 89.

32. According to a description of these events by William Prynne, a seventeenth century antiquarian and advocate of the rights of parliament, the nobles objected to Henry III's continued war with France without the consent of parliament after parliament had refused to provide aid for that purpose in 1242. Prynne had access to England's official papers, and cited these in documenting his case, but because he was attempting to prove that parliament traditionally had controlled the making of war he may have engaged in some overemphasis. His account is valuable, however, and should be consulted. See William Prynne, *The Soveraigne Power of Parliaments*

and Kingdomes (New York: Garland Publishing Co., 1979, reprint of the original edition of 1643). The section dealing with Henry III is in the second part of this volume (which consists of several parts with separate pagination), 6–7. See text below for further discussion of Prynne's views.

33. For the text of the Provisions of Oxford, see *English Historical Documents, 1189–1327*, 361–366.

34. The first use of the word Parliamentum in an official document has been traced to 1236. See Richardson and Sayles, "The Earliest Known Official Use of the Word 'Parliament'," *English Historical Review*, LXXXII (October 1967): 747. See Sayles, *The King's Parliament of England*, ch. 4, for a discussion of the Provisions of Oxford.

35. "Parliament . . . had acquired its character and role under the pressure of national war and the consequent disputes over financial obligation." Gerald L. Harriss, "War and the Emergence of the English Parliament, 1297–1360," *Journal of Medieval History*, 2 (March 1976): 35–56, at 56.

36. See G. L. Harriss, *King, Parliament, and Public Finance in Medieval England to 1369* (Oxford: Clarendon Press, 1975), 52, and Sayles, *The King's Parliament of England*, 89. Sayles notes that the maxim, *quod omnes tangit ab omnibus approbetur*, "proclaimed no popular sovereignty but openly recorded that the right to be consulted was accepted in government circles."

37. For the text of the Confirmation of Charters, see *English Historical Documents, 1189–1327*, 485–486.

38. Harriss, *King, Parliament, and Public Finance in Medieval England to 1369*, 68–69.

39. Ibid., 511.

40. For the text of the New Ordinances of 1311, see *English Historical Documents, 1189–1327*, 527–539.

41. Ibid., 529.

42. See Maude V. Clarke, *Medieval Representation and Consent* (London: Longmans, Green and Co., 1936), 7–8. Miss Clarke commented that many scholars questioned the value of the *Modus* as an accurate description of the parliament, but that as an indication of democratic concepts it is significant. For excerpts of the *Modus* see *Select Documents of English Constitutional History*, ed. George Burton Adams and H. Morse Stephens (New York: The Macmillan Co., 1918), 83.

43. Because knights of the shire and burgesses were included thereafter, eventually becoming the House of Commons, Sayles and Richardson call 1327 the "dividing line" in the evolution of the House of Commons. Sayles explains the effect of this change on the approach to law making (*The King's Parliament of England*, 115): "Under Edward I legislation had been imposed from above: prepared and propounded by the king's ministers and judges, it was submitted to the council, sometimes in and sometimes out of parliament. Under Edward II legislation originated from below, being founded upon the petition of the Commons." Sayles adds, however, that the

king with his prerogative was still in command, and could suggest, modify, or veto legislation.

44. M. H. Keen, *England in the Later Middle Ages* (London: Methuen, 1973), quoted by Harriss, "War and the Emergence of the English Parliament, 1297–1360," 42.

45. Edmund B. Fryde, "Parliament and the French War, 1336–40," in *Historical Studies of the English Parliament*, vol. I, *Origins to 1399*, ed. Edmund B. Fryde and Edward Miller (Cambridge: The University Press, 1970), 247. Fryde, however, questions the "quality" of these discussions: "Were the magnates and commons ever allowed to debate seriously the issues of peace and war or did Edward III merely seek from them a purely formal consent for policies already settled beforehand in the narrow circle of the king's closest advisers?"

46. Harriss, "War and the Emergence of the English Parliament, 1297–1360," 55. See also Harriss, *King, Parliament, and Public Finance in Medieval England to 1369*, 513–514.

47. See Powicke, op. cit., chap. XII.

48. For these developments, see selections in *The English Parliament in the Middle Ages*, ed. R. G. Davies and J. H. Denton (Manchester: Manchester University, 1981), especially A. L. Brown, "Parliament, c. 1377–1422," 109–140, and A. R. Myers, "Parliament, 1422–1509," 141–184.

49. Powicke, op. cit., 242–243.

50. Quoted by Powicke, 236.

51. Brown, "Parliament, c. 1377–1422," 138–139.

52. Powicke, op. cit., 237, and Arthur H. Noyes, *The Military Obligation in Medieval England* (Columbia: Ohio State University, 1930), 33.

53. In 1401, for example, a statute provided that no one should be made to serve without the consent of parliament; that no one should be sent out of his county except in the case of national "necessity"; that all those sent out of the county should receive wages from the king. Noyes, 37.

54. *English Historical Documents, 1327–1485*, vol. IV, ed. A. R. Myers (New York: Oxford University Press, 1969), 527–528.

55. Between 1509 and 1601, the number of seats in the Commons increased from 350 to 467, primarily because of the creation of new boroughs during a period of population growth.

56. Quoted by Edmund B. Fryde, Introduction to *Historical Studies of the English Parliament*, II: 15.
For the Jacobean period see *Faction and Parliament: Essays on Early Stuart History*, ed. Kevin Sharpe (Oxford: Clarendon Press, 1978), especially Sharpe's introduction: "Parliamentary History 1603–1629: In or Out of Perspective?" 1–42; S. L. Adams, "Foreign Policy and the Parliaments of 1621 and 1624," 139–172; and G. L.

Harriss, "Medieval Doctrines in the Debates on Supply, 1610–1629," 73–103. See also R. E. Ruigh, *The Parliament of 1624: Politics and Foreign Policy* (Cambridge: Harvard University Press, 1971).

57. From the text in J. P. Kenyon, *The Stuart Constitution, 1603–1688*, Documents and Commentary (Cambridge: The University Press, 1966), 46.

58. Ibid., 29.

59. Ibid., 47.

60. Sharpe (pp. 11–12) notes, however, that none present at the meeting disagreed with the king's statement that the Protestation had been passed by the Commons with less than a quorum of members present.

61. For these, the so-called Four Propositions, see S. L. Adams, op. cit., 167.

62. Ibid., 169.

63. For the text, see Kenyon, 82–85.

64. One of the reasons for Prynne's harsh treatment was that he had criticized stage plays for encouraging immoral and illicit behavior, thus indirectly implicating the Queen who was then taking part in a masque. In 1642, the Puritans, who controlled parliament, closed the playhouses.

65. Prynne, op. cit. According to Powicke (op. cit., p. 224n), Prynne "may be considered the father of this subject the role of parliaments in decisions on war and peace. His preoccupation with parliamentary sovereignty and the sanctity of precedent led, of course, to manifold distortions; but for the first time the marshalling of the testimony of chronicles and parliamentary rolls was opposed to the monstrous claims of the Stuart house."

66. Prynne, 2: 9.

67. Ibid., 4: 2. I have modernized spelling in this and subsequent quotations.
Prynne added that legislative control of war was common to other countries, ancient and modern. Citing Polybius, Plutarch and John Bodin, among others, he said that "in the Roman State, both under their King and Emperors, the chief power of denouncing [proclaiming] war and concluding peace was in the Senate and people. . . ." Likewise, he said, in ancient Greece, and in Sweden, Denmark and Norway, ". . . no war was begun nor peace concluded by their Kings but by the authority and preceding decrees of their Senates, Parliaments and Diets. . . ." Ibid., 2: 9–10.

68. From the text of the Propositions of Newcastle, in *The Constitutional Documents of the Puritan Revolution, 1625–1660*, ed. Samuel R. Gardiner (Oxford: The Clarendon Press, 1899), 284.

69. Ibid., 318, 320.

70. *The Leveller Tracts, 1647–1653*, ed. William H. Haller and Godfrey Davies (New York: Columbia University Press, 1944, reprinted by Peter Smith, Gloucester, Mass., in 1964), 78–79.

A year earlier, after the imprisonment for seditious writing of John Lilburne, their leading spokesman, some of the Levellers produced a pamphlet entitled "A Remonstrance of Many Thousand Citizens," attacking the monarchy, which contained this graphic complaint about the effects of the king's wars on those pressed into service:

"Wee intreat you to consider what difference there is, between binding a man to an Oare, as a *Gally-slave* in *Turkie* or *Argiere*, and Pressing of men to serv in your Warre; to surprize a man on the sudden, force him from his Calling, where he lived comfortably, from a good trade; from his dear Parents, Wife or Children, against inclination, disposition to fight for a Cause hee understands not, and in Company of such, as he hath no comfort to be withall; for Pay, that will scarce give him sustenance; and if he live, to returne to a lost trade, or beggery, or not much better: If any Tyranny or cruelty exceed this; it must be worse then that of a *Turkish Gally-slave*." *Leveller Manifestoes of the Puritan Revolution*, ed. Don M. Wolfe (New York: Thomas Nelson and Sons, 1944), 125.

71. Gardiner, op. cit., 320.

72. See the text in A. S. P. Woodhouse, *Puritanism and Liberty, Being the Army Debates* (1647–9) (Chicago: University of Chicago Press, 2nd ed., 1974).

73. For texts of the second and third agreements, as well as a discussion of each of the agreements and other Leveller tracts, see Wolfe, *Leveller Manifestoes of the Puritan Revolution*.

74. From the text of the Instrument of Government in Kenyon, op. cit., 343.

75. From the text in Gardiner, op. cit., 443–445.

76. Technically, the action was taken by an elected convention acting as a temporary parliament.

77. From the text in Adams and Stephens, *Select Documents of English Constitutional History*, 464.

78. See J. H. Plumb, *The Growth of Political Stability in England, 1675–1725* (London: MacMillan, 1967).

79. See especially Bernard Bailyn, *The Ideological Origins of the American Revolution* (Cambridge: Belknap Press of the Harvard University Press, 1967); Gordon S. Wood, *The Creation of the American Republic, 1776–1787* (Chapel Hill: University of North Carolina Press, 1969); H. Trevor Colbourn, *The Lamp of Experience* (Chapel Hill: University of North Carolina Press, 1965).

2

Not For the First Time: Antecedents and Origins of the War Powers Resolution, 1945–1970

DUANE TANANBAUM

Ever since the days of George Washington, Congress and the president have fought for control over American foreign policy. By the 1950s and 1960s, however, it looked like the fight was over, as the executive branch dominated more and more the formulation of American foreign policy. People believed that only the president could make the quick decisions that were necessary in the nuclear age, and congressional prerogatives, especially the power to declare war, seemed almost like anachronisms. The legislators had been forced on the defensive, and they appeared to be losing ground in their efforts to preserve Congress' traditional role in foreign affairs as set forth in the Constitution.[1]

Then, in the 1970s, with the presidency weakened by the war in Vietnam and the Watergate scandals, Congress reasserted its authority in foreign affairs by passing the War Powers Resolution and other measures aimed at curbing executive autonomy in foreign relations. But the legislation of the 1970s did not suddenly spring forward like Athena from the brow of Zeus. Rather, the War Powers Resolution and similar measures represented the latest in a series of efforts by Congress in the post-World War II era to rein in "The Imperial Presidency." These efforts by Congress between 1945 and 1970 to clarify and restrain presidential power are the focus of this chapter.[2]

President Harry Truman believed in a strong chief executive, one who used the powers of the presidency to their fullest extent and then passed them on, unimpaired, to his successor. Like Franklin Roosevelt before him, Truman

viewed the president's authority as commander in chief as almost unlimited
when it came to protecting or defending the United States and American
interests abroad. A former senator himself, however, Truman was well aware
of the legislators' resentment at having been ignored so often by Roosevelt.
Moreover, Republican majorities in Congress in 1947–48 and congressional
control of the purse strings gave him no choice but to work closely with
Congress in formulating the Truman Doctrine to aid Greece and Turkey, and
the Marshall Plan to revive Western Europe.[3]

Truman and his advisers also consulted with congressional leaders in
1949 when they were drafting the North Atlantic Treaty. Secretary of State
Dean Acheson realized that the agreement would need Senate approval, so
he conferred frequently with Senators Tom Connally (D-Tex.) and Arthur
Vandenberg (R-Mich.) and other members of the Foreign Relations Committee. As Senator Connally told newsmen, the senators really appreciated
having the opportunity to express their views while the treaty was being
drafted, rather than having "a finished document stuck under our noses."[4]

The senators used this opportunity to minimize any encroachments on
Congress' power to declare war. President Truman and Senator Vandenberg
agreed that the objective of the treaty was to deter a Soviet attack on Western
Europe by serving notice that the United States would defend its allies. But
Vandenberg and the senators worried that an agreement committing the United
States to go to war automatically if a member of NATO were attacked would
render superfluous the legislators' authority to declare war. Therefore, instead
of a provision requiring each signatory to take "military and other action" if
any one of them were attacked, the senators suggested an article stipulating
that in such cases each nation would take "such action as it deems necessary,
including the use of armed forces." This would leave it up to the United
States to decide how it would respond to a specific situation. The senators
also recommended that another section be inserted in the treaty specifying
that such determinations would be made by the signatories "in accordance
with their respective constitutional processes."[5]

The changes suggested by the Foreign Relations Committee ensured
that the United States could respond as it saw fit to an attack upon Western
Europe, but that still left it up in the air whether the president or Congress
or the two together would decide what action would be taken. According to
the Constitution, Congress and Congress alone has the power to declare war,
but the president, as commander in chief of the Armed Forces, possesses the
authority to act in an emergency. Senator Walter George (D-Ga.) urged his
colleagues to consider this problem now, rather than during or after a crisis,
but the Foreign Relations Committee found itself unable to draw a dividing
line between Congress' authority to declare war and the president's power as
commander in chief. In this report unanimously recommending approval of
the agreement, all the committee members could say on this point was that
"nothing in this treaty . . . increases or decreases the constitutional powers

of either the President or the Congress, or changes the relationship between them." Based in part on that assurance, senators voted eighty-two to thirteen to approve the North Atlantic Treaty.[6]

In contrast to his close cooperation with Congress in designing the Truman Doctrine, the Marshall Plan, and NATO, President Truman relied primarily on his own authority in responding to the crisis in Korea in 1950. The President did not invite any legislators to the meetings he held with representatives from the Departments of State and Defense to formulate the American response to the situation. He did meet twice during the first week of the crisis with delegations from Congress, but both sessions were merely to inform the legislators of actions he had already taken. By the time he first met with the congressmen, Truman had already dispatched American air and naval units to aid the South Koreans. Similarly, the president issued orders sending American ground troops to Korea just prior to his second meeting with the legislators, and a statement announcing that decision was released while he was still conferring with them.[7]

Most legislators supported the president's actions during the initial stages of the Korean crisis, but a small group of Republican senators, led by Robert Taft of Ohio, condemned Truman's failure to seek congressional authorization or approval for the steps he had taken. Senator James Kem (R-Mo.) charged that the President had "arrogated to himself the authority of declaring war," and Senator Arthur Watkins (R-Utah) argued that Truman should have sent a message to Congress describing the situation and "asking for the authority to go ahead and do whatever was necessary." Taft conceded that Truman may have had to move quickly, but he believed the president should still request a congressional resolution sanctioning his earlier action of sending American forces to Korea. Without such legislative approval, Taft asserted, Truman's actions constituted "a complete usurpation by the President of authority to use the Armed Forces of this country."[8]

After some consideration, President Truman decided not to ask Congress for a resolution authorizing or approving his actions in Korea. Secretary of State Acheson advised that such a measure was unnecessary because the president's authority as commander in chief provided a sufficient constitutional basis for his use of the armed forces, and a State Department study cited eighty-five previous instances in which presidents had sent American troops overseas. State Department officials also claimed that the Supreme Court's decision in 1936 in *United States v. Curtiss-Wright* had clearly established that the president had the power to conduct the nation's foreign affairs.[9]

Although there is some question as to whether Truman needed congressional sanction to use the armed forces in Korea, there is *no* question that the absence of a congressional resolution came back to haunt him politically. As the American war effort bogged down and the number of casualties rose, more and more people echoed Senator Taft's charge that "this Korean War is a Truman War." They agreed with Senator Everett Dirksen (R-Ill.) that the United States was involved in "an undeclared, unconstitutional, one-man war," and they blamed the president for getting the nation into the whole mess. The Korean War would be a major campaign issue for the Republicans in 1952, and it would also lead congressmen to try in various ways to impose or enact limits on the president's powers in foreign affairs.[10]

Truman exacerbated concern over the extent of the president's powers when he announced in late 1950 that he planned to send four additional divisions of American soldiers to Western Europe. The "Great Debate" that ensued in the Senate in early 1951 focused on both the wisdom of the president's policy and whether he had the authority to take such action without the consent of Congress. When Senator Taft and Senator Kenneth Wherry (R-Neb.) criticized the president for acting unilaterally and usurping Congress' prerogatives, Truman responded at a news conference by asserting that he had the power, "recognized repeatedly by the Congress and the courts," to send American troops "anywhere in the world." In this instance, however, he promised to consult with members of the Senate Armed Services and Foreign Relations Committees, not to seek their permission, but merely as a matter of courtesy. Senators spent much of the next three months in hearings and debates before they finally approved the president's plans to transfer the troops to Europe, but they also served notice that they disagreed with Truman on the extent of his powers as commander in chief. They adopted a resolution declaring that it was "the sense of the Senate" that no additional ground troops should be sent to Western Europe "without further congressional approval."[11]

The debate over Truman's decision to send American troops to Western Europe was more significant than it appeared. A headline in the *New York Times* minimized the controversy's impact, emphasizing that American foreign policy remained unchanged. But the *Times* also pointed out in an editorial that it had been Truman's "somewhat cavalier treatment of Congress on such a vital issue" that had precipitated the debate. Moreover, Gallup Polls taken near the end of the dispute showed that 64% of those interviewed believed the president should be required to obtain Congress' consent before sending American forces overseas, and 58% thought that Congress, not the president, should determine how many troops should be transferred to Europe. These results reflected the decline in Truman's popularity because of the stalemate in Korea, but they also revealed that public concern over presidential power was growing, as was support for congressional efforts to limit executive authority in foreign affairs.[12]

When British Prime Minister Winston Churchill visited the United States and met with President Truman in January, 1952, many legislators worried that Truman might enter into secret agreements with the British leader that impinged on Congress' power to declare war. Shortly after Churchill returned to England, Representative E. Y. Berry (R.-S.D.) introduced a resolution directing the Secretary of State to transmit to the House of Representatives:

full and complete information with respect to any agreements, commitments or understandings which may have been entered into by the President of the United States and the Prime Minister of Great Britain . . . which might require the shipment of additional members of the Armed Forces of the United States beyond the continental limits of the United States or involve United States forces in armed conflict on foreign soil.

Representative John Rankin, a right-wing Democrat from Mississippi, maintained that the resolution was necessary "to protect this country and not let it be sold out by secret agreements, such as Yalta, Teheran, Potsdam and others that have dragged America down almost to the brink of ruin," and Representative John Williams (D-Miss.) asserted that "100,000 casualties in an undeclared Korean war, undeclared by the Congress, should convince every member of this House that it is his responsibility . . . to take part in, and to know as much about foreign affairs as possible." Representative James Richards (D-S.C.) warned that the measure would set a "dangerous precedent" and limit the president's ability to negotiate with allies during a crisis, but the House ignored his advice and adopted the resolution, 189–143. With the approval of the Berry resolution, a coalition of 29 Democrats, mostly from the South, and 160 Republicans had proclaimed that they would not allow President Truman to make important agreements with other nations without consulting Congress. Only one Republican—Jacob Javits of New York—had joined with the majority of the Democrats in voting against this attempt to limit the president's powers in foreign affairs.[13]

Legislators continued their efforts to impose restraints on executive autonomy in foreign affairs by pressing for the enactment of the Bricker Amendment during both the Truman and the Eisenhower administrations. First proposed by Senator John Bricker (R-Ohio) in 1951, the Bricker Amendment was aimed primarily at limiting the effects within the United States of international agreements such as the United Nations Charter, the Genocide Convention, and the UN's draft covenant on human rights. But most versions of the amendment also included restrictions on executive agreements to ensure that presidents could not evade the limitations being imposed on treaties by using executive agreements instead. By early 1953, the Bricker Amendment had more than sixty cosponsors in the Senate, including isolationists, conservative Democrats, and almost all the Republicans, as many of the measure's supporters hoped it would prevent another Yalta and force the president to consult with Congress on important foreign policy matters. But President Eisenhower opposed the amendment, fearing that it would cripple the president's authority and make it impossible for him to conduct the nation's foreign affairs, and with the help of Senators Thomas Hennings (D-Mo.), J. William Fulbright (D-Ark.), John Sherman Cooper (R-Ky.), and others, Eisenhower was able to keep the Bricker Amendment from being adopted.[14]

Shortly after the Senate rejected the Bricker Amendment, President Eisenhower had to decide whether to intervene militarily to help the French in their fight against Communist-led rebels in Indochina. Some of the president's advisers recommended immediate American intervention to relieve the pressure on the French garrison trapped at Dienbienphu, but Eisenhower refused to commit American forces to action in Vietnam without congressional sanction. He believed Congress had a legitimate role to play in making such decisions, and remembering what had happened to Truman after he had sent American forces into Korea without congressional approval, Eisenhower was determined not to make the same mistake. If he took the nation into war, he wanted to be sure that the country was behind him, and that Congress was on the record in support of his actions. Thus, when he was asked at a press conference if the United States might become engaged in a war in Indochina, Eisenhower promised that there would be "no involvement of America in war unless it is a result of the constitutional process that is placed upon Congress to declare it." And, in a telephone conversation with Secretary of State John Foster Dulles, the president insisted that it would be "completely unconstitutional and indefensible" to use American forces to assist the French without congressional approval.[15]

In accordance with Eisenhower's wishes, Dulles and Admiral Arthur Radford, the Chairman of the Joint Chiefs of Staff, met with the congressional leaders of both parties on Saturday, April 3, 1954, to discuss whether Congress would pass a joint resolution authorizing the president to employ air and naval forces as he saw fit in Southeast Asia. Dulles and Radford both emphasized that the administration had no plans to commit ground troops, but the legislators were skeptical, fearing that "once the flag was committed the use of land forces would inevitably follow." The congressmen also sought assurances that America's allies would be involved—that this would not turn into another Korea "with the United States furnishing 90% of the manpower." If the Secretary of State could get definite commitments from the British and others that they would participate, then the leaders thought a resolution could be enacted authorizing the president to employ American forces. When the British refused to go along with the proposed intervention, however, and the French refused to make any moves toward granting real independence to the Vietnamese, the president, who had always had some misgivings about the plan, dropped the idea of direct American military involvement in Indochina.[16]

In the Formosa crisis of 1955, Eisenhower again sought congressional approval before taking steps that might lead to war. The Chinese Communists on the mainland had been shelling the offshore islands of Quemoy and Matsu for months in what administration officials feared was a prelude to an attack against Chiang Kai-shek and the Chinese Nationalists on Formosa. The president believed that he probably had the legal authority to use American forces to protect Formosa, but as he told the congressional leaders, he thought it would be "foolish to try to strain to the limit my constitutional powers" when a congressional resolution would make it clear to the Communists that the nation was united in its determination to defend Formosa. Accordingly, on January 24, 1955, Eisenhower asked Congress to pass a joint resolution authorizing the president to employ the armed forces as he deemed necessary to protect Formosa and the Pescadores against armed attack. As Dulles explained to members of the Senate Armed Forces and Foreign Relations Committees, congressional approval of the resolution would show widespread support for the president's policy and increase its chances for success. Since there was "some doubt and uncertainty" over the respective powers of the executive and the legislature in such matters, the secretary recommended that Congress and the president "work together to clarify and remove any such possible doubts from the arena."[17]

Most legislators praised the president for consulting with Congress in this situation. Walter George commended Eisenhower for coming to Congress with his request, and John Bricker claimed that the joint resolution under discussion "fully vindicates the constitutional arguments of Bob Taft, myself, and others when the Senate debated the legality of the intervention in Korea and the sending of troops to Europe." By explicitly authorizing the president to commit American troops in this case, Bricker asserted, Congress would "demolish . . . the fallacious theory that the President, as Commander in Chief, has exclusive power to send Armed Forces of the United States anywhere in the world for the defense of any possible victim of aggression." This resolution, Bricker stressed, would repudiate

> lock, stock, and barrel any theory that the Congress' power to declare war is only a ministerial function—an act involving little more discretion than that of the recorder of deeds in recording a sale of real estate in the District of Columbia.[18]

A number of lawmakers argued, however, that the president already had the authority to act to protect the United States and its allies. Senators Hubert Humphrey (D-Minn.), Mike Mansfield (D-Mont.) and Estes Kefauver (D-Tenn.) all maintained that the president had the power under the Constitution to do whatever was necessary to safeguard vital American interests, and thus they would have preferred a simple sense of the Congress resolution expressing the legislature's support for the president's policy. Nonetheless, they believed they had no choice but to back the president in such a crisis, and they voted for the joint resolution.[19]

In the Senate, only William Langer (R-N.D.), Herbert Lehman (D-N.Y.), and Wayne Morse (I-Ore.) opposed the Formosa Resolution. Langer and Morse both complained that the bill was so vague that it might even be construed as authorizing the bombing of the Chinese mainland if the President decided it was necessary to do so to protect Formosa. Morse and Lehman insisted that the president already had the power to defend the United States and its interests, and they were reluctant, as Lehman explained, to give the president "a blank check of authority for acts which might be beyond his constitutional powers." Morse warned his colleagues that Congress should never "in any way delegate its power to declare war," and the senator from Oregon promised that so long as he was in the Senate, he would oppose any advance attempts "to give blanket approval to the President of the United States to proceed to commit an act of war against another nation."[20]

Langer, Lehman, and Morse were in a small minority, though, and Congress quickly passed the joint resolution that Eisenhower had requested. The measure was introduced in the House of Representatives on 24 January 1955, and that body approved it the following day by a vote of 410–3. After a short debate, the Senate went along three days later, adopting the proposal 85–3. Thus, even though a few critics had raised some important questions about the bill's implications, most lawmakers concluded that Eisenhower's asking for congressional authorization represented a tremendous improvement over Truman's unilateral decisions to send American troops to Korea and Western Europe.[21]

When the situation in the Middle East deteriorated in 1956 and 1957, President Eisenhower again consulted with Congress before taking any action. In the aftermath of the Suez crisis of 1956, administration officials feared that communist influence was growing in the Middle East, especially in Egypt, and the president hoped to stabilize the situation by serving notice that the United States would not sit by idly while the Soviet Union gained a foothold in the region. But rather than relying solely on his powers as president and commander in chief, Eisenhower chose to work with Congress, and on 5 January 1957, he asked the legislature to approve a joint resolution authorizing him to send military and financial aid and use the armed forces "as he deems necessary" to help any nation in the Middle East requesting American assistance in resisting communist aggression.[22]

Most legislators praised the president for working with Congress in this situation rather than acting unilaterally. Senator Jacob Javits (R-N.Y.) commended Eisenhower for giving Congress the opportunity to influence foreign policy in a constructive way, and Arthur Watkins emphasized that this president, in contrast to his predecessor, understood the Constitution and the limits it imposed on his prerogatives. John Bricker asserted that if the United States ended up in a war in the Middle East, at least this time there would be "unity at home and no suggestion that the war is 'unconstitutional.' "[23]

A number of legislators raised questions, however, about the Eisenhower Doctrine, as the proposal came to be known. J. William Fulbright, John Sparkman (D-Ala.), and Hubert Humphrey all argued that the president already had the authority to use the armed forces to protect American interests in the Middle East, and Fulbright charged that the resolution was really an attempt to have Congress share the blame for any disasters that might ensue.

Fulbright, Wayne Morse, Sam Ervin (D-N.C.), and Herman Talmadge (D-Ga.) also warned that the resolution, in Talmadge's words, "amounts to an undated declaration of war—a blank check to be signed by Congress and handed to the Chief Executive to fill in the date and place as he sees fit." They urged their colleagues to retain for themselves the power to decide if and when the United States would go to war.[24]

Concerned about the respective powers of Congress and the president over the armed forces, the Senate Armed Services and Foreign Relations Committees modified the measure to minimize any controversy over this issue. Instead of authorizing the president to deploy American forces as he saw fit, the senators changed the bill so that it now proclaimed that "if the President determines the necessity thereof, the United States is prepared to use armed forces" to help any nation in the Middle East resisting communist aggression. The revised resolution made clear the importance that the American government—both the president and Congress—attached to the Middle East, and it showed the readiness of the United States to intervene there militarily if necessary. It did so, however, by avoiding the question of whether the president could take such action under his own authority, or if he needed the consent of Congress.[25]

When the amended resolution reached the floor, Senate Majority Leader Lyndon Johnson (D-Tex.) explained the changes the committees had made in the bill. Johnson emphasized that the resolution submitted on behalf of the administration had "raised grave questions about the constitutional relationship between the President and the Congress." He reported that the committees had found it impossible to draw a line between the president's authority as commander in chief and Congress' power to declare war, and thus they had altered the measure to remove this problem while still warning the Communists to keep out of the Middle East.[26]

Most legislators endorsed the revised resolution. Mike Mansfield hailed it as a fine example of "responsible cooperation in foreign policy," and John Bricker maintained that "the amended text overcomes the objection that Congress is giving the President a blank check to declare war." Theodore Francis Green (D-R.I.), the chairman of the Senate Foreign Relations Committee, stressed that the new language had "the 'virtue' of avoiding a constitutional debate which might have the effect of getting an important foreign policy statement lost in a lengthy discussion of constitutional interpretation." With these sentiments predominating, Congress approved the Eisenhower Doctrine for the Middle East by an overwhelming majority.[27]

As the 1950s drew to a close, congressmen could look back with some satisfaction at the steps they had taken during the decade to strengthen their role in formulating foreign policy. In 1950 and 1951, President Truman had decided without consulting Congress to send American forces into combat in Korea and increase the number of American troops in Western Europe. Over the next few years, however, the legislators had served notice that they would not allow themselves to be bypassed or ignored on foreign policy issues. Senators had passed a resolution declaring that congressional approval would be required before additional troops could be dispatched to Europe; the House of Representatives had directed President Truman to disclose any agreements he had entered into with Churchill; and the Senate had almost adopted the Bricker Amendment to limit the use and effects of treaties and executive agreements. Subsequently, President Eisenhower had asked Congress for authorization before committing American forces in Indochina, Formosa, and the Middle East, and at the time most legislators saw the use of congressional resolutions as a major improvement over Truman's unilateral decisions to deploy American forces overseas. Only after the Gulf of Tonkin Resolution was passed in 1964 and the American commitment escalated rapidly in Vietnam would it become apparent that such resolutions were inadequate and really afforded Congress very little opportunity to influence American foreign policy.[28]

After the escalation in Vietnam in the mid-1960s, however, Senator Fulbright, Senator Javits, Senator Clifford Case (R-N.J.), and others realized that new measures were needed to restore the constitutional balance between congressional authority and presidential prerogatives in foreign affairs. President Johnson's use of the Gulf of Tonkin Resolution as a basis for sending five hundred thousand American troops to Vietnam without a declaration of war showed that congressional resolutions could in fact be utilized by presidents as "blank checks." When administration officials also cited the SEATO treaty, congressional appropriations, and the president's powers as commander in chief as additional bases for Johnson's escalation of the war, and Johnson sent twenty thousand American troops to the Dominican Republic in 1965, Fulbright feared that the president and his advisers had concluded that they could, on their own initiative, commit American forces anywhere in the world. Fulbright decided that something had to be done to reestablish Congress' role in formulating foreign policy, and in the summer of 1967, he introduced a sense of the Senate resolution declaring that "a national commitment by the United States" to another nation could only be made by the president and Congress acting together through a treaty or legislation "specifically intended to give effect to such a commitment." With this resolution, Fulbright was challenging the view that the president could unilaterally commit the nation to act in various contingencies, and arguing instead that congressional concurrence was necessary before any binding commitments could be made.[29]

In 1969, in an attempt to reaffirm and reestablish Congress' constitutional responsibilities and prerogatives in foreign affairs, the Senate approved a modified version of Fulbright's National Commitments Resolution. The final bill defined a national commitment as "a promise to assist a foreign country, government, or people by the use of the Armed Forces or financial resources of the United States," and proclaimed that it was the sense of the Senate that such a commitment required legislative sanction by means of a treaty, statute, or concurrent resolution specifically endorsing the commitment. Senators Fulbright, Javits, Ervin, and others all emphasized that this measure was needed to ensure that executive agreements, presidential letters and statements, or the presence of American troops or military bases in such places as Spain and Thailand, could not later be cited as American commitments to defend various nations. Senator Javits described the resolution as an expression of the Senate's "determination not to yield" its constitutional powers in foreign affairs, and Senator John Stennis (D-Miss.) urged his colleagues to support this effort "to reassert the congressional responsibility in any decision to commit our Armed Forces to hostilities abroad." Most senators agreed with Stennis that this was a necessary first step if Congress were to regain its "coequal role in foreign relations," and they voted seventy to sixteen to adopt the National Commitments Resolution.[30]

Congress took the second step in December, 1969, when it approved an amendment sponsored by Senator Frank Church (D-Idaho), Senator Javits, and others that prohibited the expenditure of funds to introduce American ground combat troops into Laos or Thailand. As Church explained to his colleagues, the amendment was designed to reassert Congress' authority "as a part of the constitutional process in determining questions of war and peace and the nature of the foreign policy of the United States." Specifically, he stressed, the measure would protect the country against getting involved in a war in Laos or Thailand without the consent of Congress. Unfortunately, the Cambodian incursion in 1970 would show that Congress had picked the wrong countries, but nonetheless, the enactment of the Church Amendment represented another attempt by Congress to reestablish its role in formulating the nation's foreign policy.[31]

Subsequently, when Senator Javits first proposed the War Powers Resolution in June, 1970, he was not working in a legislative vacuum. There were various precursors and precedents from the last twenty years, as senators ranging from Robert Taft and John Bricker to Frank Church and J. William Fulbright had tried during the 1950s and 1960s to limit executive autonomy in foreign affairs. For a while during the Eisenhower years their efforts had succeeded, but the escalation in Vietnam, the intervention in the Dominican Republic, and the growing tendency of presidents to make commitments on behalf of the nation had made it clear by the late 1960s that new measures were needed to restore the original balance of power between the president and Congress that the Founding Fathers had intended. Under the leadership of Senator Fulbright, Senator Javits, Senator Church, and others, the Senate by 1970 had already adopted the National Commitments Resolution, and Congress had prohibited the introduction of American ground troops into Laos or Thailand. These moves to reassert Congress' constitutional role in the foreign policy-making process helped pave the way for the introduction of the War Powers Resolution.

NOTES

1. In 1967, for example, Under Secretary of State Nicholas Katzenbach, testifying before the Senate Committee on Foreign Relations, asserted that Congress' power to declare war was "outmoded in the international arena." See U.S., Congress, Senate, Committee on Foreign Relations, *U.S. Commitments to Foreign Powers, Hearings*, before the Senate Committee on Foreign Relations, 90th Cong. 1st sess., 1967, p. 81. By 1969, most of the members of the Senate Committee on Foreign Relations were complaining that there had developed in recent years a "dangerous tendency toward executive supremacy in foreign policy." See U.S., Congress, Senate, Committee on Foreign Relations, *National Commitments*, 91st Cong. 1st sess., 16 April 1969, S. Rept. 91–129, 10.

2. Arthur Schlesinger, Jr., popularized the phrase "The Imperial Presidency" with his book so entitled in 1973. See Arthur Schlesinger, Jr., *The Imperial Presidency* (Boston: Houghton Mifflin Company, 1973).

3. See Arthur Vandenberg, Jr., ed., *The Private Papers of Senator Vandenberg* (Boston: Houghton Mifflin Company, 1952), 337–52, 373–98; Dean Acheson, *Present at the Creation: My Years in the State Department* (New York: W. W. Norton & Company, Inc., 1969), 217–35; and Joseph Jones, *The Fifteen Weeks* (New York: Viking Press, 1955).

4. See *New York Times*, 6 Feb. 1949, 1, 37.

5. Acheson, *Creation*, 280–81; Vandenberg, *Private Papers*, 476–80; and *New York Times*, 21 Jan. 1949, 4; 10 Feb. 1949, 1, 7; 16 Feb. 1949, 1; 17 Feb. 1949, 4; and 19 Feb. 1949, 1, 4. See also Article 5 and Article 11 of the North Atlantic Treaty, reprinted in *Department of State Bulletin*, XX (20 Mar. 1949), 339–42.

6. *New York Times*, 26 Mar. 1949, 4; 5 June 1949, 12; 7 June 1949, 1, 3; and 8 June 1949, 1, 4; U.S., Congress, Senate, Committee on Foreign Relations, 81st Cong. 1st sess., 6 June 1949, S. Exec. Rept. 8, printed in 95 *Congressional Record* 9816–9824, 1949, esp. 9820; 95 *Congressional Record* 9915–16; and *New York Times*, 22 July 1949, 1, 2. (All citations to the *Congressional Record* are to the bound volumes.)

7. See Glenn Paige, *The Korean Decision* (New York: Free Press, 1968); Acheson, *Creation*, 402–15; and George Elsey's Notes of the Meeting on Korea with the Congressional Leaders, 30 June 1950, Elsey Papers, Box 71, Harry S. Truman Library.

8. 96 *Congressional Record* 9228 (Kem), 9233 (Watkins), and 9323 (Taft), 1950.

9. Acheson, *Creation*, 414–15; and U.S., Department of State, "Authority of the President to Repel the Attack in Korea," 3 July 1950, reprinted in U.S., Congress,

House, Committee on Foreign Affairs, *Background Information on Korea*, 81st Cong. 2d sess., 11 July 1950, H. Rept. 2495, 61–68. See also *United States v. Curtiss-Wright Export Corporation et al.*, 299 U.S. 304 (1936).

10. For the quotations from Taft and Dirksen, see *New York Times*, 23 Oct. 1951, 12, and 11 July 1952, 6. See also Senator Vandenberg to Senator Lodge, 26 Feb. 1951, in Vandenberg, *Private Papers*, 572–73; and Dean Acheson to Felix Frankfurter, 30 July 1953, Frankfurter Papers, Box 19, Library of Congress. On the importance of Korea as an issue in the 1952 election, see Barton Bernstein, "Election of 1952," in Arthur Schlesinger, Jr. and Fred Israel, eds., *History of American Presidential Elections* (4 vols.; New York: Chelsea House Publishers, 1971), IV: 3260; Angus Campbell, Philip Converse, Warren Miller, and Donald Stokes, *The American Voter*, abridged ed., (New York: John Wiley and Sons, Inc., 1964), 20; and Ronald Caridi, *The Korean War and American Politics: The Republican Party as a Case Study* (Philadelphia: University of Pennsylvania Press, 1968), 209–45.

11. *New York Times*, 10 Sep. 1950, 1, and 20 Dec. 1950, 1; 97 *Congressional Record* 54–61 (Taft), and 94 (Wherry), 1951; S. Res. 8, 82d Cong. 1st sess., 8 Jan. 1951; President's News Conference, 11 Jan. 1951, in *Public Papers of the Presidents: Harry S. Truman, 1951*, 18–22; *New York Times*, 12 Jan. 1951, 1, 8; U.S., Congress, Senate, Committee on Foreign Relations and Committee on Armed Services, *Assignment of Ground Forces of the United States to Duty in the European Area, Hearings*, before the Committee on Foreign Relations and the Committee on Armed Services, Senate, 82d Cong. 1st sess., 1951; U.S., Congress, Senate, Committee on Foreign Relations, *Executive Sessions of the Senate Foreign Relations Committee* (Historical Series), Vol. III, Part 1, 82d Cong. 1st sess., *1951* (made public in 1976), 1–7, 63–100, 103–258, and 299–342; *New York Times*, 26 Feb. 1951, 1, 10, and 9 Mar. 1951, 1, 4; S. Res. 99, 82d Cong. 1st sess., 14 Mar. 1951; U.S., Congress, Senate, Committee on Foreign Relations and Committee on Armed Services, *Assignment of Ground Forces of the United States to Duty in the European Area*, 82d Cong. 1st sess., 14 March 1951, S. Rept. 175; 97 *Congressional Record* 3075, 3096, and 3282; and *New York Times*, 3 April 1951, 1, 4, and 5 April 1951, 1, 12, 13. See also David Kepley, "The Senate and the Great Debate of 1951," *Prologue*, XIV (Winter 1982): 213–226.

12. *New York Times*, 8 April 1951, IV, 3; Editorial, *New York Times*, 4 April 1951, 24; and Gallup Poll results reported in *Washington Post*, 4 April 1951, 5.

13. H. Res. 54, 82d Cong. 2d sess., 31 Jan. 1952; 98 *Congressional Record* 739 (Berry), and 1205–15 (Rankin, Williams, and Richards), 1952; and *New York Times*, 21 Feb. 1952, 1, 3. See also S. Res. 371, 81st Cong. 2d sess., 6 Dec. 1950; 96 *Congressional Record* 16173 (Senator Kem); S. Res. 246, 82d Cong. 2d sess., 14 Jan. 1952; and 98 *Congressional Record* 110–11 (Senator Hugh Butler) for similar resolutions proposed in the Senate in 1950 and 1952.

14. See S. J. Res. 102, 82d Cong. 1st sess., 14 Sep. 1951; S. J. Res. 1, 83d Cong. 1st sess., 7 Jan. 1953; Dwight Eisenhower to Edgar Eisenhower, 27 Mar. 1953, and 12 Jan. 1954, Dwight Eisenhower Papers, Diary Series, Dwight D. Eisenhower Library; U.S., Congress, Senate, Committee on the Judiciary, *Treaties and Executive Agreements, Hearings,* before the Senate Committee on the Judiciary,

83d Cong. 1st sess., 1953; U.S., Congress, Senate, Committee on the Judiciary, *Constitutional Amendment Relative to Treaties and Executive Agreements*, 83d Cong. 1st sess., 15 June 1953, S. Rept. 412; 100 *Congressional Record* 2262, 2374–75, 1954; and *New York Times*, 27 Feb. 1954, 1, 8. See also Duane Tananbaum, "The Bricker Amendment Controversy: Its Origins and Eisenhower's Role," *Diplomatic History* IX (Winter 1985): 73–93; and Tananbaum, "The Bricker Amendment Controversy: The Interaction Between Domestic and Foreign Affairs" (Ph.D. diss., Columbia University, 1980).

15. President's News Conference, 10 Mar. 1954, in *Public Papers: Eisenhower, 1954*, 306; and Memorandum of telephone call, Dulles to the President, 5 April 1954, in U.S., Department of State, *Foreign Relations of the United States, 1952–54*, XIII, *Indochina*, 1241–42. See also George Herring, *America's Longest War: The United States and Vietnam, 1950–1975* (New York: John Wiley & Sons, 1979), 28–36.

16. See Dulles, Memorandum of conversation with the president, 2 April 1954, and Draft of Joint Resolution, 2 April 1954; Memorandum for the file of the Secretary of State, 5 April 1954, *Re*: Conference with Congressional Leaders Concerning Crisis in Southeast Asia, 3 April 1954; and Memorandum of telephone conversation between the president and the Secretary of State, 3 April 1954; all in *Foreign Relations, 1952–54*, XIII, 1211–12, 1224–25, and 1230. See also Memorandum of discussion at the 192d Meeting of the National Security Council, 6 April 1954, in *Foreign Relations, 1952–54*, XIII, 1250–65, esp. 1254; James Hagerty Diary, April 26 and June 28, 1954, in Robert Ferrell, ed., *The Diary of James C. Hagerty: Eisenhower in Mid-Course, 1954–1955* (Bloomington: Indiana University Press, 1983), 48–49 and 79–80; Chalmers Roberts, "The Day We Didn't Go to War," The *Reporter*, 14 Sep. 1954, 31–35; Herring, *America's Longest War*, 28–38; and Stephen Ambrose, *Eisenhower*; Vol. II: *The President* (New York: Simon and Schuster, 1984), 173–185.

17. Hagerty Diary, 25 Jan. 1955, in Ferrell, ed., *Hagerty Diary*, 173–74; and U.S., Congress, Senate, Committee on Foreign Relations, *Executive Sessions of the Senate Foreign Relations Committee* (Historical Series), Vol. VII, 84th Cong. 1st sess., 1955 (made public in 1978), 87, 127. See also S. J. Res. 28, 84th Cong. 1st sess., 24 Jan. 1955; Summaries of telephone calls, Senator Knowland to the President, 21 Jan. 1955, and Secretary Dulles to the President, 25 Jan. 1955, both in Eisenhower Papers, Diary Series; and Ambrose, *Eisenhower: The President*, 212–14, and 231–45.

18. See 101 *Congressional Record* 819–21 (George) and 953–54 (Bricker), 1955. See also the comments by Senator H. Alexander Smith (R-N.J.) in ibid., 823; and by Representatives Charles Halleck (R-Ind.) in Hagerty Diary, 25 Jan. 1955, in Ferrell, ed., *Hagerty Diary*, 174.

19. 101 *Congressional Record* 929–30 (Humphrey); 974–75 (Mansfield); and 991 (Kefauver). See also Summary of telephone call, House Minority Leader Joseph Martin and Speaker of the House Sam Rayburn to President Eisenhower, 20 Jan. 1955, Eisenhower Papers, Diary Series.

20. 101 *Congressional Record* 940 (Langer); 929 and 841 (Morse); and 992 (Lehman).

21. See H. J. Res. 159, 84th Cong. 1st sess., 24 Jan. 1955; S. J. Res. 28, 84th Cong., 1st sess., 24 Jan. 1955; U.S., Congress, Senate, Committee on Foreign Relations, *Authorizing the President to Employ the Armed Forces of the United States for Protecting the Security of Formosa, the Pescadores, and Related Positions and Territories of that Area*, 84th Cong. 1st sess., 26 Jan. 1955, S. Rept. 13; and 101 *Congressional Record* 680–81 and 994.

22. See Eisenhower to Dulles, 12 Dec. 1956; and Summaries of telephone calls, Eisenhower to Dulles, December 8 and December 28, 1956; all in Eisenhower Papers, Diary Series; White House Press Release, 1 Jan. 1957, Eisenhower Papers, OF99Q; U.S., Congress, House, *Middle East Situation*, Address of the President of the United States delivered before a Joint Session of Congress, 5 Jan. 1957, 85th Cong. 1st sess., 5 Jan. 1957, H. Doc. 46; H. J. Res. 117, 85th Cong. 1st sess., 5 Jan. 1957; and President's News Conference, 23 Jan. 1957, in *Public Papers: Eisenhower, 1957*, 86–87. See also Ambrose, *Eisenhower: The President*, 314–18, 328–34, 338–40, 350–54, 356–73, and 381–88.

23. See 103 *Congressional Record* 2594–98 (Javits) and 3023–26 (Watkins), 1957; and John Bricker, Memorandum on the Eisenhower Middle East Doctrine, 5 Mar. 1957, Bricker Papers, Box 128, Ohio Historical Society.

24. See 103 *Congressional Record* 1855–59, 1868–69 (Fulbright); 1859 (Sparkman); 1864 (Humphrey); 1858–59, 2310 (Morse); 2314 (Ervin); and 2518 (Talmadge).

25. See U.S., Congress, Senate, Committee on Foreign Relations and Committee on Armed Services, *To Promote Peace and Stability in the Middle East*, 85th Cong. 1st sess., 14 Feb. 1957, S. Rept. 70, esp. 8–9.

26. 103 *Congressional Record* 2230–31.

27. 103 *Congressional Record* 3129 (Mansfield) and 2232 (Green); and Bricker, Memorandum on the Eisenhower Middle East Doctrine, 5 Mar. 1957, Bricker Papers, Box 128. For approval of the resolution in the House and the Senate, see 103 *Congressional Record* 1323–24, 3129.

28. On the Gulf of Tonkin Resolution, P.L. 88–408, see S. J. Res. 189, 88th Cong. 2d sess., August 5, 1964; U.S., Congress, Senate, Committee on Foreign Relations and Committee on Armed Services, *Southeast Asia Resolution, Hearing*, before the Committee on Foreign Relations and the Committee on Armed Services, Senate, 88th Cong. 2d sess., 1964; U.S., Congress, Senate, Committee on Foreign Relations, *Promoting the Maintenance of International Peace and Security in Southeast Asia*, 88th Cong. 2d sess., 6 Aug. 1964, S. Rept. 1299; U.S., Congress, Senate, Committee on Foreign Relations, *The Gulf of Tonkin: The 1964 Incidents, Hearings*, before the Senate Committee on Foreign Relations, 90th Cong. 2d sess., 1968; Herring, *America's Longest War*, 122–23; and John Galloway, *The Gulf of Tonkin Resolution* (Rutherford, N.J.: Fairleigh Dickinson University Press, 1970).

29. See S. Res. 151, 90th Cong. 1st sess., 31 July 1967; and Senator Fulbright's remarks in U.S., Congress, Senate, Committee on Foreign Relations, *U.S. Commitments to Foreign Powers, Hearings*, before the Senate Committee on Foreign Relations, 90th Cong. 1st sess., 1967, p. 1. On administration officials citing the Gulf of

Tonkin Resolution, the SEATO treaty, appropriations bills, and the president's authority as commander in chief as bases for Johnson's escalation of American involvement
in the war in Vietnam, see President Johnson to the Speaker of the House of Representatives, 19 Jan. 1966, and Attorney General Nicholas Katzenbach to the president, 19 Feb. 1966, both in Lyndon Johnson Papers, White House Central File ND19/
CO312, Lyndon B. Johnson Library; Testimony of Secretary of State Dean Rusk
before the Senate Committee on Foreign Relations, reported in *New York Times*,
19 Feb. 1966, 1–3; Leonard Meeker, Legal Advisor, Department of State, "The
Legality of United States Participation in the Defense of Viet-Nam," *Department of
State Bulletin,* LIV (28 Mar. 1966), 474–89, esp. 484–88; and President's News
Conference, 18 Aug. 1967, in *Public Papers: Johnson, 1967,* 794–95. Testifying
during the hearings on Fulbright's proposal, now Under Secretary of State Katzenbach
claimed that the Gulf of Tonkin Resolution, combined with the SEATO treaty, constituted "the functional equivalent" of a declaration of war. See *U.S. Commitments
to Foreign Powers, Hearings*, before the Senate Committee on Foreign Relations,
90th Cong. 1st sess., 1967, p. 82. On Senator Fulbright's opposition to American
policy in the Dominican Republic and his growing concern over executive domination
of American foreign policy, see also *New York Times*, 16 Sep. 1965, 1, 16, and
20 July 1967, 5; and J. William Fulbright, *The Arrogance of Power* (New York:
Vintage Books, 1966), esp. chaps. 2–4.

   30. See 115 *Congressional Record* 17245, 1969 for the final text of S. Res.
85 as approved by the Senate, and the vote on the resolution. See also U.S., Congress,
Senate, Committee on Foreign Relations, *National Commitments*, 91st Cong. 1st sess.,
16 April 1969, S. Rept. 91–129; Mike Mansfield to Everett Dirksen, 20 May 1969,
copy in George Aiken Papers, Crate 19, Box 1, University of Vermont Library; and
115 *Congressional record* 17214–45 for the final debate on the measure, esp. 17214–
18 (Ervin), 17218–19 (Javits), 17228–33 and 17239 (Fulbright), and 17241–42 (Stennis).

   31. See 115 *Congressional Record* 39145–73 for the debate on the Cooper-
Mansfield Amendment to H.R. 15090, the 1970 Defense Appropriations Bill, esp.
39160 and 39168–72 for the remarks by Senator Church and the debate on his amendment to the original amendment. Senators Javits, Allott (R-Col.), Cranston (D-Cal.),
McClellan (D-Ark.), and Baker (R-Tenn.) joined with Senator Church in offering the
amendment.

3

The Debate over the War Powers Resolution

SENATOR JACOB K. JAVITS

Thank you very much Dean Neuberger and thank you Professor Tananbaum for a magnificent exposition of a precedent which dictated my own activity, which had many partners and is, however, my proudest achievement in 32 years in the Congress, although history may decide otherwise. I give you my opinion of my own work, and I am very grateful to Dr. Sullivan for joining us to assess the impact of that U.S. law to exactly what I emphasize that it is. The president who violates that law is violating a law he or she has sworn to uphold and that is a very important point.

Whatever one says about the War Powers Resolution, it is there on the books as much a law of the United States and the president who violates it runs the same risk that Richard Nixon took when he violated the law and became the first president who had to resign. As a result, I have no other message to leave to those who follow than that one.

Now to be elementary I wish to restate what the War Powers Resolution, passed over the veto of President Nixon in the fall of 1973, states. In effect, it says "that the President of the United States as Commander-in-Chief does not have the power to commit the nation to war except with the consent of a majority of both Houses of the Congress and the debate begins there."

Professor Tananbaum has vividly described the struggle of other senators and myself, to somehow balance the authority given by the Constitution for the Congress to declare war and for the president to direct the Armed Forces.

In my judgment there is no other umpire in this struggle than the people. It is a political struggle. I do not believe it can be settled in the Supreme Court but only in the forum of the voting public to whom both the Congress and the president are responsible. The Constitution leaves this question in exactly that twilight zone, and I am entirely satisfied that is where it should be. My efforts, so long as I live, will be to persuade the Congress that the people, who suffer and pay and die in war, are entitled in this awesome question of peace and war to have a joint decision of the Congress and of the president. That's the long and the short of it.

The reason I have lent myself over all those decades to sustaining the power of the president to negotiate in foreign affairs is because I believe that to uphold the power of the Congress in its domain as the Constitution provides, I must also uphold the power of the president as to foreign policy negotiations in his domain as well. I pay great tribute to Senators like Church, Fulbright, Case, Cooper, McGovern, Taft and others, who have been men of Congress like I have, who will fight for and support these principles.

Now the subject of my presentation is the debate that took place over the War Powers Resolution and that includes why I compromised, because I did, and I will explain the compromise and why I decided to do it. The origin of a resolution introduced by me in 1970 was the failure of what we had done before to enable us to, as Lincoln said, "disenthrall ourselves" from the Vietnam disaster. Aside from the precedent of the Fulbright and Case Commitments Resolution, the Congress saw the oncoming disaster militarily as well as socially, politically and economically of the Vietnam War—which President Johnson, otherwise responsible for great things like the war on poverty, did not realize was dangerously jeopardizing our country—a conviction to which I had come in 1967 after first believing in the ideal of supporting resistance to communist adventurism under the rubric "Wars of National Liberation."

In the period between 1969 and 1971, we tried in the Congress two approaches to end the bloodletting and the other dangers of Vietnam. By the way, I spoke of the social and political danger because the escalation of inflation was very heavily attributable to the enormous expenditure of that war for which there was no adequate taxation. Now this was a great error by President Johnson. In that time we had tried two alternatives in the Congress to stop the war. One was to deny authority and that was the approach of the so-called Church-Cooper Amendment. The other was to cut off the money and that was the approach of the Hatfield-McGovern Amendment. The president was able to frustrate both. He did command our troops and it would be anarchy to assume otherwise, so he either disregarded or circumvented our effort to cut off his authority and that was true of both Johnson and Nixon. He had other money in the pipeline so when we cut it off at position A, he dipped into the public purse from position B.

We were frustrated and I devoted my thinking and that of my wonderful staff to a way out. I chose a methodology and that was to prescribe by statute the means by which the Constitution could be implemented with the Congress having the veto and the president having the power to make war when Congress let him do so and not before. Now this takes a good deal of adjusting and the Senate passed in 1971 an admirable version of the War Powers Resolution. This version spelled out what were the president's powers as commander in chief in the deployment of our Armed Forces and gave his power under four headings: to defend our nation in its states and possessions; to defend our Armed Forces wherever they were; to implement the directions of Congress as to initiating war; and to protect, defend and rescue U.S. citizens in danger wherever they might be.

Now the House was ambivalent on this subject and the furthest they went was to author a resolution requiring consultation and report by the president, as to whether he was deploying our armed forces under circumstances which could lead to conflict. This was completely unsatisfactory to the Senate and a great number of senators had lined up with me on the Senate bill.

Senator Stennis of Mississippi who was then Chairman of the Armed Services Committee, Senator Spong of Virginia, as well as Cooper and Case and many others felt, as I did, that the Senate's was our best version. The sequel was that in 1971 and in 1972 nothing happened, not even a House or Senate conference got anywhere, but by 1973, the situation surrounding President Nixon began to get worse and when the disaster of the Vietnam War began to shake government itself, the matter was brought to issue between the Senate and the House.

Clement Zablocki, then Chairman of the House Foreign Affairs Committee and Dante Fascell, who was a congressman from Florida, who is now the Chairman, acting as the focal point of the House position, offered a compromise. The compromise was to accept the House bill insofar as reporting to the Congress was concerned and to accept the Senate bill, as to the power to implement congressional authority to veto war but to omit, in effect, the specification of the powers of the president in respect to defending the country and the Armed Forces, etc., which were in the Senate bill. The best I could do with that was to get a recital of those facts in the preliminary Section 2 of the law. I had to decide at that time whether I would be for it or against it. It was a hard decision but in consultation with my principal cosponsor in the Senate, Senator Stennis, we agreed to do it and for the first time in the history of our country to put such a law upon the books.

Obviously, the fashion of declaring war as we did in World Wars I and II may be obsolete. Nowadays and since World War II, conflict does not happen that way. There is no formality about it. We slip into it slowly but surely and it gets very fuzzy at the end. As Professor Tananbaum has already told us, no president wants to give up that power. Eisenhowers or generals who understand the dreadful penalty, cruelty and barbarism of war don't come along every Wednesday and so some new definition of authority is essential and that is what the War Powers Resolution is about.

Now presidents, since Jefferson sent the U.S. Navy after the Barbary pirates in the early years of the nineteenth century, don't like to give up any power and that goes up until today with our very popular President Reagan in Nicaragua. Congress has only very recently understood this question of authority but we now have a law which we never had before. I will do everything I can to see that Congress has the guts to use it as I believe the Founding Fathers intended in protecting our people in accordance with modern demands against the scourge of war. That is what it is all about and that is how it came to be.

4

The Impact of the War
Powers Resolution

JOHN H. SULLIVAN

More than twelve years after the final passage of the War Powers Resolution, the Vietnam War is the subject of memory and memoirs. Watergate for most of our university students is not a personal trauma but a topic for American history class. Three other men have held the presidency since Congress overrode President Nixon's veto of the War Powers Resolution and made it law. The intervening years also have wrought significant changes in the U.S. Congress. Gone from the Senate are such major figures as Senators Javits and Mansfield, Fulbright and Muskie. In fact, of the seventy-five senators who voted to override the Nixon veto, only twenty-six still serve. The House of Representatives presents the same picture: Gone are most of the men who made the War Powers Resolution—Zablocki, Findley, and Bingham—along with seventy-two percent of the 244 who voted "aye" on the veto override.

Given the passage of time and major changes in personnel and circumstances, other landmark enactments of the same period have been expunged. The Hughes-Ryan Amendment of 1974, which required congressional notification of secret CIA operations, had been repealed by 1980. The 1975 Clark Amendment forbidding clandestine U.S. aid to rebels in Angola was struck by Congress just last summer. We live in an era in which the House can decide by sizeable majority one day that it does not wish to aid the *contras* in Nicaragua and within a month reverse itself completely. As with glory, these days "sic transit" legislation.

Since the War Powers Resolution was enacted in 1973, critics have predicted its demise. A *Washington Star* editorial suggested that the resolution was reminiscent of the frown of a vanished Cheshire cat, as the mood that produced it faded from memory.[1] (Ironically, the *Star* is now defunct; the resolution is not.) In an article entitled "The War Powers Flop," two political scientists observed that "the . . . act has seemingly been forgotten since the resignation of President Nixon."[2] Yale University law professor Charles L. Black, Jr. labeled it "a museum piece."[3] And former President Gerald Ford has told audiences, "the day will come when the Congress will regret that legislation."[4]

These critics have had their allies on Capitol Hill. Senator Tower of Texas, writing in *Foreign Affairs* called the resolution "the most potentially damaging of the 1970's legislation." His Arizona Republican colleague Barry Goldwater has seen it as "probably the most unconstitutional measure Congress has ever passed . . ."[5]

Despite the passage of the time and personalities, the arguments of its detractors, the intentions of those who would amend it, the action of the courts, and perceived vagaries in its application, the War Powers Resolution remains today exactly as it was enacted twelve years ago. My thesis is that it has survived because it has had a clearly demonstrable impact in three closely related areas:

- First, as durable symbol of congressional resurgence in the exercise of war-making powers;
- Second, as a mechanism to facilitate congressional reaction to international crisis; and
- Third, as an effective, if erratic, constraint on presidential decisions to commit U.S. armed forces into combat.

Let us review each of these impacts:

THE WAR POWERS RESOLUTION AS SYMBOL

The symbolic importance of the War Powers Resolution has been noted by many observers. To James Sundquist of the Brookings Institution, the resolution is a "symbol of the Congressional resurgence" in foreign affairs, an event of major political significance: "Viewed in the perspective of history," Sundquist said, "the changes wrought by a single Congress—the 93rd—are truly momentous."[6] In their book on Congress and foreign policy, Franck and Weisband saw it having "major symbolic and institutional significance."[7] In his 1975 book Senator—soon to be Vice President—Walter Mondale stressed the symbolic importance of the War Powers Resolution to a Congress "seeking to reassert its coordinated power over the basic decisions affecting the course of our Nation."[8] Perhaps the most evocative testimonial to the symbolic importance of the resolution has come, not from one of its supporters, but from a longtime, avowed opponent. "The War Powers Act," Senator John Tower of Texas told the Senate in 1980, ". . . is like motherhood and Sunday school and apple pie, something you just cannot vote against."[9]

Tower spoke from experience, having seen the Senate—over his opposition—repeatedly reaffirm the symbolism of the resolution. Several notable occasions warrant review:

1. The Exon Amendment

The first is an amendment offered in the Senate to the fiscal 1981 military procurement authorization bill. Strongly supported by the Carter administration, this legislation contained funds to create a rapid deployment force, capable of projecting American military power into areas long distances from traditional U.S. military bases. This mobile strike force had been a controversial item in Congress for a number of years and had been opposed successfully by the former Chairman of the Senate Armed Services Committee, Richard Russell, on the grounds that, "If Americans find it easy to go anywhere and do anything, they will always be going there and doing something."[10] Seen from that perspective, the bill was a test of continued congressional interest in placing checks on presidential war making.

James Exon, a freshman Democrat from Nebraska who had not been in Congress in 1973, warned his colleagues that authorizing the force was tantamount to giving the president new war-making instruments. Prudence, he suggested, warranted a reaffirmation of the War Powers Resolution. His amendment language called the resolution a "significant safeguard" against misinterpretation of U.S. foreign and defense policies and expressed the sense of Congress that its provisions be "strictly adhered to" and that its consultation processes be used meaningfully.[11]

The resolution's traditional opponents like Senator Tower vigorously opposed the Exon Amendment: "I cannot think of a more supine and cowardly signal to send to friend and foe alike," the Texan averred.[12] Even Senator Javits had doubts about the utility of the provision.[13] As he often had with the original War Powers Resolution, Senator John Stennis of Mississippi carried the day. As a supporter of the 1973 Resolution, Stennis said, he believed the concept should be reaffirmed again and again: "The way to keep it bright is like . . . the plow that becomes rusted if it is not used. If you plow the soil with it, it will become bright and shine."[14] The Exon Amendment would keep the War Powers Resolution bright and shiny, Stennis suggested, and he supported it. A few minutes later the Senate also did, 54 to 35. Subsequently the House agreed and the Exon Amendment became law.

2. The Sinai Multinational Force

One year later, the War Powers Resolution was reaffirmed once again as the Congress faced a decision to contribute American military units to a multinational force (MFO) to monitor the Israeli withdrawal from the Sinai under the Camp David agreements. A central issue in congressional consideration of the force was its relationship to the War Powers Resolution. On both sides of Capitol Hill, witnesses were questioned closely on the issue. The House accepted administration reassurances; the Senate did not. Senator Charles Percy, Chairman of the Senate Foreign Relations Committee, championed an amendment stating explicitly that the MFO authorization in no way affected "the responsibilities of the President or the Congress under the War Powers Resolution . . ."[15] Chairman Percy defended the amendment on the grounds that it was necessary to make clear that the MFO bill did not supersede or otherwise affect the resolution. The Senate agreed on a voice vote, House conferees readily accepted it, and the version passed both bodies on December 16, 1981. Stennis' plow was being kept shiny.

3. The Lebanon Resolution

More recent demonstrations of the symbolic importance of the War Powers Resolution occurred during the 1983 confrontation between Congress and the executive branch over the use of U.S. armed forces in Lebanon in the wake of the Israeli invasion. During the summer of 1982 President Reagan had provided a contingent of some 800 Marines to a Multinational Force (MNF) that was to undertake peace-keeping activities in Beirut. At the time, the president emphasized that there was "no intention or expectation that U.S. Armed Forces will become involved in hostilities."[16] Months passed without significant hostilities but by August 1983 fighting involving the Marines was escalating rapidly. The president sent another message to Congress on August 30 reporting the death of two Marines and the wounding of 14, victims of small arms fire.[17] Within two weeks the U.S. rules of engagement had been broadened to permit the Marines to call in artillery and air strikes to defend their positions. The White House, however, failed to send Congress the kind of report that triggers the War Powers Resolution. Almost immediately strong reactions resulted on Capitol Hill. Significantly, the congressional debate was not primarily about *whether* to enforce the resolution, but *how*. One group favored a cutoff of funds for the Lebanon peace-keeping activities unless the president invoked it; another group wanted to negotiate new legislation under the resolution that would let Congress codetermine policy. At first the Executive balked, but facing threats of a congressional revolt, agreed to what became known as the "Multinational Force in Lebanon Resolution."[18] I will deal with that resolution and its relationship to the War Powers Resolution in more depth later. Its importance here is the vehicle it provided for the symbolic celebration of the War Powers Resolution as each camp sought to embrace it more faithfully than the other. As a result, the debate, particularly in the Senate, made for some unusual bedfellows and sometimes tortured reasoning. Senator Stennis, a coauthor of the War Power Resolution and the advocate of its reaffirmation, opposed the Lebanon Resolution which reaffirmed the War Powers Resolution. On the other hand, his fellow Democrat Thomas Eagleton of Missouri—a strenuous foe of the War Powers Resolution as enacted—applauded its application but then voted against the Lebanon Resolution. Senator Howard Baker of Tennessee, acknowledging that he had been one of eighteen senators in 1973 voting against the War Powers Resolution, said he now respected it as law and believed in the Lebanon Resolution ". . . we have done something precious . . ." because it invoked the earlier War Powers Enactment.[19] Senator Goldwater, an unremitting opponent of the War Power Resolution, joined Baker in voting for the Lebanon Resolution, which passed the Senate 54 to 46. Clearly other political dynamics also were involved; yet the verbal endorsements of the War Powers Resolution from many sides is striking: they recall Senator Tower's allusions to motherhood and Sunday school and apple pie.

THE WAR POWERS RESOLUTION AS MECHANISM

Clearly, however, a law can have enormous symbolic importance and yet be impotent. Witness the Logan Act. Passed in 1799 to punish private U.S. citizens who treat politically with foreign powers and rediscovered periodically in Congress as a way to deal with the likes of Jane Fonda and Jesse Jackson, the law never once has been enforced. Is the War Powers Resolution, as some critics have suggested, a similar toothless tiger?

Part of the answer lies in the efficacy of the mechanisms the Congress established in the legislation to insure timely consultation and codetermination of policy. The resolution's sponsors—men like Jacob Javits and Clem Zablocki—recognized that its importance would be in putting in place the legislative machinery to permit Congress to respond in an appropriate and timely fashion to its constitutional responsibilities in future crisis situations. The reputed success or failure of that machinery has been discussed in dozens of books, monographs, newspaper items and articles in political science quarterlies and legal journals.[20] Many of them have contained detailed prescriptions for improving the language, content and impact of the statute. In fact, the resolution seems to have spawned a minor cottage industry of self-ordained reformers.

When the smoke of the rhetoric has cleared, nevertheless, the War Powers Resolution has emerged intact, the durability of its machinery evidenced by:

- Its frequent emulation in other legislative enactments.
- The unwillingness of the courts to tamper with its processes.
- The lack of success of critics in repealing or amending it, and
- Its frequent use to reassert congressional war powers.

1. Emulation In Other Legislation

Since its passage the War Powers Resolution repeatedly has been cited in both Houses of Congress for setting a standard for subsequent enactments, particularly those designed to recapture power for the Congress away from the executive branch. While critics of the resolution are questioning its constitutionality and practicality, majorities in Congress have repaired to it as a model.

The most important of these enactments is the Budget and Impoundment Act of 1974, which some observers[21] have seen as ranking with the War Powers Resolution as the two most important congressional actions of 1970s. The budget act clearly "went to school" on the resolution and incorporates at least five of its mechanisms. Most important of the budget act's provisions is the recision clause. It permits the president to rescind spending for projects Congress has authorized, but he must send to Capitol Hill a special message that sets a 45-day clock running. His impoundment of the funds must end after that period unless Congress passes a resolution—brought to a vote under specified accelerated procedures—repealing its earlier authorization. So striking are the parallels that House Judiciary Committee Chairman Peter Rodino in 1974 devoted a lengthy law journal article to an exploration of their parallelisms—including their similar purpose. Both acts, Rodino said, were aimed at limiting the exercise of unbridled Executive power.[22] Other emulative legislation includes the Reserve Call-up Bill of 1975, the National Emergencies Act of 1976, the International Economic Emergency Powers Act of 1977, and the Nuclear Non-Proliferation Act of 1978. In virtually every instance, the references to the War Powers Resolution were explicitly drawn.

2. Court Action

Although Senator Arlen Specter of Pennsylvania is reported as saying that the Republican leadership in the Senate and the White House had discussed some type of Supreme Court test of the resolution,[23] the courts have it left unchallenged. In *Drinan vs. Ford*, a 1975 case aimed at halting U.S. defense aid to Cambodia, and *Crockett vs. Reagan*, a 1981 case with the same purpose for El Salvador, the courts, in effect, told liberal members of Congress who brought the suits that judicial remedies were denied them so long as political remedies available through the War Powers Resolution had not been availed. Although the *Chadha* case called into question the legitimacy of the concurrent resolution veto, that mechanism is not central to the War Powers Resolution nor is it entirely clear that the Supreme Court ruling affected its use in the resolution.[24] Furthermore, because the Supreme Court does not issue purely advisory opinions, a legal test is not likely to occur soon.

3. Failure to Amend

The durability of the resolution's mechanism also is demonstrated by its having remained unaltered in text for the past dozen years. In each Congress since 1973 bills and resolutions have been introduced to repeal it or alter it significantly. None has ever been approved, even at the subcommittee level. When in 1977, congressional critics succeed in gaining a series of hearings before the Senate Foreign Relations Committee to reconsider the War Powers Resolution, a package of amendments proposed by Senator Eagleton received so little support that he never formally introduced it.

4. Use of the Mechanism

The willingness of Congress to make use of the War Powers Resolution mechanisms in crisis situations to codetermine policy—while not predictable— generally has demonstrated their utility. In 1973, as the Indochina War was being lost, President Ford asked Congress for legislation "clarifying" his authority to carry out an evacuation of Americans and Vietnamese. Both Houses passed bills citing the resolution that sought to codetermine policy. Senator Javits was among those who hailed the effort as a landmark. The bills, he said, vindicated the War Powers Resolution as a "methodology" through which Congress could join in decisions of war and peace, rather than have the president act unilaterally. Ultimately, however, the hopes of Senator Javits and other resolution supporters were dashed when events in Indochina outran even an accelerated legislative effort. The bills were considered moot and the House ultimately rejected a conference report.[25]

In the 1983 Lebanon situation, by contrast, the Congress used mechanisms provided by the resolution to codetermine policy. When the president failed explicitly to trigger the sixty-day provision of the act, the Congress provided its own finding in the Lebanon Resolution that American armed forces has been introduced into hostilities and that the sixty-day authorization period was running. (As an aside, it should be noted that the provision permitting the substitution of a congressional trigger for a recalcitrant Executive was a particularly insightful contribution of Senator Javits to the War Powers Resolution.) Final passage of the Lebanon Resolution and its signing by President Reagan on October 13, 1983, marked the high point of the resolution's effectiveness as a mechanism—on three counts:

First, as contemplated under the resolution, the Congress for the first time since its passage actually provided an authorization for the use of American forces in hostilities abroad.

Second, the authorization was no Tonkin Gulf Resolution-style "blank check" for the commander in chief, but a carefully crafted statement of policy; and

Third, passage of the Lebanon Resolution marked the first time the president actually had signed legislation whose roots and effects were sunk deep in the letter and spirit of the War Powers Resolution.

Those are meaningful achievements even though the executive-legislative consensus that underlay passage of the Lebanon Resolution broke down almost immediately as a result of changed circumstances, and despite the inability of Congress to effect a similar outcome in the next crisis—the Grenada invasion.

In the Grenada situation, the Executive retreated to a customary posture on war making: There was no consultation with Congress, no attempt at codetermination, and no willingness to invoke the War Powers Resolution by reporting under the "trigger clause" of Section 4 (a) (1). Again, however, the Congress responded immediately. On the day following the landing of American forces on the Caribbean island, House Foreign Affairs Committee Chairman Zablocki introduced a resolution declaring that the War Powers Resolution had become operative on the invasion day and that the sixty-day authorization was in effect and time was running. A similar resolution was introduced in the Senate. The House passed the Zablocki resolution 403 to 23;[26] the Senate passed similar legislation as a "rider" to the Debt Ceiling Authorization.[27] In the waning days of the first session of the 98th Congress, neither Grenada provision was brought to conference, and each ultimately died—but not before the Reagan Administration promised to remove all combat troops before sixty days. It delivered on the promise.[28]

To the legal purist, the descriptions of the War Powers Resolution being applied in Indochina, Lebanon and Grenada, may appear to be a litany of failure. In practical fact, however, it is not. While the mechanisms admittedly have been employed fitfully, they have given Congress a vehicle for codetermination of policy. In their absence, the Congress would be forced in each new crisis to invent a means of dealing with presidential war making or, more likely, to do nothing. The resolution provides a context and set of procedures for permitting Congress in a focussed way to exercise its responsibilities as it sees them in a given situation. While the mechanism is not perfect, it has proven its utility and flexibility.[29]

THE WAR POWERS RESOLUTION AS RESTRAINT

Whatever its significance as a symbol, whatever its usefulness as a mechanism, the value and success of the War Powers Resolution ultimately will depend upon how well it achieves its purpose of introducing restraints on presidential war making.

That objective was central to the resolution's passage. Its major purpose, Senator Javits has suggested, was to impose on the presidency ". . . the necessity to stop, look, and listen, and to take prudent counsel when a military operation is suggested."[30] Former Senate Foreign Relations Committee Chairman William Fulbright has said that to the extent the resolution can introduce elements of restraint into national security planning, it succeeds.[31]

The resolution's proponents have seen this restraint working in two ways: practically and legally.

1. Practical Restraints

When the War Powers Resolution was under consideration in 1973, Congressman Les Aspin of Wisconsin predicted that it would have an enormous impact on the decision-making process of the executive branch. A former Pentagon planner himself, Aspin suggested that, with the resolution in force, a president and his advisors would know that a decision to send American troops into fighting would provoke an intense debate that would focus on a concrete decision to be made by Congress within a sixty-day period:

> Congressmen will hold hearings, editorial writers will write editorials, columnists will construct columns, *Meet the Press* and *Face the Nation* will cross-question government spokesmen, there will be network specials, demonstrators will demonstrate, and most important, constituents will write mail—telling Congressmen they should say yea or nay to the President's action. This foreknowledge is bound to strengthen the hand of those in the President's council who might otherwise find it more politic to stifle their dissents.[32]

2. Legal Restraints

Other observers have seen the resolution's restraining influence in the fact that, whatever presidents may think or say about it, it remains the law of the land. Into what previously had been a "zone of twilight" of concurrent and uncertain authority between president and Congress, the legislative branch wrote into law the principle that it can compel the president to withdraw troops he has committed to action without a declaration of war or other congressional authorization. Future presidents, George Reedy has suggested, would be reluctant to test the law to determine if it really works: "No one will battle for the distinction of being the second Chief Executive to lose his job," said Reedy.[33] The fundamental premise of the resolution then becomes, as political analyst Alan Frye has noted, that "future conflicts must find this country either quickly united or promptly disengaged. If there is a sounder prescription for use of force by a democratic government, no one has yet advanced it."[34] Remarking on this need for unity and partnership, Senator Javits predicted that the resolution would modify the tendency of modern presidents to "shoot from the hip." If the collective judgment of the president and Congress is required for the nation to go to war, he said, the result inevitably will be more responsible action and ". . . restraint by both the Congress and the President."[35]

It is one thing for proponents of the War Powers Resolution to proclaim their handywork a restraint, quite another for actual practice to prove it so. At least one observer has declared invalid all assertions that within its limited testing the resolution has worked as a restraint. "In fact it did not," Professor John T. Rourke has declared: "It did not significantly alter the pattern of executive-legislative liaison which has evolved since World War II."[36]

Let's look at the record for the past twelve years. Certainly there were instances in which the resolution's impact was minimal. Examples are the rescue of the *Mayaguez* crew in 1975, the 1980 abortive rescue of the U.S. hostages in Iran, and the Grenada invasion of 1983. At the same time, however, at least three instances exist in which the restraining effects of the resolution have been evident:

1. The Fall of Indochina

In subsequent statements both Presidents Nixon and Ford have blamed the outcome of the Indochina War on the effects of the War Powers Resolution.[37] Although the resolution imposed no direct legal bar to U.S. direct reintervention with armed forces in 1975, its elaborate and explicit statutory provisions insured that any military action ordered by the president would be subject to intense and, because of the times, hostile congressional review. Unwilling to risk potential outcomes, President Ford passed up a military response to the Communist advances.

Former Vice President Mondale is among those who have suggested that Ford acknowledged the resolution's impact when he stated publicly that any reintroduction of American troops into Southeast Asia required advance congressional approval. Said Mondale:

> Any temptation to introduce American troops or bombing into Cambodia or South Vietnam in early 1975 to help "save" those governments was effectively removed by the War Powers Act. Without the Act, the President might have felt obliged to once again escalate involvement and possible once again plunge our Nation into a major military involvement in Southeast Asia.[38]

While Mondale may put more emphasis on the resolution as a direct restraint than serves our memories, it is certainly true that it played a role, one large enough to attract blame from the former presidents most directly involved.

2. The 1978 Zaire Airlift

It seems clear that the United States might have projected its force into the Zaire civil war of the late 1970s had there been no War Powers Resolution. According to former Congressman Charles W. Whalen, Jr., the statute caused a "chilling effect" on potentially more ambitious plans within the Carter administration for rescuing Americans and Europeans trapped by the conflict.[39]

In that conflict U.S. transport planes assisting in the evacuation of foreigners from Zaire ultimately landed in secure staging areas more than one hundred miles from the sites of the conflict. The surmise by Whalen and others that this cautious approach to hostilities in Zaire was occasioned by the War Powers Resolution was confirmed by Douglas J. Bennet, who was assistant secretary of state for congressional affairs at the time. He has said that the War Power statute definitely conditioned the executive branch's decision-making process in the Zaire crisis. Because the resolution demands congressional participation if a U.S. military initiative is to succeed, Bennet said, it inhibits "extralegal and covert activities. It makes bold adventures less feasible."[40]

3. Strife in El Salvador

Following a guerrilla offensive in El Salvador in January 1981, the newly installed Reagan administration escalated U.S. involvement in that conflict by sending significantly enhanced numbers of security assistance advisors into the country. Almost immediately a flurry of questions about the U.S. commitment and the War Powers Resolution were engendered. In a letter of 13 March 1981 from Deputy Secretary of Defense Carlucci to Foreign Affairs Committee Chairman Zablocki, the administration emphasized the limited role those forces would play in the civil conflict:

> Every possible precaution has been taken, and will be taken, to ensure that U.S. military personnel will not become engaged in, or be exposed to, the hostilities . . . The possibility that U.S. military personnel would become engaged or endangered by the hostilities is remote.[41]

About the same time a State Department memorandum was made public stating that U.S. military representatives "will not act as combat advisors, and will not accompany Salvadoran forces in combat, on operational patrols, or in any other situation where combat is likely."[42]

Those statements clearly were reflecting the Reagan administration mandated "rules of engagement" for U.S. advisors in El Salvador. The rules clearly frustrated those bound by them; U.S. advisors frequently complained

to American reporters that the limitations made it impossible for them to
observe how aggressive Salvadoran soldiers were being on combat patrols or
in fire-fights with the enemy.

When three armed U.S. military advisors in El Salvador were video
taped by one of the networks accompanying their students into a guerrilla
contested area of El Salvador in February 1982, the administration quickly
asserted the seriousness of its purpose. President Reagan himself called for
an investigation stating that: "The policy is we do not engage in combat."[43]
The following day the ranking officer of the offending three was ordered out
of the country by the U.S. ambassador and the other two soldiers were
reprimanded.[44]

It seems clear that the rules of engagement in El Salvador were established exactly to prevent a need to report under the War Powers Resolution.
In all such situations, the attempt to avoid the letter of the law can lead to
some strange byways: *The Washington Post* reported in October 1984, for
example, that in order to avoid violating the resolution—which prohibits
battlefield coordination betwen American advisors and Salvadorans without
congressional concurrence—information gathered by U.S. reconnaissance
planes over El Salvador was being sent through U.S. facilities in Panama to
listening posts in the United States and from there back down to U.S. advisors
based in El Salvador. Salvadoran military officials were said to know which
frequency to listen to as the messages reached the U.S. advisors an hour or
so after the intelligence was gathered. Thus a direct connection was avoided.[45]

When this use of American reconnaissance in support of Salvadoran
troops was revealed, the news occasioned the Speaker of the House, Thomas P.
(Tip) O'Neill, to write a highly publicized letter to Chairman Fascell of the
House Foreign Affairs Committee asking for an investigation into whether
the War Powers Resolution was being complied with by the administration.[46]

Fascell's inquiry forced the White House to review the situation and
although it ultimately denied any breach of the War Powers Resolution, the
entire affair put pressure on the Executive to move more carefully. By focuss-
ing public opinion on the Central American situation, the policy makers in
the White House were compelled to consider congressional and public opinion
before expanding the U.S. commitment. To an important extent, therefore,
the resolution was serving as a restraint without being invoked.

One only need superimpose this situation on the escalation that occurred
in the Indochina War to appreciate the impact that the War Powers Resolution
appears to have had. The Reagan administration could have put combat advisors
into El Salvador. Because of the War Powers Resolution—and the convictions
that lay behind it—it did not. As the situation gradually improves there, the
restraints increasingly seem wise. Is the fact that we have major exercises in
Honduras but no permanent stationing of troops there a response to the resolution? Is our circumspection about a direct military confrontation with the

Sandinistas in Nicaragua due in part to the resolution? Perhaps, and time may tell.

Clearly no administration lightly will set in motion the processes of the War Powers Resolution in search of some tactical advantage in a foreign civil conflict. Once triggered, a national debate is certain to ensue. Further, if the U.S. participation in the conflict is protracted, the president would be faced with the need for a positive congressional authorization or see U.S. participation in danger of being terminated in sixty to ninety days. While falling short of a national referendum on undeclared wars, the resolution nevertheless provides an opportunity for national opinion to be expressed and affected by congressional action. If the American public and its representatives believe the president was right in committing U.S. Armed Forces into hostilities, the Chief Executive and commander in chief have nothing to fear from the resolution. If the president acts unilaterally and without public and congressional support, he runs the risk of being disavowed. That consequence alone counsels prudence and restraint.

Perhaps the most eloquent testimonial to the reality of the restraint has come from those whom it has frustrated. In the wake of the U.S. withdrawal from Lebanon, administration spokesmen used the War Powers Resolution as their whipping boy. Secretary of State Shultz charged in a major statement that the resolution had usurped the president's constitutional role as commander in chief.[47] Expanding on the theme to the Trilateral Commission several days later, the secretary charged that the act sets "arbitrary sixty days deadlines that practically invite an adversary to wait us out."[48] About the same time the Navy's top officer, Admiral James Watkins, chief of naval operations, told an audience in Baltimore that the War Powers Resolution had crippled the president's ability to use military force rapidly in time of crisis, the first time—according to a Pentagon spokesman—that a top-ranking military officer had spoken out publicly against the resolution.[49]

If a coordinated campaign was underway against the resolution aiming at congressional or court review, the effort fizzled. Asked at his subsequent press conference just how much problem he had with the resolution and whether he wished a Supreme Court test of its constitutionality, President Reagan plainly avoided a direct answer, speaking rather in generalities about the burden of 150 restrictions on the president's power in foreign affairs that the Congress had imposed during the past decade.[50]

With that nonanswer, the campaign to review the War Powers Resolution flagged and little more has been heard of it to this very day. Critics of the resolution, perhaps unwittingly, had testified twice to its potency: once for attacking it as a restraint on Executive power and again for backing down against the reality of its continuing durability.

Symbol . . . mechanism . . . restraint. Through a dozen years the War Powers Resolution has served each role. In so doing, it has lived up to the labors and hopes invested in it by proponents like Jake Javits and Clem Zablocki and dozens of others who sought a dozen years ago to reassert for Congress its constitutionally-given rights and responsibilities in making peace and war.

NOTES

1. "War Powers Irresolution," 5 May 1980.

2. W. Stuart Darling and D. Craig Mense, "The War Powers Flop," *The Washington Post*, 6 March 1977, C3.

3. "The Presidency and Congress," *Washington and Lee Law Review* 4 (Fall 1975): 850.

4. *Five Virginia Papers Presented at the Miller Center Forums, 1979, by Four Distinguished Americans* (Washington, D.C.: University Press of America, 1980), 11.

5. "Congress vs. the President: The Formulation and Implementation of American Foreign Policy," *Foreign Affairs* (Winter 1981/1982): 238;*Congressional Record*, 28 September 1983, S13073.

6. *The Decline and Resurgence of Congress* (Washington, D.C.: The Brookings Institution, 1976), 272.

7. Thomas M. Franck and Edward Weisband, *Foreign Policy by Congress* (New York: Oxford University Press, 1979), 82.

8. *The Accountability of Power: Toward a Responsible Presidency* (New York David McKay Inc., 1975), 138.

9. *Congressional Record*, 1 July 1980, S9092.

10. Cited, ibid., S9088.

11. Ibid.

12. Ibid., S9089.

13. "Whenever there is a law on the books, an effective law, which I think the War Powers Resolution represents," Javits said, "normally speaking, we do not add anything by reiterating or by saying we mean it 'to be strictly adhered to.' " Ibid.

14. Ibid., S9090.

15. Sec. 5, S.J. Res. 100, *Congressional Record*, 97th Cong. 1st Sess., 7 October 1981, S11336.

16. "Report Dated August 24, 1982, From President Ronald Reagan to Hon. Thomas P. O'Neill, Speaker of the House of Representatives, Consistent with the War Powers Resolution, Relative to Use of United States Armed Forces in Lebanon," *The War Powers Resolution: Relevant Documents, Correspondence, Reports*

(December 1983 Edition), House Committee on Foreign Affairs, 98th Cong. 2d sess., Committee print, 61.

17. "Report Dated August 30, 1983, from President Ronald Reagan to Hon. Thomas P. O'Neill, Speaker of the House of Representatives, in Further Reference to the Use of United States Armed Forces in Lebanon and Consistent with Section 4 of the War Powers Resolution," Ibid., 65.

18. H.J. Res 364, 98th Cong. 1st sess., Text in ibid., 67.

19. *Congressional Record*, 28 September 1983, S13073.

20. See, for example, Richard M. Pious, *The American Presidency* (New York: Basic Books, Inc., 1979) 403–415; Darling and Mense, *Washington Post*, 6 Mar. 1977, C8; and King and Leavens, "Curbing the Dog of War: The War Powers Resolution." *Harvard International Law Journal*, vol. 18, no. 1 (Winter 1977): 55–96.

21. Former Speaker of the House Carl Albert said that the two enactments represented the two major accomplishments of the Congress in his memory. Quoted in Lock Johnson and James McCormick, "Foreign Policy by Executive Fiat," *Foreign Policy* (Fall 1977): 138.

22. "Congressional Review of Executive Action," *Seton Hall Law Review* (Spring 1974): 507.

23. *Washington Post*, 30 March 1984, A-9.

24. *Jagdish Rai Chadha vs. Immigration and Naturalization Service,* Appeal No. 77–1702 (9th Cir., Dec. 22, 1980). In addition, despite the court's disapproving use of the veto in the *Chadha* case, Congress since has enacted more than fifty legislative-veto provisions in score of laws. "Legislative Veto Called 'Alive and Well' " *Washington Post*, 6 August 1985, A13.

25. The debate on the conference report on H.R. 6096 took place on 1 May 1975. See the Congressional Record for that date, H3540–H3551.

26. *Congressional Record*, 31 October 1984, H8887.

27. Ibid., 28 October 1983, S14876–S14877.

28. *New York Times*, 17 November 1983, I3. Statement of White House spokesman Larry Speakes.

29. An important exposition of this point appears in an article by Rep. Clement J. Zablocki, published posthumously in the *Loyola of Los Angeles Law Review*, Vol. 17, No. 3, 579–598 (1984).

30. James William Fulbright, *Fulbright of Arkansas*, ed. by Karl E. Meyer (Washington: R. B. Luce, 1963), 414.

31. Interview, 14 April 1981.

32. *Congressional Record*, 31 October 1973, E6915.

33. *The Omniscient President: A Myth Collapses*, A Poynter Pamphlet, the Poynter Center, Indiana University (Bloomington, 1975), 10.

34. Congress and Foreign Policy Hearings, 23.

35. Ibid., 198.

36. "The Future is History: Congress and Foreign Policy," *Presidential Studies Quarterly* (Summer 1979): 280.

37. Nixon, *Memoirs* (New York: Grosset and Dunlap, 1978), 899 and *The Real War* (New York: Warner Books, 1980), 117; Ford, *A Time to Heal: The Autobiography of Gerald F. Ford* (New York: Harper and Row, 1979), 249–250.

38. *The Accountability of Power*, 137–138.

39. "A Decade of Reform in the U.S. House of Representatives, 1969–1979: Its Impact on American Foreign Policy," A paper prepared for a colloquium, The Woodrow Wilson International Center for Scholars (November 1980): 16–17.

40. "Congress in Foreign Policy: Who Needs It?" *Foreign Affairs* (Fall 1978): 49.

41. Copy in House Committee files.

42. *Congressional Record*, 5 March 1981, E901.

43. *The Washington Post*, 13 February 1982, A1.

44. Ibid., 14 February 1982, A1.

45. Ibid., 27 October 1984, A1.

46. 30 March 1984. Copy in House Committee files.

47. *The Washington Post*, 30 March 1984, A9.

48. Ibid., 4 April 1984, A1.

49. Ibid., 4 March 1984, A9.

50. Ibid., 5 April 1984, A14.

PART TWO

Congress and Arms
Limitation

Introduction

As with the war power provision, the Constitution is likewise a model of brevity on another aspect of congressional control over foreign policy: treaty making. Professor Wayne Cole points to a host of circumstances that arose to complicate the treaty process, from the rise of partisanship to a country with sectional, racial, ethnic, and economic interests more pluralistic than the nation's founders could have anticipated. The result, Cole writes, was nevertheless a surprising degree of consensus between the Executive and Congress. Wilson's failure to secure Senate approval of the Treaty of Versailles after World War I was spectacular, but a spectacular exception to a record of cooperation, one due more to Wilson's failings than the Senate's churlishness.

Professor Robert Schulzinger provides an intriguing confirmation of Cole's picture. The Anti-Ballistic Missile Treaty, part of the SALT I package, sailed through the Senate. Why did the agreement—not a treaty—limiting offensive arms provoke such rhetorical fury? The issue was not partisanship, nor competing sectional or other interests. Democrats and Republicans, north and south, alike questioned the wisdom of deploying an ABM system and going forward with the Trident submarine and B-1 bomber. The chief source of opposition to SALT I, in fact, came from Henry Jackson of Washington state. Fellow Democrats, such as J. William Fulbright and Alan Cranston, stoutly defended the agreement.

Despite (perhaps because of) the acrimony in the Senate, Schulzinger concludes that the upper house fundamentally shaped the nature of SALT I and the ABM treaty. Jackson's vituperativeness also critically affected the course of SALT II negotiations, as Dr. Stanley Heginbotham demonstrates. Heginbotham is especially sensitive to the ways in which Congress performs its 'shaping' role—not as a codeterminer and constant partner with the Executive, but as an antibureaucratic body presenting any president with the problem of how to cope with its powers of the purse, of ratification, of war, and of investigation in his conduct of foreign policy. In stressing the failure of the Carter administration to cope successfully as the chief cause of SALT II's nonratification, Heginbotham echoes Cole's assessment of Wilson. As well, in his analysis of the Senate Foreign Relations Committee's handling of the SALT II treaty, he reinforces Cole's insistence on Congress' willingness to cooperate with the president whenever possible.

5

With the Advice and Consent of the Senate: The Treaty-Making Process Before the Cold War Years

WAYNE S. COLE

The American treaty-making process under the Constitution may be a bit like the bumble bee; technically the bumble bee should not be able to fly—but it does. America's cumbersome treaty-making process should not work—but it does. Furthermore, whether through the foresight of the Founding Fathers, or through good fortune, or through the endless adaptive capacities of the human animal, that treaty-making process has taken on profoundly vital roles in the twentieth century that America's early statesmen did not fully envisage.

The Constitution is quite brief on the subject, asserting that the president "shall have Power, by and with the Advice and Consent of the Senate, to make Treaties, provided two-thirds of the Senators present concur." (Article II, Section 2) President George Washington's initial efforts to get the advice of the Senate proved so unsatisfactory that he abandoned that part of the process early on, as did his presidential successors most of the time.[1]

In still other ways the history of the treaty-making process did not evolve quite the way the Founding Fathers had intended or expected. Political parties emerged on the American scene, and initially they were rooted deeply in foreign policy differences. From the beginning political partisanship, sectional conflicts, and clashes between urban commercial interests and rural agrarian interests disrupted foreign policies and treaty making. Contrary to Washington's advice, "permanent, inveterate antipathies against particular nations and passionate attachments for others"[2] did develop and complicate the treaty-making process. The ethnic heterogeneity of America extended emotional variables into the process and made compromises difficult. Chronic tensions developed in contests between the presidency and the legislators for control of foreign affairs—tensions so powerful that they immobilized the United States in particular situations in world affairs.

At times the personal and political alienation of congressional leadership from the presidency virtually assured defeat for treaties submitted to the Senate. Such was the case after the Civil War with a succession of expansionist treaties considered or proposed by Secretary of State William H. Seward under the unpopular President Andrew Johnson.[3] There were secretaries of state whose relations with the Senate were so deplorable that senators almost delighted in making life difficult for them. Such was the experience of the haughty John Hay as he served as secretary of state under Presidents William McKinley and Theodore Roosevelt. The Senate's disenchantment with Secretary Hay was exceeded only by his contempt for the Senate—especially when it intruded into his domain of foreign affairs.[4]

That alienation between the presidency and the Senate in the treaty-making process culminated with the rejection of President Woodrow Wilson's Versailles Treaty and its League of Nations Covenant by the Senate under the leadership of Republican Senator Henry Cabot Lodge of Massachusetts in 1919–1920. That traumatic experience, with its worldwide ramifications, produced a storm of protests among statesmen, diplomats, pundits, journalists, political scientists, and historians that dominated American thought and writing on the subject for a generation. In hundreds of books and thousands of articles some of America's finest minds called for signficant changes in the treaty-making process to make certain that that sort of impasse would not occur again, and to make it possible for the United States, under enlightened executive leadership, to play a constructively responsible role in guarding world peace and security.

Those same tensions were highlighted in the controversies surrounding enactment of the neutrality legislation adopted by Congress in the 1930s as war clouds loomed ominously in Africa, Asia, and Europe. In shaping those neutrality laws the Franklin D. Roosevelt-Cordell Hull administration wanted to limit the legislative role and to provide the president with discretionary powers to guide the United States constructively in world affairs. In opposition, the Senate, under isolationist and pacifist influences, determined to restrict the president's freedom of action in foreign affairs and to impose legislative restraints in the interests of noninvolvement by the United States in foreign wars.[5] Those differences in the 1930s underscored the continuing controversy set off by the defeat of the Versailles Treaty more than fifteen years earlier.

In the midst of the passions aroused by the controversies surrounding the Versailles Treaty and the neutrality laws, however, careful scholars using quantitative methods made some surprising discoveries. The Senate did not defeat any treaty with a foreign government during the first thirty-five years under the Constitution, despite heated differences between political parties and sections on policies toward the wars raging in Europe much of that time, and despite controversies over American involvement in those wars. The Senate approved five-sixths or eighty-six percent of the 786 treaties submitted to it during the one hundred and forty years from 1789 to 1928. Many had urged that the Constitution be amended so that treaties might win approval by simple majorities in both houses of Congress rather than by a two-thirds vote in the Senate. But careful study revealed that most of the treaties rejected by the two-thirds vote in the Senate would have been rejected by majority rule as well.[6]

The Senate approved most of the treaties quickly and with no reservations or amendments. Generally when the Senate attached reservations or amendments they concerned technical or drafting details that had no real political significance. In a few instances the Senate's amendments were in response to presidential guidance, as when the Senate essentially rewrote the Gadsden Purchase Treaty of 1853 with Mexico, partly in accord with the wishes of President Franklin Pierce. In other instances the amendments insisted upon by the Senate forced the diplomats to return to their task and negotiate a better treaty. That was the case with the Hay-Pauncefote treaties of 1900–1901 with Great Britain concerning building, control, and fortification of an isthmian canal across Central America. To keep matters in perspective, one should also note that it was not the Senate alone that blocked treaties involving the United States. In a surprisingly large number of instances (eighty-seven of them between 1789 and 1928) the presidents of the United States either did not submit a signed treaty to the Senate, or withdrew a treaty from consideration before the Senate could act on it, or failed to ratify or exchange ratifications even after the Senate had approved it without amendments or reservations.[7]

One must not mask the seriousness of Senate rejection of the Treaty of Versailles. One should also note the negative role that the Senate played in blocking particular kinds of treaties—including some involving reciprocity, expansion, arbitration, and international organization.[8] And it is impossible to know how many worthy treaties were never negotiated or signed because statesmen knew they could never win Senate approval. Nonetheless, a careful examination of the Senate performance on treaties during the first one hundred and fifty years of American constitutional history provides a less negative picture than one might get from the uproar that raged after the defeat of the Versailles Treaty. And in those instances when sharp differences between the presidency and the Senate manifested themselves, it did not necessarily follow that the presidency was always right or that the Senate was always wrong.

Ninety percent of the time Senate actions on treaties conformed to the recommendations from its Foreign Relations Committee. Consequently its composition and performance were of major importance in the treaty-making process. Initially treaties were referred to temporary select committees, but in December 1816 the Senate created the Foreign Relations Committee as a permanent standing committee. Procedures changed over time, but the majority party in the Senate filled a comparable majority of positions on the Foreign Relations Committee. Each political party through its Committee on Committees determined its members. Committee assignments took geographic sections into account to provide national distribution, but from urban perspectives that distribution often seemed to overrepresent sparsely populated states.[9]

Senators won assignments to the committee for widely disparate reasons not necessarily related to knowledge of foreign affairs. Nonetheless, senators with special interest or experience in foreign affairs often won positions. That prestigious committee normally included some of the more powerful senators, including chairmen of other Senate committees. Members tended to be older and more experienced than the average senator.[10]

The chairman of the Foreign Relations Committee generally was the most powerful member of Congress on foreign policy matters. Normally the chairmanship went to the member of the majority party who had served on the committee longest, though no senator served as chairman of more than one major committee. That seniority system did not assure that the best qualified person would be chairman, but generally it produced chairmen who had had long experience dealing with foreign policy matters as members of the committee. The forty senators who served as chairmen of the committee between 1816 and 1945 included many of the more famous, able, and powerful senators in American history. Charles Sumner of Massachusetts had been a member only two years before he became chairman in 1861, but he chaired the committee for a decade before his ouster in 1871; Republican Henry Cabot Lodge of Massachusetts served on the committee for twenty-nine years, and was chairman from 1919 until his death five years later in 1924; progressive Republican William E. Borah of Idaho was a member from 1913 until his death twenty-seven years later a few months after World War II erupted in Europe, and he was chairman during the presidential administrations of Calvin Coolidge and Herbert Hoover from 1924 to 1933; Democrat Key Pittman of Nevada was a member for nearly a quarter of a century until his death late in 1940, and he was chairman most of Franklin D. Roosevelt's first two terms in the White House; Democrat Walter George of Georgia ultimately served nearly twenty-nine years and was chairman when Congress passed lend-lease in 1941; and Democrat Tom Connally of Texas was a member of the committee nearly twenty-two years, and was chairman throughout America's military participation in World War II. Sumner, Lodge, and Borah were exceptionally powerful chairmen of the Foreign Relations Committee. Pittman's political caution on dealings with Europe and his hard-line urgings against Japan in the Pacific could not lightly be disregarded by President Roosevelt in those perilous times. Senator George's even-handed guidance of the committee, and Tom Connally's aggressive internationalism helped assure Roosevelt the support he needed from the Senate on foreign affairs during America's greatest war.[11]

The Senate Foreign Relations Committee and its varied chairmen confronted America's presidents and secretaries of state with powerful legislators who often had had years of experience treating Senate dimensions of developments in American foreign policies. And those senators were drawn from all sections of the United States, providing something of a national mosaic of American hopes, fears, and aspirations in their country's relations with other parts of the world.

The operation of America's constitutional treaty-making process during the century and one-half that preceded the end of World War II was affected not only by the performances of senators, but by those of presidents and secretaries of state as well. If mistakes were made (and they were), one must look to the Executive as well as to the legislature. Given human frailty and imperfection, one must make certain allowances for human error. And timing may affect the degree of error or imperfection that may be tolerated. Nonetheless, the operation of the American treaty-making process under the Constitution was heavily dependent on the political skills of the presidency, as well as of the legislature.

Woodrow Wilson made more mistakes in his handling of the Versailles Treaty than the difficult times and circumstances would tolerate. In admittedly more favorable circumstances and times, both at home and abroad, Franklin D. Roosevelt and Cordell Hull (and, more briefly, Harry S. Truman and Edward R. Stettinius, Jr.) learned from the mistakes of their predecessors, and performed much more skillfully in guiding the United States toward a positive leadership role in the United Nations Organization at the close of World War II. The quality of presidential leadership and political skills (and the nature of the times) made a difference.

Woodrow Wilson properly ranks as one of America's greatest presidents. He helped shape and inspire an idealistic and promising agenda for America and the world. He brought impressive abilities to bear in his efforts to guide the United States and the world in hopeful paths for the future. For all of his brilliance, however, Wilson made mistakes, and those mistakes helped account for the failure of the United States in general and the Senate in particular to follow the course he had set for them in world affairs.

After the reasonably supportive performance by Republicans in and out of Congress during World War I, and given the certain need for support from both Republicans and Democrats for any peace settlement, it was a mistake for Wilson to appeal for the election of Democratic majorities in Congress in the elections of 1918. That appeal may not have been responsible for the Republican victories and the Democratic reverses. But neither did it produce the results that Wilson wanted and needed. Republicans won slim majorities in both houses of Congress, and made Henry Cabot Lodge both Senate majority leader and chairman of the Foreign Relations Committee. Wilson's appeal removed the wartime political wraps, and unleashed the vigor with which Republicans turned to partisanship in the elections and after.[12]

Under the circumstances Wilson reasonably may have considered it necessary to lead the American delegation personally in the peace negotiations in Paris. Personal and political alienation, along with sharp ideological differences, may have made it impractical and unrealistic for Wilson to have named Henry Cabot Lodge or any of the other powerful Republican senators to the delegation. And to have bypassed Lodge while naming a Democratic senator would not have eased the difficulty. Nonetheless, for Wilson to name only one minor Republican to the delegation was a mistake. William Howard Taft was a former president; Charles Evans Hughes was a distinguished jurist and former presidential candidate; and Elihu Root was a former secretary of state. All were respected Republicans. All favored creation of a world organization and American membership in that organization. Two of them had had experience in diplomatic negotiations, and the third later was to demonstrate impressive diplomatic skills. If Wilson's conceptions of the peace settlement and League of Nations were too rigid and inflexible to tolerate the degree of bipartisanship that the appointment of one of those distinguished Republicans to the delegation would have represented, he was certain to have major political difficulties when his treaty was introduced to the rough-and-tumble of Senate politics where it had to win two-thirds approval.[13] In that same context, Wilson's failure to confer with Senate leaders in the course of naming the delegation and in preparations for the mission to Paris helped make certain that they would feel like outsiders to the process and feel no special responsibility to share in commitments to the treaty that Wilson's efforts in France would produce.[14]

No one can doubt the earnestness with which President Wilson battled to win Senate approval for the Versailles Treaty and League Covenant that he brought back to America with him in June 1919. And one must feel deep sadness for the man, the nation, and the world as physical exhaustion, emotional difficulties, and strokes damaged the president's abilities to cope. One could wish that Wilson had had a stronger reed to depend upon for Democratic leadership in the Senate than Gilbert Hitchcock of Nebraska—particularly in contesting with such powerhouses as Lodge, Borah, Robert M. LaFollette, George W. Norris, and Hiram W. Johnson. But it became increasingly clear that approval of the treaty required compromise, including both face-saving cosmetic compromises and the substantial Lodge reservation on Article 10. That reservation explicitly determined to guard the powers of Congress under the Constitution "to declare war or authorize the employment of the military or naval forces of the United States." It seems probable that the major states would have accepted Lodge's reservations, even on Article 10, if that had been the price they had had to pay for America's participation. But on that matter Wilson would not yield. He insisted on all or nothing—and he got nothing. As Professor Thomas A. Bailey correctly wrote forty years ago, "In the final analysis the treaty was slain in the house of its friends rather than in the house of its enemies." Wilson "delivered the final stab."[15]

Franklin D. Roosevelt and Cordell Hull had a less difficult task in guiding the Senate to approve the United Nations Charter than Wilson had had with his Versailles Treaty and League of Nations a quarter of a century earlier. Changes both at home and abroad had eroded traditional bases for American isolationism. On the world scene the further decline of British and French power, the terrifying military might and aggressiveness of Hitler's totalitarian Nazi Germany and Mussolini's Fascist Italy, the increased destructiveness and mobility of modern military planes and ships, and the Japanese attack on Pearl Harbor, all made the seriousness of foreign threats to American security more credible than they had been in World War I. Similarly, within the country American industrial capacity and capital accumulations increased phenomenally. Urban growth accelerated, and rural and small-town America dwindled. Network radio and metropolitan news publications, along with schools and colleges, chipped away at parochialism and apathy. Isolationism hung on tenaciously, but internationalism triumphed while Roosevelt was president of the United States.[16]

In addition, Roosevelt and Hull consciously learned from Wilson's mistakes. Over the years, in dozens of speeches, they tried to educate the people away from their traditional isolationism toward a more positive multilateral leadership role for the United States in world affairs. In June 1940, Roosevelt pressed his efforts to build bipartisan support for his foreign policies with the appointment of interventionist Republicans Henry L. Stimson as Secretary of War and Frank Knox as Secretary of the Navy.[17]

Roosevelt and members of his cabinet (particularly Republican Secretary of the Interior Harold L. Ickes) indulged in a certain 'overkill' in warring against isolationists by blurring the distinction between patriotic American critics of the administration's foreign policies on the one hand, and subversive agents of Hitler's Nazi Germany on the other. That guilt-by-association tactic represented considerably less than the best in American traditions of freedom of speech and right of dissent. And it probably was not necessary to accomplish the president's foreign policy goals. But it so thoroughly discredited the isolationists that they were but a remnant of their prewar power by the time the Senate gathered to consider the United Nations Charter in July 1945.[18]

Secretary Hull was proud of his efforts to build bipartisanship in foreign affairs during World War II. Initiatives from both houses of Congress, cautiously watched and guided by the administration, led to adoption of the Fulbright and Connally resolutions in the fall of 1943. Those resolutions were designed to make clear that the United States would not reject membership in the United Nations after World War II as it had rejected membership in the League after World War I. The Connally Resolution in the Senate sought the broadest possible base by proclaiming that the treaty creating that organization would "be made only by and with the advice and consent of the Senate of the United States, provided two-thirds of the Senators present concur." With that assurance, the resolution was approved by the overwhelming vote of eighty-five to five in the Senate.[19]

Hull also called into being a bipartisan committee of eight senators to confer with him on developing plans for the postwar organization. That secret committee had four Democrats, three Republicans, and one Progressive— including at least three who had been isolationists before Pearl Harbor. It was not just a token group; in its many sessions with Hull its members conducted thoughtful, responsible discussions. Its contributions were evident in the United States positions at the Dumbarton Oaks conference in 1944 and at the United Nations Conference in San Francisco in 1945.[20] Hull also worked out an agreement with Republican John Foster Dulles designed to prevent postwar peace from becoming a political football in the 1944 presidential campaign.[21]

Like Wilson earlier, President Roosevelt planned to attend and address the San Francisco conference called to negotiate the United Nations Charter. But he named his new secretary of state, Edward R. Stettinius, Jr., to head the American delegation. FDR included two senators on the delegation (Democrat Tom Connally and Republican Arthur Vandenberg), as well as two congressmen. Vandenberg would not accept the appointment until he won written assurances from the president that he would be free to speak his own mind at the conference and in the Senate after the conference. With Roosevelt's death on 12 April 1945, the new president, Harry S. Truman, retained the same persons FDR had named earlier to the American delegation. He directed Stettinius to consult with Senators Connally and Vandenberg on all issues, and told the delegates that he "wanted them to write a document that would pass the U.S. Senate and that would not arouse such opposition as confronted Woodrow Wilson." They followed his instructions.[22]

By the time President Truman submitted the completed United Nations Charter to the Senate, the outcome was no longer in doubt. In the final vote on 28 July 1945, eighty-nine senators voted yea, and only two voted nay.[23] It could be done—if it were done right.

That carries the history of the Senate and the treaty-making process chronologically as far as this chapter was to take it. But perhaps one may be permitted a tiny excursion beyond the end of World War II. In the cold war, America's involvement in world affairs has become immeasurably larger and more complex than ever before; responsible citizens can feel overwhelmed as they try to keep up with developments and to understand them. Secrecy hides essential parts of that incredibly complicated involvement in world affairs from legislators and citizens alike. Executive agents and executive agreements short-circuit the constitutional treaty-making process. The foreign policy bureaucracy has become almost impossible for the ordinary citizen to penetrate.

If foreign affairs in the cold war are not to become the 'tail wagging the dog' of American democracy and freedom, an active and responsible Senate role (including its role in the treaty-making process) may be more essential now than ever before in American history. Now more than ever the Senate (and especially members of the Foreign Relations Committee) need to 'watch-dog' foreign policy and the conduct of foreign affairs. The Senate and its members need to serve as essential conduits helping to explain America's policies to the man and woman in the street, and helping to channel public sentiment to those who shape and implement American foreign policy. It may be an impossible task. But the future of American representative government may well depend on the Senate's capacity and determination to perform those vital functions in this time of bureaucracies, secrecy, and thermonuclear weapons.

NOTES

1. Edward S. Corwin, *The President's Control of Foreign Relations* (Princeton: Princeton University Press, 1917), 3, 85–92.

2. Ruhl J. Bartlett, ed., *The Record of American Diplomacy*, 4th edition enlarged (New York: Alfred A. Knopf, 1964), 86.

3. W. Stull Holt, *Treaties Defeated by the Senate: A Study of the Struggle Between President and Senate Over the Conduct of Foreign Relations* (Baltimore: Johns Hopkins Press, 1933), 100–20.

4. Ibid., 178–95.

5. Robert A. Divine, *The Illusion of Neutrality* (Chicago: University of Chicago Press, 1962), passim. See also Wayne S. Cole, *Roosevelt and the Isolationists, 1932–45* (Lincoln: University of Nebraska Press, 1983), 163–86, 230–34.

6. Royden J. Dangerfield, *In Defense of the Senate: A Study in Treaty Making* (Norman: University of Oklahoma Press, 1933), xvi, 91–92, 305–13; Denna Frank Fleming, *The Treaty Veto of the American Senate* (New York: G. P. Putnam's Sons, 1930), 50–51.

7. Fleming, *Treaty Veto of American Senate*, 37–39; Dangerfield, *In Defense of the Senate*, 89–96, 111, 193–99; Paul Neff Garber, *The Gadsden Treaty* (Philadelphia: University of Pennsylvania Press, 1923), 116.

8. Fleming, *Treaty Veto of American Senate*, 50–116; Dangerfield, *In Defense of the Senate*, xvi, 117, 153–70, 183–245, 258–71.

9. Dangerfield, *In Defense of the Senate*, 72–86; Eleanor E. Dennison, *The Senate Foreign Relations Committee* (Stanford University: Stanford University Press, 1942), 1–53.

10. Dangerfield, *In Defense of the Senate*, 80–84; Dennison, *Senate Foreign Relations Committee*, 4–11.

11. Dennison, *Senate Foreign Relations Committee*, 11–20, 172–96; David N. Farnsworth, *The Senate Committee on Foreign Relations* (Urbana: University of Illinois Press, 1961), 22, 27; David H. Donald, *Charles Sumner and the Rights of Man* (New York: Alfred A. Knopf, 1970); John A. Garraty, *Henry Cabot Lodge: A Biography* (New York: Alfred A. Knopf, 1953); Robert James Maddox, *William E. Borah and American Foreign Policy* (Baton Rouge: Louisiana State University Press, 1969); Fred L. Israel, *Nevada's Key Pittman* (Lincoln: University of Nebraska Press, 1963); Wayne S. Cole, "Senator Key Pittman and American Neutrality Policies, 1933–1940," *Mississippi Valley Historical Review* 46 (March 1960): 644–62; Tom Connally, as told to Alfred Steinberg, *My Name is Tom Connally* (New York: Thomas Y. Crowell Co., 1954).

12. Ralph Stone, *The Irreconcilables: The Fight Against the League of Nations* (New York: W. W. Norton & Co., 1973), 27–30; Wilfred E. Binkley, *American Political Parties: Their Natural History*, 2d ed. (New York: Alfred A. Knopf, 1947), 370–71; Seward W. Livermore, *Politics Is Adjourned: Woodrow Wilson and the War Congress, 1916–1918* (Middletown: Wesleyan University Press, 1966), 224–47.

13. Arthur S. Link, *Woodrow Wilson: Revolution, War, and Peace* (Arlington Heights, Illinois: AHM Publishing Corp., 1979), 105 and 105n; Daniel M. Smith, *The Great Departure: The United States and World War I, 1914–1920* (New York: John Wiley and Sons, 1965), 111–17; Richard W. Leopold, *Elihu Root and the Conservative Tradition* (Boston: Little, Brown and Co., 1954), 123–34.

14. Smith, *Great Departure*, 116–17.

15. Link, *Woodrow Wilson*, 109–13, 122–27; Smith, *Great Departure*, 184–98; Edwin A. Weinstein, *Woodrow Wilson: A Medical and Psychological Biography* (Princeton: Princeton University Press, 1981), passim; Thomas A. Bailey, *Woodrow Wilson and the Great Betrayal* (New York: Macmillan, 1945), 148–279.

16. Cole, *Roosevelt and the Isolationists,* passim, but see especially 1–14.

17. Ibid., 367–70.

18. Ibid., 315, 322, 397, 412–13, 430–31, 460–64, 484–87.

19. Ibid., 519–25; Robert A. Divine, *Second Chance: The Triumph of Internationalism in America During World War II* (New York: Atheneum, 1967), 89–153; *Congressional Record*, 78th Cong. 1st sess., 1943, 89:7662, 7728–29, 9221–22.

20. Cole, *Roosevelt and the Isolationists*, 525–26; Divine, *Second Chance*, 194–203; Cordell Hull, *The Memoirs of Cordell Hull*, 2 vols. (New York: Macmillan Co., 1948), 2:1656–85; Arthur H. Vandenberg, Jr., with the collaboration of Joe Alex Morris, eds., *The Private Papers of Senator Vandenberg* (Boston: Houghton Mifflin Co., 1952), 90–125.

21. Cole, *Roosevelt and the Isolationists*, 544–45; Divine, *Second Chance*, 216–20; Hull, *Memoirs*, 2:1689–94; Vandenberg, *Private Papers*, 111–13.

22. Cole, *Roosevelt and the Isolationists*, 527; Divine, *Second Chance*, 270–72, 279–83; Vandenberg, *Private Papers*, 139–40, 146–59, 165–69.

23. Cole, *Roosevelt and the Isolationists*, 527–28; Divine, *Second Chance*, 304–14; Vandenberg, *Private Papers*, 218–19; *Congressional Record*, 79th Cong. 1st sess., 1945, 91:8188–90.

6

The Senate, Detente
and SALT I

ROBERT D. SCHULZINGER

At the Moscow summit of May 1972, United States President Richard Nixon and Soviet Communist Party Secretary Leonid Brezhnev signed three important documents: The Anti-Ballistic Missile Treaty, the Interim Agreement on the Limitations of Strategic Arms, and the Basic Principles of U.S.-Soviet Relations. Taken together, the three set the ground rules for détente between the United States and the Soviet Union.

Only one of these documents was an actual treaty of the sort requiring constitutionally mandated action. Curiously, though, the obligatory ratification of the ABM treaty went smoothly, with little senatorial debate and less rancor. On 3 August 1972 the treaty breezed through the upper House with an affirmative vote of eighty-eight to two. On the other hand, the interim agreement, or SALT I accord, and the Basic Principles, neither of which required congressional approval, set off a sulphurous debate. By the time both houses of congress adopted a joint resolution favoring SALT I at the end of September, much of the original congressional and public euphoria over the fruits of the Moscow summit had dissipated.

What role did the U.S. Senate play in the negotiations leading to the May 1972 agreements? How did the early Senate interest in ABM systems affect the eventual treaty? How did hawkish sentiment, voiced most by Henry Jackson (D.-Wash.), affect future developments of SALT? Finally, how did the Senate's contribution to the debate over détente affect relations between the secretive Nixon administration and an assertive congress?

Briefly, congressional opposition to the development of an ABM system grew after the summit meeting between President Lyndon Johnson and Soviet Premier Alexei Kosygin in June 1967. In 1969 the *Congressional Quarterly* observed that "it was [at that time] the only occasion since World War II on which a substantial part of the public and their representatives in congress questioned the wisdom of the Defense Department on a major issue."[1] A bipartisan group of senators including John Sherman Cooper (R.-Ky.), J. William Fulbright (D-Ark., Chairman of the Foreign Relations Committee), Clifford Case (R.-N.J.), Mike Mansfield (D.-Mont., Majority Leader), Joseph Clark (D.-Pa.), Philip Hart (D.-Mi.), Gaylord Nelson (D.-Wisc.), Edward Brooke (R.-Mass.) and Jacob Javits (R.-N.Y.) concluded that further work on the ABM system endangered deterrence and hence stability. An awareness that its adversary was attempting to protect its own cities or its nuclear launchers might encourage either the United States or the Soviet Union to unleash a preemptive strike. In the words of Senator Brooke's principal adviser on arms control, "these senators were acting on the basis of a high-level political judgment that the United States could best serve its long-term security interests through attempts to negotiate a standstill in the strategic arms race."[2]

In the Nixon administration, anti-ABM senators forced substantial revisions in the original system. In March 1969, the president shifted the focus of the program from a "thin defense" of U.S. cities against a potential Chinese attack (the Sentinel system favored by former Secretary of Defense Robert McNamara) to a "hard defense" of U.S. missile launchers against Soviet assaults (the Safeguard system). This alteration did not satisfy the critics. Senator Albert Gore (D.-Tenn.) derided the change in names and targets as proof that the ABM was "a weapon in search of a mission."[3] By the summer of 1969 the Senate came within one vote of passing the Cooper-Hart amendment deleting funds for construction of any ABM system.

Development of the ABM therefore went forward with the barest possible congressional approval. The Nixon administration managed to keep support for it only by begging senators not to deprive its diplomats of a "bargaining chip" in the negotiations with the Soviet Union over limitations of offensive nuclear weapons. "Negotiations through strength" became the slogan of administration lobbyists.

Over the next three years a team of American diplomats led by Arms Control and Disarmament chief Gerard Smith met with their Soviet counterparts in Helsinki and Vienna. The Senate played a subsidiary role in these Strategic Arms Limitation Talks. Two unofficial observers represented the Foreign Relations and Armed Services Committees at the plenary meetings. Senator John Sherman Cooper, an ardent advocate of an end to the arms race, came from Foreign Relations and Senator Henry Jackson, and equally fervent supporter of the anti-ballistic missile system, spoke for Armed Services. Consequently, the Senate presented highly ambivalent positions at the negotiations. Cooper favored SALT and feared ABM, while Jackson's position was exactly the reverse.

Neither senator, however, was greatly influential in the actual negotiations. They could not spend much time at the talks, so the technical experts worked at their own pace. Moreover, the public negotiations slipped into irrelevance as the "backchannel" conversations between National Security

Adviser Henry Kissinger and Soviet Ambassador to the United States Anatoly Dobrynin emerged. While the public talks stalemated in 1970, Kissinger and Dobrynin went to work.[4]

They divided the issue of ABMs (the primary Soviet concern) and offensive arms (the foremost American issue). In May 1971 the two countries announced that they would "concentrate this year on working out an agreement for the limitation of the deployment of anti-ballistic missile systems. They have also agreed that, together with concluding an agreement to limit ABMs, they will agree on certain measures with respect to the limitation of offensive strategic weapons." In other words, Kissinger and Dobrynin decided that it was easier to reach a firm commitment banning the deployment of ABMs, which did not yet exist, than it was to draft a treaty setting limits on nuclear weapons already deployed. As one observer put it, "left unresolved in the 'backchannel' discussions were the specific limitations to be placed on offensive arms."[5]

Over the next year diplomats on both sides worked feverishly to fill in the details. ABM proved more tractable than SALT. The public negotiators arranged an ABM treaty limiting each side to two deployments, one protecting their capital city and one protecting an ICBM field. Kissinger, however, short-circuited Gerard Smith's team in working out a SALT agreement. He went by himself to Moscow in April 1972 to determine the agenda of the summit meeting the next month between President Nixon and Party Secretary Brezhnev.

When Nixon reached Moscow in May, the national security adviser once more cut the public negotiators out of the process in four days of bargaining. On May 26, the two leaders signed the ABM treaty worked out by the public negotiators. They also put their signatures to an Interim Agreement on Strategic Arms. In it they agreed to limit their offensive ballistic missiles to the same number they had deployed to date. The agreement had a term of five years, with a stipulation that they would try within that period to develop a full fledged treaty. Finally, Nixon and Brezhnev ended their summit on the 29th with a statement of "Basic Principles of U.S.-Soviet Relations." In this, the framework of détente they observed that "there is no alternative to. . . peaceful coexistence." They acknowledged "the principle of equality and the renunciation of the use or threat of force."[6]

When the treaty, interim agreement, and basic principles reached congress in June they revealed disagreements among lawmakers over the organization of American foreign policy and détente. The role of the national security adviser in drafting the treaty stood out in sharp relief to the inactivity of the Secretary of State or Defense. Members of Congress wondered where the SALT process might lead. If the interim agreement had been short on specifics and was not a full-fledged treaty, would the final arrangement satisfy United States interests?

Observing the formal courtesies, Kissinger stepped back and let Secretary of State William Rogers present the case publicly for ABM and SALT.

The official report to Congress on the two agreements came from the secretary's office, and Rogers testified in the public session before the Senate Foreign Relations Committee. Secretary of Defense Melvin Laird, who like Rogers had had little direct input into drafting the agreements, presented the case before the open sessions of the Armed Services Committee. But Kissinger, relishing his role as the wizard who had brokered the final accord, offered the closed door, executive session briefings on the administration's positions.

Both supporters and skeptics revealed ambivalent positions about the agreements at the hearings. Senator Fulbright, an influential advocate of arms control, opened discussion with the observation that "it would have been better for the security of the world had we been able to hold this hearing some time ago." Besides berating the Republican administration for waiting too long to reach an agreement with Moscow, Fulbright also worried that the very lack of specifics in SALT encouraged the acceleration of the arms race. He lamented that "already there have been sounds of alarm and cries to abandon any euphoria. Some [most notably Defense Secretary Laird and Sen. Jackson] say we must have an accelerated program for the development of a new type of missile submarine called Trident and a new supersonic bomber to replace our B-52 fleet, as well as other offensive weapons not covered by the Moscow agreements."[7]

Fulbright and other supports of arms control used the remainder of the hearings to rebut charges that the interim agreement put the United States at a disadvantage. The sticking point was the part of the Basic Principles calling for "equality" between the United States and the Soviet Union. Acknowledgment that the Soviet Union was fully the equal of the United States in international relations had long been a goal of Soviet diplomacy. Moscow expected that a recognition of equality would give the Soviets the right to express their opinions on the same issues as did the United States.

Equality, however, meant different things to different people in different contexts. Senate supporters of arms control tried to demonstrate that the United States and the Soviet Union did not have to match each other missile for missile, warhead for warhead, plane for plane or submarine for submarine. "Sufficiency" to deter an attack or an "equivalency" between the two forces was all that was needed. Senator Javits stressed this point to Secretary Laird. Quoting Kissinger's briefing, Javits asked if Kissinger accurately expressed administration policy when he announced to the Foreign Relations Committee: "Beyond a certain level of sufficiency, differences in numbers therefore are not conclusive." Laird grudgingly admitted that "I believe that we have that sufficient deterrent today." He wanted Congress, however, to go forward with the Trident submarine and the B-1 bomber. Senator Claiborne Pell (D.-R.I.) also made a pitch for substituting "sufficiency" for "superiority" or mechanical equality. He noted that "some years ago we used to talk about negotiating from strength. Then, as we studied the problem more we agreed that if we are dealing with pretty much a man of equal strength we must accept parity, or as President Nixon put it, sufficiency."[8]

These arguments made little headway with Senator Jackson, the chairman of the Arms Control Subcommittee of the Armed Services Committee. Jackson had carried water for the administration in the 1969 debate over the Safeguard ABM system. Now that Kissinger and Nixon had accepted the Soviet position that work stop on ABMs, he had little interest in supporting SALT. He seized upon the vagueness of the numerical limits of the agreement. At the Armed Services Committee hearing he lectured Secretary Laird that "the total number of ICBM missiles [listed in the treaty] represents a unilateral position on our part and does not represent a bilateral understanding with the Russians. . . . In all of my experience, I must say that I have not heard of an agreement which involves such a serious substantive matter as the whole land-based strategic force not being set out in detail in the agreement. This kind of ambiguity can breed suspicion and lead to an unstable situation rather than to a more stable one. So if I do nothing else, I am going to try to nail down, line by line, the exact meaning of these agreements."[9]

Over the next several days of hearing Jackson hammered away at what he considered to be the deficiencies in the SALT interim agreement. He insisted that Kissinger, in his haste to reach an understanding before Nixon left Moscow, had specified the number of missiles the United States would maintain without demanding that the Soviets do the same. He berated Paul Nitze, the Defense Department's expert on arms control, "All you are saying is that there is no ambiguity about the fact that the number is not specified. That is not the point. Without a specific number, there is definitely uncertainty and ambiguity because the Soviets cannot be held to a specific number of ICBM launchers."

SALT I was not a treaty, however, so it would have taken more than the votes of one third of the Senate to prevent its ratification. Jackson probably did not have a majority of the upper house who would oppose any future SALT talks. Besides, arms control had a popular constituency outside of Congress. Therefore, instead of trying to halt SALT, Jackson sought to make sure that future American negotiators followed his design for American force structure. He developed an amendment to the Joint Resolution expressing congressional support for SALT. In it Jackson seized upon the Basic Principle of "equality" to mold the SALT process to his liking.

Jackson turned the notion of equality from a Soviet phrase denoting Western acknowledgment that Moscow was a legitimate state with rights equivalent to those enjoyed by the United States, to an affirmation that the missile forces of the two powers be equal in every particular. His amendment to the Joint Resolution insisted that the standard for the forthcoming set of SALT negotiations was to be "the principle of United States-Soviet equality reflected in the Anti-Ballistic Missile Treaty."[10] It warned that pending a permanent limit on offensive weapons, the United States would consider new

Soviet deployments endangering American weapons to be contrary to U.S. interests. It also called for continuation of research and development of the next generation of American missiles.

Some forty senators joined Jackson in sponsoring these amendments. For those concerned that SALT might promise more than it could deliver, the amendment seemed a good way of hedging a bet. Moreover, what could be more innocent than an appeal to "equality" between the United States and the Soviet Union?

Yet supporters of SALT, led by Senators Fulbright and Cooper, perceived that the Jackson amendment altered Kissinger's arrangements. They resisted the language and forced some modifications in it. For example, the amendment as passed did not specifically mention the new weapons that the United States would develop in response to new Soviet deployments. Nonetheless, Jackson's objections turned the debate away from the accomplishments of the Moscow summit into a discussion of the future of arms control. In it the lawmakers came closer to Jackson's skepticism than to Fulbright's optimism.

On the floor, Fulbright and Alan Cranston (D.-Calif.) took the lead in opposing Jackson's request that the United States match the Soviet Union launcher for launcher. According to Fulbright, the general public had a better, intuitive understanding of equality than did the senator from Washington. This common sense approach meant "overall equality, and that is overall equality of nuclear weapons—equality of capacity to develop new ones. . . . I do not believe that what the Senator from Washington is really saying is that—regardless of the degree of superiority we may have in the fields of airplanes and the capacity to deliver nuclear weapons from forward bases, or our superiority in other areas—these are excluded from his concept of equality, and that all the senator is contemplating when he uses the word 'equality' is in the number of intercontinental missiles." Jackson shot back that "it is amazing for the Chairman of the Foreign Relations Committee to tell over forty members of the Senate that they do not know what equality in intercontinental forces is about."[11]

In the end, much of Jackson's language remained in the Joint Resolution. Congress went on record favoring equality in negotiations between the United States and the Soviet Union. It did not, however, threaten specific weapons systems if the Soviets did not accept the American understanding of equality. The resolution also chided the administration for not going very far toward *reducing* armaments. It called for the beginning of Strategic Arms Reduction Talks (a Jackson locution now popular with the Reagan administration). Finally Congress insisted that any new treaties be "concrete agreement," an obvious recognition of Jackson's concern over the slipperiness of the numbers.[12]

The Senate's participation in the ABM-SALT negotiations and ratification reveals the extent and limits of congressional advice during the Nixon-Kissinger era. This was an administration notoriously reluctant to share power.

In the SALT negotiations the national security adviser effectively cut the
Secretary of State and the Arms Control and Disarmament Agency out of the
crucial decisions. What hope, therefore, was there for effective policy emerging from another branch of the government?

Yet despite this suspicion from the White House, many of the contours
of arms control came from the Senate. Without senatorial skepticism over the
anti-ballistic missile system, the administration would not have been as willing
to cut a deal on ABM. That backchannel breakthrough led to the treaty. But
the ABM debate also brought Henry Jackson into the center of the SALT
process. It was Jackson's skepticism, or what his adversaries would describe
as his obtuse nit-picking, which helped erode support for SALT. As long as
supporters of arms control could focus attention on the fact that the United
States and the Soviet Union, despite their difference, were actively engaged
in a *process* which *could* slow the race, they held the upper hand. When
Jackson managed to turn attention to specific details, however, the arms
control consensus broke down. The results were obvious six years later when
exactly that sort of skepticism or nit-picking prevented the ratification of
SALT II, the only arms limitation treaty negotiated on the principles outlined
in the Joint Resolution of September 1972.

NOTES

1. *Congress and the Nation*, vol. II (Washington: Congressional Quarterly
Service, 1969), 869. See also Alton Frye, *A Responsible Congress: The Politics of
National Security* (New York: McGraw Hill, 1975), especially 15–46.

2. Frye, 22.

3. U.S. Senate, Commitee on Armed Services, *Authorization for Military
Procurement, Research and Development, Fiscal Year 1970 and Reserve Strength*,
Part 2, April 22 and 23, 1969.

4. The negotiations are covered in: John Newhouse, *Cold Dawn: The Story of
SALT* (New York: Holt, Rinehart and Winston, 1973); Mason Willrich and John B.
Rhinelander, eds., *SALT: The Moscow Agreements and Beyond* (New York: Free
Press, 1974); Henry Kissinger, *White House Years, 1969–1973* (Boston: Little, Brown,
1979); and Gerard Smith, *Doubletalk: The Story of the First Strategic Arms Limitations
Talks* (New York: Doubleday, 1980).

5. Roger P. Labrie, "Overview," in Labrie, ed., *SALT Handbook* (Washington:
American Enterprise Institute, 1979), 13.

6. "Basic Principles of Relations Between the United States of America and
the Union of Soviet Socialist Republics," *Department of State Bulletin*, 26 June 1972,
898.

7. United States Senate, Committee on Foreign Relations, *Strategic Arms Limitation Agreements* June 19–22, 1972. 92d Cong. 2d sess.

8. Ibid.

9. United States Senate, Committee on Armed Services, *Military Implications of the Treaty on the Limitations of Anti-Ballistic Missiles and the Interim Agreement on the Limitations of Strategic Offensive Arms*, June 20–July 18, 1972. 92d Cong. 2d sess. See also Henry M. Jackson, "Weapons Agreements: A Senator Questions U.S. Concessions," *Los Angeles Times*, 25 June 1972, F7.

10. Public Law 92–448, as amended by Senator Jackson. Approved by House on 25 September 1972 and Senate on 30 September 1972.

11. United States Congress, Senate, *Congressional Record*, 92d Cong. 2d sess., 1972. Vol. 118, no. 138, S14280.

12. PL 92–448.

7

Constraining SALT II: The Role of the Senate

STANLEY J. HEGINBOTHAM

On January 3, 1980, nine days after the Soviets invaded Afghanistan, then-President Jimmy Carter asked the Senate to delay further consideration of the SALT II Treaty. It had been under consideration by the Senate for 191 days, but its approval for ratification had been in serious doubt from the beginning. Even before the invasion of Afghanistan, SALT II had been under serious attack from a broad range of quarters within the Senate on grounds that it:

- perpetuated a Soviet advantage in numbers of "heavy" ICBMs;
- failed adequately to assure U.S. monitoring of Soviet compliance;
- allowed the Soviet Union to build strategic forces that would not be adequately matched by the strategic and conventional forces the Carter administration planned to acquire;
- represented excessive, unnecessary, and unwise compromise of U.S. advantages in order to perpetuate an arms control negotiating process; and
- represented unwarranted reward and recognition for the Soviet Union, which had in recent years behaved irresponsibly in the Third World by exporting revolution to Ethiopia and Angola and by moving combat forces into Cuba.[1]

SALT II, whose provisions expired on 31 December 1985, never received further Senate consideration. Some maintain that, absent the invasion of Afghanistan, the Senate would eventually have consented to ratification of SALT II; others are skeptical.[2]

What, in retrospect, is so extraordinary, however, is that despite the absence of Senate support for it, and despite the subsequent election of Ronald

Reagan, many of whose major defense policy advisors vigorously opposed it, the major provisions of SALT II continued to be observed by the U.S. government until late 1986. Some cynics, of course, write this paradox off to the hypocrisy and inconsistency of the president and his supporters. Others bemoan the fact that the Senate became so deeply enmeshed in the details of the treaty and in issues only tangentially related to it. In this view a responsible Senate would have consented to its ratification following a much more expedited review of its provisions. A third conclusion, however, shapes this chapter. It is that the process of congressional-executive relations leading to advice and consent by the Senate failed to reflect the public will. In this view, failure to achieve ratification was not a product of public opposition to the substance of the treaty, but to the way it was negotiated. If this is the case, it should be useful to reexamine that experience in order to understand both what went wrong and how it might be better managed on future occasions.

UNDERSTANDING THE PROCESS AND THE CONTEXT OF SENATE ACTION ON SALT II

Those of us who become engrossed in the role of Congress in foreign policy need to be clear about the fundamental features of SALT II. It was a treaty negotiated by the president of the United States with his counterpart in the Soviet Union. It is not to demean the role of the Senate to recall that it is one of review: to determine whether or not to consent to the ratification of the president's treaty. Clearly the Founding Fathers, by requiring that at least two thirds of senators voting support the president in order to permit ratification, reflected their concern that any treaty have broad public support if it were to enter into force.

Nuclear arms control, however, is not a free-standing policy area. It is one instrument of what is known as strategic policy. A credible nuclear force posture based on military weapons systems designed to avoid nuclear war while protecting American interests vis-à-vis the Soviet Union is the other primary instrument of strategic policy. Here the role of the Senate, working in conjunction with the House of Representatives, is equally vital: it must vote to fund or not to fund the individual components of the president's research, development, and procurement programs to deploy those weapons systems.

The dynamics that flow from this basic statement of the relationship between the president and the Soviet leadership on the one hand, and between the president and the Senate on the other hand are extensive and important to understand. First is the perspective of president as negotiator. Second the perspective of Senate as part of the negotiator's funding and approving constituency. And third is the notion of a presidential strategy for managing the complex political and substantive process that must be followed to achieve three competing ends:

- the vigorous protection of the national security interest, including arms control agreements with the Soviets (if any are to be had on terms that benefit American national security interests);
- the approval of Congress to fund appropriate weapons systems and to consent to ratification of any arms control agreements he concludes; and
- electoral success for himself and his party.

A. *The President as Arms Control Negotiator*

Negotiations as Zero-sum and Expanding-sum Games. Strategic policy provides a classic illustration of the proposition that negotiation situations are a mix of what theorists call zero-sum and expanding-sum elements. For some observers, the critical features of strategic policy are zero-sum, i.e., those in which any Soviet gain is produced at the expense of a comparable U.S. loss, and vice versa. These observers tend to ask questions such as:

- Can one side create perceptions of nuclear superiority that would lead the other to suffer in conventional military, diplomatic, economic, or public opinion arenas?
- Could one side survive nuclear conflict in a way that would give it a significant advantage over the other in a post-conflict world?

For other observers, the critical features of strategic policy are expanding-sum, i.e. those in which a change can produce gains for both the Soviet and the American sides. For those who emphasize this perspective, the key questions tend to be:

- Can nuclear forces of the two sides be managed so that they deter either side from resorting to military force?
- Can mutual distrust and fear be contained so that the financial, organizational, and human resources spent on nuclear weapons systems can progressively be reduced?

The problem for the president is to maintain a reasonable balance between the two perspectives, recognizing that excessive emphasis on either perspective will create dynamics for compensatory attention to the other. The president who is concerned with avoiding nuclear conflict to the exclusion of concern with limiting Soviet expansion and global influence promotes Soviet behavior and responses in the American public that force greater attention to containing Soviet gains made at the expense of the United States. The president who focuses on containing the Soviets without regard for the need to reduce the destructive potential of our forces and the incentives to use them promotes public pressures for strengthening procedures for reducing the risk of war.

The Tactics of Negotiating. Negotiating is, by nature, risky. The negotiator who lets it be known that he is not prepared to risk failure of the negotiations is at a distinct disadvantage in negotiating over zero-sum elements with an adversary who convincingly takes the position that he could prosper with or without an agreement. Thus, the skilled and practiced negotiator goes to considerable length to create and sustain uncertainty in the mind of his adversary as to what the negotiator really wants, what he would accept, and how anxious he is for an agreement, especially with respect to those aspects of the negotiations that he sees to be zero-sum in character. He avoids appearing too anxious for an agreement, and tries to create the impression that delay disadvantages him less than it does his adversary. He suggests bargains that reflect significant advantages to his side, recognizing that his adversary is likely to do the same and that the final agreement is likely to be very close to the mid-point between the two initial positions. He emphasizes the political constraints as well as the objective interests that limit his flexibility in accommodating to the demands of his adversary. Away from the bargaining table his behavior suggests his readiness to thrive or even prosper in the absence of an agreement.[3]

The negotiator recognizes the risks in such posturing. His bluff can be called; his actual position can be exposed by dissidents on his own negotiating team; his political support base can desert him if he seems too inflexible; his opponent can conclude that he isn't seriously interested in an agreement and terminate negotiations; his opponent can take actions that reduce his dependence on a successful outcome of the negotiations.

Risk taking in strategic policy making and arms control negotiating has a quality all of its own because miscalculation and failure can quite conceivably lead to nuclear holocast. The predisposition of a president to take risks by posturing in arms control negotiations seems primarily to depend on his sense of confidence in his ability to handle negotiating situations and on the extent to which he views strategic policy issues as zero-sum or expanding-sum. For the president who feels that reducing the risk of nuclear war is vastly more important than preventing the Soviets from obtaining advantages over the United States, the incentives for risky posturing in negotiations seem minimal. As the analysis of the experience of SALT II will suggest, however, *failure* to adopt somewhat risky postures in negotiations involves its own dangers.

Stages and Timing of Negotiations. Time management is perhaps the most crucial aspect of negotiations. Because neither side is anxious to make concessions, the pace of events in negotiations is usually forced by some kind of external event. In strategic policy negotiations, the dominant forcing event is the quadrennial American presidential election. Both sides recognize that the American negotiating team is assured only of four years of tenure and will be in place for a maximum of eight. Whether to play for a four or an eight year negotiating cycle is a key decision. Beyond that, each side must figure out how to pace developments so that they can complete the negotiations and allow adequate time for Senate action before the cycle ends or the political climate of national elections makes conclusion of the process impracticable.

Negotiations predictably go through four major stages. *First* is establishing the context and atmosphere for the negotiations. This is an important period that is often not associated with negotiations because frequently both parties are emphasizing their disinterest in negotiations on any terms that would be of interest to their adversary. In strategic policy, emphasis might be on force structure development and on public presentation of positions designed to embarrass the other side more than provide a basis for serious negotiation. *Second* is shaping initial negotiable bargaining positions and a strategy for reaching an agreement. This is generally a period of intense bargaining within each side's national security bureaucracy. *Third* is a process of mutual and incremental adjustment of positions leading to conclusion of an agreement. This is the phase that most observers think of when they consider negotiations. And *fourth* is ratification, when the agreement is subjected to approval by political authorities.

The negotiator who wants to pursue higher risk strategies can disguise the extent of his interest in negotiations by dictating relatively slow movement through these stages, gambling that last-minute difficulties won't derail an agreement. The less risk-oriented negotiator can use external events other than quadrennial election benchmarks (such as summit meetings or decisions to fund, test, or deploy new weapons systems) as forcing mechanisms to accelerate the pace of negotiations.

B. The Senate as Funder of Weapons and Consenter to Ratification

It is well to recall that the Senate is a deliberative body that is organized to pass judgments through a series of votes on legislative proposals. Despite the size of its supporting staffs, its organizational characteristics are not those of a bureaucracy. Indeed, if anything, it is quintessentially antibureaucratic in structure, lacking hierarchy, functional differentiation based on mutual exclusivity, continuing monitoring capability, selection and promotion through merit systems, and clear distinction between person and position. It is, as a result, quite incapable of producing the kinds of broad and integrated policy proposals that a bureaucracy can. Nor can it formulate elaborate negotiating positions or conduct the kinds of sustained and orchestrated negotiations that a bureaucracy can.[4]

The point is important here because it helps to delineate the role that the Senate can realistically be expected to play in strategic policy and arms control. The Senate is not organized to work with the executive branch to codetermine defense and arms control policy. Rather it is organized to do what the constitution asks it to do: to either affirm or deny the executive branch the authority it asks for to acquire weapons systems and to ratify treaties. In providing advice and consent, its members may suggest or require modifications on the margin to accommodate its concerns. Indeed, a foresighted administration may attempt to craft a legislative proposal or treaty in order to anticipate the concerns of key senators. To speak, as is the fashion, of a reassertive Congress or Senate, however, is to speak of a Congress or Senate that performs its affirming or denying role with thoroughness and vigor, not to speak of a structure of government that had transformed itself into a bureaucracy that can replicate the activities of the executive branch.

The Senate is also a body of generalists. Each member must confront the full scope of federal legislation in addition to extensive and complex political problems and heavy demands for servicing the needs of individual constituents. When faced with a problem of the complexity of SALT II, most senators must look for simplifying devices that make their decisions more manageable. Where a decision is reasonably clear cut, they can often limit the extent of their involvement in the issue.

A common and effective simplifying device for senatorial scanning of strategic defense policy and arms control is built around questions as to the extent to which the United States is and should be flexible and accommodating toward the Soviet Union. Those favoring relative inflexibility generally emphasize the zero-sum character of the relationship, support extensive military expenditures, and are dubious about the prospects and promise of arms control. Those who are inclined to greater flexibility stress the importance of avoiding nuclear conflict, tend to see military expenditures as contributing to a spiraling of defense spending, and view arms control as central to strategic policy.

In order to pursue successfully his strategic policy, a president must cope with two threats from the Senate:

- the threat of opposition to his defense spending from a majority who see the president as too inflexible toward the Soviets;
- the threat of opposition to his arms control agreements from a one-third plus one minority who see the president as too flexible toward the Soviets.

If one assumes that senators vote exclusively on the basis of their perceptions of presidential flexibility toward the Soviets, the president faces a peculiar and disturbing gap. If he adopts a posture toward the Soviet Union that is slightly on the flexible side of the spectrum in order to assure support for his defense program, his arms control proposals are likely to be seen as too flexible by a slight majority, perhaps 51, of the Senate. He can secure ratification of an agreement, however, only if he can reduce the number of opponents below thirty-four. Though the numbers are hypothetical and the assumptions are unrealistic, they nevertheless suggest the character and magnitude of the problem facing a president when he contemplates taking a treaty before the Senate.

Two other features of the Senate deserve brief note. The first is that its voting, like that of many representative bodies, is characterized by frequent linkage across issues. When a president's defense appropriation request or an arms control treaty is under consideration, the president can either use, or have used against him, leverage on other issues. He can count on a shift in his favor when his military procurement proposals are being considered because of his ability to influence decisions that will determine the distribution of the economic benefits from the contracts. When his arms control proposals are considered, however, he must count on a shift against him because he is in need of Senate votes and has little of substance to offer in return. Senators who place higher priority on aspects of U.S.-Soviet relations other than arms control are particularly likely to seek policy changes in those areas in return for their support of arms control. Though the shift favors the president in the case of appropriations and works against him on arms control treaties, in both cases the president must position himself somewhat to the more inflexible side of the spectrum than he otherwise would in order to account for the shifts.

Finally, those who are especially troubled by the increased assertiveness of the Senate often fail to see the self-restraint that goes with that assertiveness. Though many in the Senate are prepared to press presidents to the point of concession and compromise, few relish the thought of facing a president with the outright repudiation of international commitments he has already made. Thus, behind all of the posturing in opposition to a president lies a widespread interest in and desire for ultimate compromise with him.

C. Presidential Strategies for Management of the Senate

The analysis thus far leads to the following conclusion: The president, who represents the national interest in complex and extended negotiations with the Soviet Union on arms control, must devise a strategy for managing those negotiations that not only promises reasonable results at the bargaining table but also reasonable prospect of approval for ratification in the Senate. His problem in doing so is complicated by the electoral cycle and the peculiar requirement for the support of sixty-seven senators for treaty ratification. This is largely a problem of positioning along the flexibility-inflexibility continuum toward the Soviet Union within the Senate. If he appears as flexible and accommodating as about half of the Senate, he has good prospects of gaining support for his strategic weapons programs. He needs to appear as inflexible as more than two-thirds of the Senate, however, to be assured of relatively easy assent to any arms control treaty he presents.

Only a president who is extraordinarily fleet of foot or extraordinarily lucky is likely to be able to negotiate the transformation across perhaps 15–18 percent of the senatorial spectrum on attitudes toward the Soviet Union while progressing from defining his force structure requirements to defining and then negotiating an arms control proposal. He then has, however, other resources which he can use to bring his support among senators to the necessary sixty-seven: the resources he commands as head of his party; the resources he commands as president; the appeal of his need as commander in chief to avoid the international humiliation of having a treaty he had signed rejected by the Senate; and the logic of the benefits of the treaty he had negotiated.

The dilemma for a president, then, is how to position himself so that he can sustain congressional support for his strategic weapons systems program, achieve a satisfactory arms control agreement (if the Soviets are prepared to accept an agreement that is on balance of benefit to the United States), and have sufficient senatorial support for the agreement to make it feasible to use his political and personal resources to reduce the number of opponents to thirty-three.

PRESIDENTIAL POSITIONING FOR THE NEGOTIATING AND SELLING OF SALT II

The president begins to position himself along a spectrum of flexibility-inflexibility toward the Soviet Union through actions and statements on a wide range of topics. Carter, for example, gave early and strong signals of flexibility toward the Soviets by his nominations of Ted Sorenson to head the CIA and Paul Warnke to head the Arms Control and Disarmament Agency and be chief SALT negotiator. This section, however, focuses on four elements in presidential positioning that were of special significance for SALT II. First was *timing*. How rapidly did the president try to press forward the progress of negotiations? How successful was he in conveying the impression that the Soviets had more to lose from delay than the U.S.? Second was *military force requests*. How strong a force did the president seem to want? Was it perceived as providing adequate protection in the absence of arms control? Third was *linkage policy*. How did the president and his spokesmen describe the relationship between arms control and other aspects of U.S.-Soviet relations? Did they try to insulate arms control from conflictual issues? Did they suggest that progress in arms control would depend on satisfactory Soviet behavior in other arenas of concern to the United States? And fourth was *arms control policy*. How tough a negotiating position did the president seem to take? Did he seem to hold firm on key issues in order to assure the achievement of significant American advantage on zero-sum elements in the negotiations?

A. Timing

SALT II negotiations began in a difficult context for the Carter administration. Substantial progress had been made under the second Nixon and the Ford administrations toward a SALT II agreement. Indeed the Vladivostok agreement of November 1974 had seemed to provide the major ingredients of an agreement. As the 1976 presidential primaries approached, however, and Ford was challenged from the right by Ronald Reagan, the political consequences of making necessary accommodations with the Soviets to conclude an agreement seemed increasingly unmanageable.[5]

Thus, when Carter came to power, he was faced with the major elements of an arms control agreement that had been negotiated by a man he had just defeated in national elections. From the substantive perspective, an agreement seemed close at hand. From the political perspective, however, an effort to achieve a quick agreement would be problematic. It could blur the distinction between Ford and Carter approaches to arms control.

From the perspective of the negotiating tactician who was prepared to take some risks, Carter seemed to have two options. The first was to present an essentially new proposal as a signal of willingness to set aside the Vladivostok process and to wait for Soviet responsiveness. The second was to try to arrange a forcing event that would lead to a quick tying up of the remaining pieces of the Vladivostok agreement and then establish a distinctive Carter approach in a subsequent initiative.

Carter in fact presented a proposal to the Soviets that was seen as a radical departure from the step by step progress that had been made on the Vladivostok road. The proposal, which called for "deep cuts" in both sides' strategic forces, was developed within a very small group in the bureaucracy and then announced with a great deal of public fanfare shortly before it was presented to the Soviets. The various accounts of the period suggest that the proposal was calculated to move the administration boldly and expeditiously toward significant arms control achievements, distinguish dramatically the Carter from the Ford approaches, and neutralize the danger from conservative Senate Democrats.[6]

The Soviet rejection of the Carter position came quickly and unambiguously. What is interesting about the incident, however, is not the Soviet reaction, but the effect that reaction had on the Carter administration. The presentation of the proposal had many of the earmarks of a signal of disinterest in rapid progress on arms control in favor of pushing the Soviets to make compromises on a new and more ambitious approach. Part of such a signal, well accepted in international negotiation, would be to present a first proposal in a highly public way in order to gain as much propaganda value from it as possible. Viewed from this perspective, the Soviet response seemed appropriate: firm and unambiguous rejection with vigorous public accusations and strong indications of willingness to outwait the United States. The United States could then have adjusted its positions to counter Soviet propaganda points, moving eventually toward positions that would provide the bases of serious detailed negotiations.[7]

The insider accounts of the period make clear, however, that the comprehensive proposal was not a negotiating tactic, but a very serious proposal designed to speed negotiations toward a rapid conclusion. Senior administration negotiators were shocked, surprised, and distressed by the Soviet response. They thought that their proposal had been crafted so as to contain at least one alternative that could draw a positive Soviet response.

When they recovered from their shock at the Soviet reaction, administration officials felt that they had fallen seriously behind schedule and would have to try to force the pace of negotiations to catch up to their original schedule. The Soviets, meanwhile, had adjusted their sights to a much longer timeframe. The results were a set of signals to both the Soviets and to the SALT-sensitive Senate that the administration was now anxious to move quickly toward agreement. Zbigniew Brzezinski, who shared neither the high priority that Carter gave to arms control in U.S.-Soviet relations nor the impatience of Vance and Warnke for an agreement, commented of this period, "The Soviets were making every effort to obtain from President Carter a quick SALT agreement on terms favorable to the Soviet Union. . . . The Soviets must have assumed that Carter's public commitment to SALT gave them bargaining leverage which could be exploited to obtain these ends." Carter writes in his memoirs, "[The Soviet leaders] refused to submit any counter-offers, except a proposal to meet again in May to consider much more limited options and resolve some of the issues left over from Vladivostok. It was obvious that they wanted to move slowly and in small increments. I was angry over the Soviet attitude, and disappointed because we would have to set back our timetable for an agreement."

Secretary of State Vance was candid about his own views of timing the SALT negotiations:

> . . . some of the president's political advisors were worried about the attacks from the Right, and were concerned about the SALT head count in the Senate. They recommended that we deliberately slow down the negotiations and toughen our positions. It was suggested that this was necessary to undercut the opponents who were claiming that the administration was in too much of a hurry.
>
> I disagreed emphatically. We should be under no artificial sense of urgency in the negotiations, and we should not compromise our security interests for the sake of an agreement. But I wanted to keep moving steadily ahead without any self-imposed delay. A responsible administration could not allow so fundamental an objective to be sidetracked. I need not have been concerned about the president. He rejected all such advice.[8]

It was well into 1978 before prospects for an agreement again began to seem promising. The Soviets had been showing a great deal of inflexibility and impatience and, though demand for progress in the administration was palpable, the interagency process of developing and presenting positions limited its flexibility. In his account of these frustrating months, Strobe Talbott describes the end of what seemed like a potentially climactic Vance-Gromyko negotiating session:

> The meeting had gone so well that a number of American officials hoped that Vance and Gromyko might be able to tie up the loose ends in SALT in a matter of days. [Then, when Gromyko returned to Moscow abruptly] Carter himself was disappointed and angry. He commented in a meeting with his staff that the Soviets seemed to be "dragging it out" and that he was "impatient and frustrated—do the Russians want it or don't they?"[9]

The negotiations did indeed drag out for an additional nine months. What seemed like little issues became the focus of prolonged haggling. The U.S. felt under increasing pressure not to compromise further as the magnitude of the forthcoming Senate debate became clear; the Soviets seem to have wanted to extract any advantage they thought they could get as the Americans became increasingly nervous about the limited time available for ratification before the presidential campaign season arrived.

The Carter negotiating approach seems clearly then to have positioned the administration as being highly flexible toward the Soviets. In part this was a product of its firm commitment to obtain an early agreement. Its anxiety for an agreement was increased, however, by Soviet misreading of its comprehensive proposal as a bargaining ploy designed to slow the pace of negotiations. It is indeed ironic that in the final analysis it was timing that killed prospects for SALT II ratification. The agreement was reached in June of 1979 and observers generally agreed that Senate action would have to be completed by the end of 1979 to allow Republicans who were up for election in 1980 time to recover from having supported a Democratic president's treaty (for those who voted for the Panama Canal treaties, the burden would be a doubly difficult one). In order to understand why six months was inadequate time for this process, however, we need to look at how the president's actions and rhetoric on force structure, linkage policy, and arms control policy served to position him along the dimension of flexibility toward the Soviets.

B. Military Force Requests

Both conventional and nuclear force structure issues became embroiled in the SALT II debate. When Jimmy Carter took charge of the country's national security in 1977, defense spending had declined, in real terms, from $256 billion in 1968 to $171 billion (in constant 1985 dollars). Though much of that decline was from the abnormal peaks of the Vietnam War, defense spending had not been as low as it was in 1976 and 1977 since 1951. Many steps that had been taken to hold down defense spending in the post-Vietnam war years had cost the services heavily in terms of the readiness and sustainability of their forces. Nuclear force modernization had also been deferred during much of this period so that development and funding decisions for a new strategic bomber and a new land-based missile would be awaiting the administration.[10]

The public mood of the period, however, seemed more impressed by the magnitude of defense spending and the need to keep that spending under control. Carter came to power in part on the basis of his commitment to achieving arms control agreements with the Soviets and avoiding unnecessary defense spending. Negotiating theory suggests that Carter might have improved his bargaining positioning vis-à-vis the Soviets had he, during an initial phase of positioning and context setting, begun significantly to request increases in defense spending and especially in strategic systems. For Carter to have done so, however, would clearly have been to fly in the face of his natural constituency. Far more comfortable were the steps that he did take during his first two and one-half years in office: the pursuit of defense budgets that left defense spending in fiscal year 1980 less than 1 percent higher than it had been in fiscal year 1977, the cancellation of the major strategic modernization program up for consideration, the B-1 bomber, and the deferral of work on enhanced-radiation nuclear warheads.

As with Carter's approach to timing of negotiations, his action and rhetoric served to position him well to the side of flexibility in the spectrum of Senate approaches to the Soviets. Both the B-1 and the neutron bomb decisions were particularly striking because attempts could have been made in negotiations with the Soviets to gain some concessions in return for the cancellations. The Carter administration saw these as decisions to be made on their own merits, however, independent of arms control negotiations. It was only in the months immediately proceeding the signing of SALT II that the major strategic modernization proposal of the administration was announced: the development of the MX missile in complex "racetrack" settings designed to provide mobility, invulnerability to attack, and accessibility to Soviet inspection.[11]

C. Linkage Policy

Perhaps the single most significant tactical problem in negotiating SALT was that of managing linkage. At issue was the relationship between the SALT negotiations and other aspects of the U.S.-Soviet relationship: to what extent should progress on SALT depend on reasonable Soviet behavior on other matters? It was an issue of negotiating tactics because linkage policy was a major factor in defining how important SALT would seem to be to the administration. Negotiating theory suggests that the U.S. bargaining position could have been enhanced, at some risk to the prospects for agreement, had we used a policy of linkage to persuade the Soviets that arms control issues were of lesser importance to us than to them. A stated policy of linking arms control to Soviet behavior on other issues says, in effect, that we are prepared to risk failure of negotiations in the belief that the Soviets are sufficiently concerned with arms control that they will constrain their behavior in other areas in order to improve prospects for arms control agreements. We are, we suggest, prepared to live without arms control if they fail to cooperate in other aspects of the bilateral relationship. A policy of delinking arms control negotiations from Soviet behavior, on the other hand, says that the mutual advantages of arms control (i.e. its positive-sum features) are so dominant that it is neither appropriate nor necessary to try to gain tactical advantage from the Soviets by linking them to other aspects of the relationship.

Though there were differences within the Carter administration, the latter approach dominated during most of the pre-ratification period, again contributing to a positioning of the administration toward the side of flexibility in its dealings with the Soviets. The president himself saw linkage, which he defined as "basing progress on arms control to [sic] good behavior by the Soviets," as an obstacle to success created by anti-SALT groups. Vance was most articulate, consistent, and outspoken in his opposition to linkage of arms control to other issues in the bilateral relationship. "When cooperation could enhance our security, as in limiting the nuclear arms race, it should be pursued without attempting to link it to other issues." Marshall Shulman, his senior advisor on U.S.-Soviet relations, saw a two-track model, with those aspects of the relationship involving mutual interests such as crisis stability and avoidance of nuclear war being pursued independently of competitive aspects of the relationship.[12]

Though the linkage issue first arose with respect to human rights in the Soviet Union, it soon became focused around Soviet behavior in the Third World. As Soviet and Cuban actions in Zaire, Angola, the Horn of Africa, and elsewhere on the continent raised concerns among American observers, the administration was more and more frequently asked how arms control negotiations could go forward in the face of such Soviet behavior. On 1 March 1978, Brzezinski, who was generally thought to be more concerned about Soviet actions in Africa than many of his colleagues, said, in answering a press question, that "if tensions [with the Soviets over Africa] were to rise . . . then that will inevitably complicate the context not only of the negotiating process itself but also of any ratification that would follow. . . ." Vance, the next day, said to the Senate Foreign Relations Committee, "There is no linkage between the SALT negotiations and the situation in Ethiopia." Brzezinski quotes from notes of a meeting of the Special Coordination Committee of the National Security Council later that same day:

BRZEZINSKI: The President said in response to a question this noon that there is no linkage but Soviet actions may impose such linkage.

VANCE: I think it is wrong to say that this is going to produce linkage, and it is of fundamental importance.

BRZEZINKSI: It is going to poison the atmosphere.

VANCE: We will end up losing SALT and that will be the worst thing that could happen. If we do not get a SALT treaty in the President's first four years, that will be a blemish on his record forever.

BRZEZINSKI: It will be a blemish on his record also if the treaty gets rejected by the Senate.[13]

This was, of course, a debate over negotiating tactics. Vance was concerned primarily with sending a message to the American people that it was legitimate and proper to move forward on SALT, events in Africa notwithstanding. Brzezinski was more interested in sending a message to the Soviets warning that they could pay consequences in the delay or failure of SALT II if they persisted in their behavior in Africa. Ironically, the message that probably mattered most was the unintended one drawn by some Senate moderates: that, in a badly divided administration, key policymakers were so publicly anxious for an arms control agreement that they did not want the success of that agreement to be jeopardized by any other problems, even though such a posture weakened the U.S. bargaining position.

D. Arms Control Policy

The Substance of the Agreement. The history of SALT II can be, of course—and usually is—written as a story of the substance of the agreement. The substantive issues have been widely discussed and analyzed. They are certainly of fundamental importance to a thorough understanding of the treaty and of the Senate's review of it. It is the thesis of this chapter, however, that focus on the specific issues can draw attention away from the broader context within which the Senate debate needs to be understood. What is important to understand, in short, is why the detailed provisions of a treaty that has been observed with virtually unanimous consent for over five years should have faced such detailed, hostile, and potentially fatal questioning in the Senate. Rather than cover the substantive issues in detail, it is helpful to illustrate some general points by drawing on one example.

One of the features of U.S. and Soviet strategic forces has been their asymmetry. The Soviets have relied very extensively on land-based systems and on very large but not necessarily highly sophisticated or accurate missile delivery systems. The strategic inventory of the United States has been better balanced among bombers and land- and sea-based missiles. We have also relied more heavily on accuracy than sheer size in order to achieve destructive potential and have had the advantage of being able to use bases in Europe and elsewhere in Eurasia from which to target parts of the Soviet Union.

Asymmetric forces typically require asymmetric bargains if they are to be constrained through arms control. In SALT I, for example, the five year interim agreement allowed the Soviets 40 percent more ICBM launchers than the United States, and 308 launchers of so-called "heavy" ICBMs to our 54. The agreement looked good to our negotiators because, in return for these concessions to the Soviets, it allowed us to pursue those areas in which we were ahead—bombers, sea-launched cruise missiles, the use of multiple, separately guided warheads on individual missiles, and improvements in accuracy—relatively unimpeded.[14]

When the agreement was presented to the Senate for approval, however, it did not look good to Senator Henry Jackson, who argued that intercontinental missiles, and especially the capacity of those missiles to deliver warheads—know as their "throwweight"—was too important to have been bargained away as it had been in SALT I. Jackson voted for the resolution, but only after the Senate had added his amendment, which reflected Senate guidance that:

> future treaties on offensive weapons not limit the United States to levels of intercontinental strategic forces inferior to those of the Soviet Union.[15]

When Carter's consultation with Jackson during the first month of his administration drew the Perle-Jackson memo of advice on SALT II, among its suggestions were that further cuts be made in limits on heavy Soviet missiles and that much more extensive cuts be made in overall ceilings. These approaches were included in the Carter administration's comprehensive proposal, which it presented in Moscow several months later. Though many other factors shaped the administration's proposal and some of the Perle-Jackson recommendations were not included in it, a distinct argument in favor of the proposal was seen to be that it would improve the prospects of gaining Jackson's support for an eventual treaty.

After both sides recovered from the trauma of the Moscow sessions at which the Soviets rejected the comprehensive proposal, however, a process of incremental adjustment of positions began. Press accounts suggested that the administration had removed the limit on heavy missiles from their negotiating position and had raised their ceiling on MIRVed missiles—those with multiple independent warheads—by 45 percent. Jackson and his supporters felt that the administration had made crucial concessions in its rush to reach an agreement. When the administration argued that the restrictions on "heavy" missiles were less important than the ceiling on MIRVed missiles that it had achieved because a new MIRVed Soviet missile, the SS-19, was of greater concern than the "heavy" SS-18, Jackson and Perle seemed particularly outraged because they had argued that Carter should have negotiated to redefine "heavy" missiles to include the SS-19. "Hell," Strobe Talbott quotes Perle as saying, "Scoop himself had been warning the arms controllers about the SS-19 ever since SALT I failed to define the SS-19 as a heavy!"[16]

Before the end of the first year of the Carter administration, then, the White House effort to co-opt and neutralize Jackson and those who supported him had failed. A bitter kind of conflict involving leaks and counterleaks and charges and countercharges evolved. As Talbott described it: "The battle lines were drawn. . . . Jackson and other critics of SALT declared war on the treaty to which the Carter administration had now committed itself."[17]

Both participants in and observers of the experience with the American comprehensive initiative and our subsequent withdrawal from its provisions have concluded that one of its worst consequences was that it provided opponents with a bench mark against which they could mercilessly attack SALT II. Vance wrote:

> Perhaps the most serious cost of the Moscow discussions was to be felt later in the domestic battle over SALT ratification. The comprehensive proposal gave a weapon to anti-SALT and anti-détente hard-liners, who held up the deep-cuts proposal as the only standard against which to measure the success of the ultimate agreement.

"By such a measure," Talbott suggested:

> any reasonable, negotiable agreement would seem to be an ignominious retreat. Thus, the yardstick of the ill-conceived, ill-fated comprehensive proposal was destined to become, in the jaundiced eyes of the skeptics, a bench mark of failure. . . .[18]

This view reflects one side of the dilemma faced by negotiators whose agreements must be ratified by independent publics. Since eventual agreements usually are close to the midpoint between the initial positions of the two sides, an effective bargainer must usually present an initial position that is disproportionately favorable to his side and then progressively back away from it as his adversary does the same. He thus sets up, as the Carter administration did with the comprehensive proposal, a more favorable initial position "bench mark" which those in his public constituency can use to demonstrate his concessions.

What this line of analysis fails to recognize, however, is that the negotiator whose going-in position is accepted essentially intact by his adversary is equally susceptible to the criticism that because he failed to take a hard enough initial position, he extracted too little in concessions from the other side. The problem, in short, is an inevitable one; it cannot be avoided, it can only be managed by the negotiator.

In fact, the reality of the Carter negotiating team's performance in achieving significant Soviet concessions on zero-sum issues probably reflected substantially greater toughness and inflexibility than its handling of timing, procurement, and linkage issues would have led one to expect. In contrast to Kissinger's use of backchannel efforts to circumvent normal bureaucratic practice, Carter's team developed and modified positions after intensive inter-agency review. The capacity of different parts of the bureaucracy to delay or even veto action reduced the risk of ill-considered or hasty compromises. They made progress in small steps and were sometimes unduly optimistic about the resolution of remaining issues. When negotiations broke down, however, the interagency process imposed a degree of patience and discipline that paid off in further Soviet concessions.

The Ratification Debate

Cyrus Vance approached the ratification debate in the Senate with full recognition of the extent of the opposition the administration had to overcome, but with excessive confidence in the effectiveness of facts, logic, and argumentation as instruments of change. Commenting on testimony that the administration had given throughout most of the negotiating period, he wrote:

> SALT was a complex set of issues filled with technical terms and acronyms. It was easy to get lost in a jungle of technical detail. . . . I was sure we were succeeding in putting SALT into a clearer perspective. I was also convinced that once we had an agreement in hand, SALT's supporters would come forward. Our security policies and programs were sound. Politically and economically we were much stronger than the Soviet Union; militarily we were at least equal.

Looking back over the unsuccessful effort to win approval for ratification, he wrote:

> The record of the congressional hearings shows that opponents of the treaty failed to prove their case. Ratification was blocked because the opponents were successful in creating political linkage between the treaty and the problem of restraining Moscow's attempts to expand its influence.

The SALT II ratification process was not, however, a trial or a debate. The Senate was—and is—above all a political body, attuned to broad public currents of opinion as much as to proof, and concerned as much with the context of an issue as with the facts that would be considered relevant in a debate or a court of law.[19]

When the treaty was signed and laid before the Senate, the widespread skepticism to it stemmed primarily from skepticism about the way it had been negotiated. Reflecting on the decline in Carter's popularity in opinion polls a year before the treaty was signed, Strobe Talbott wrote:

> The deftly drafted provisions of the treaty would be seen as no stronger, no more purposeful, no more enlightened and vigilant than the administration that negotiated them. Any ambiguities, no matter how well-intentioned, would be' seen as in the interests of the Soviet Union if the strategic wisdom and the political resolve of the U.S. administration were themselves in question.[20]

The lack of public and political support for the Carter administration by mid-1979 was a product of many different elements. Among the factors that made approval of SALT II such an uphill battle, however, was the political positioning of the administration along the dimension of flexibility-inflexibility toward the Soviet Union. If the great majority of members of the Senate—and the articulate public—had had a clear sense that the president and his negotiators had taken tough positions with the Soviets, extracted significant concessions from them without excessive compromises on the U.S. side, and reduced the prospects of global conflict, the treaty could have been ratified, I believe, relatively expeditiously, even in the context of poor and worsening Soviet relations.

The Carter administration conveyed, instead, an aura of excessive flexibility in managing the timing of the negotiations, the development of U.S. military posture, and the linkage between arms control and other issues in the U.S.-Soviet relationship. It should be clear that there is an important distinction between suggesting that the Carter administration was excessively flexible and saying that it conveyed an aura of excessive flexibility. Even if one believes that arms control is so dominantly an expanding-sum game that the relative advantages of an agreement to the U.S. and the Soviets are of much less consequence than the benefits of getting an agreement, the constitution weighs very heavily the need to protect against giving away too much to another country in a treaty. It is the veto power of the thirty-four most inflexible Senators that provides that protection. Only if a president can penetrate that group can he gain consent to ratification of his treaty. Part of his strategy must be, therefore, to pursue a bargaining approach that persuasively suggests that he is bargaining with skill, determination, and full awareness of the zero-sum features of the negotiations.

Developments during the 191 days that SALT II lay before the Senate suggest the pitfalls that await the president who finds himself positioned near the center of the Senate's spectrum of flexibility-inflexibility toward an adversary. Though some of the developments reflected ill-fortune, others seem, in retrospect, to have been a predictable result of the situation.

First, linkage was invoked in time-honored Senate tradition. The debate within the Carter administration notwithstanding, it was a well established principle of legislative behavior that members would try to work trades across issues so that they could have greater influence on issues of disproportionate interest to them. The movement led by Senator Nunn to gain a commitment to increased defense spending in return for support for SALT II was a classic exercise of this approach. Having lost any hope of Senator Jackson's support, Carter very much needed help from a senator who commanded respect as a defense expert. Nunn was skeptical about certain provisions of the treaty, but seemed more concerned about the lack of growth in the conventional forces budget. His negotiations with administration officials drew an agreement to present a preview of a five-year defense plan that would call for something approaching 5 percent annual real growth in defense spending in return for his support of the treaty.[21]

Linkage between SALT II and a Soviet brigade in Cuba also delayed the Senate's vote on approval of ratification. In late July, 1979, intelligence evidence of Soviet military units in Cuba began to accumulate. Forces in both the Senate and the administration made sure that the matter was pursued vigorously and by the end of August, the presence of a brigade-sized unit was reasonably clearly established. Senator Church, Chairman of the Foreign Relations Committee, made these findings public in order, he argued, to preclude partial leaks of the story. He also called on the Carter administration to demand immediate withdrawal of the brigade and suggested that, failing withdrawal, SALT II probably could not be ratified. The Soviets were firm in their refusal to withdraw the brigade, however, and subsequent evidence made it clear that the forces had been in Cuba for over a decade and had been noted and tacitly accepted by earlier administrations. The ratification debate, though not derailed by this diversion, was clearly delayed while posturing and negotiating went on.[22]

Second, the administration was subjected to predictable attack on the compromises it had made in the course of negotiations. Jackson and others attacked the advantages in land-based missile "throwweight" the treaty would give the Soviets. Senator Glenn questioned whether treaty provisions would reasonably protect our need to monitor Soviet activities to assure their compliance. His concerns took on special significance when the Iranian revolution led to the departure of American intelligence from two important monitoring stations in Iran. Most galling to the administration, however, was the alliance of those to its left and right around the argument that SALT II was not really arms control because it did not provide for significant cuts in force levels. It seemed not to matter that one part of the alliance would in the end certainly vote for the treaty whereas the other part might not.[23]

The predictable forces operating to the advantage of those favoring limited flexibility to the Soviet Union made the administration's task a near-impossible one. The unpredictable ones finished the job. Clearly a president benefits from having a public that moves from relative inflexibility toward the Soviet Union when he wants to build up his defense forces to relative flexibility when he wants approval of an arms control treaty. Carter experienced precisely the opposite phenomenon. Samuel Huntington has compiled poll data that show growing public belief, beginning in 1976 and 1977, that the military balance was beginning to favor the Soviets and that U.S. defense spending was inadequate. Support for SALT II was relatively strong during the early Carter years, but fell off sharply beginning in 1978. Soviet and Cuban activities in Africa clearly fostered these shifts in attitudes; the invasion of Afghanistan, however, crystallized them and foredoomed any prospect for Senate approval of SALT II.[24]

Despite the powerful structural and situational forces operating in favor of those who believed that the Carter administration had given up too much to the Soviets for too little in return, prospects for ultimate Senate acceptance were reasonably good prior to the Afghanistan invasion, because Carter had one very powerful force in his favor: the great majority of members of the Senate seemed to want to find a way to avoid the embarrassment and damage to the international credibility and respect of the United States that would have resulted from Senate rejection of a treaty negotiated by its president. The problem was to do so in a way that was at least politically tolerable and perferably politically advantageous. For some this involved keeping their options open while negotiating with the president for his support on allied issues. For others it involved staking out claims to positions that clearly distanced them from what seemed to be the Carter administration's excessive flexibility toward the Soviet Union but did not force them to oppose the treaty.

This was the remarkable achievement of the Foreign Relations Committee during the period between June 25th, when it received the treaty, and November 9th, when it voted out a resolution of ratification: that it provided, through carefully crafted reservations, declarations, and understandings, a sufficient range of means by which moderate senators could effectively distance themselves from the Carter administration and still support the resolution, that it had reasonable prospects for passage in the Senate and for acceptance by the Soviets.

It is for his key part in this process that we owe Senator Javits a special debt of gratitude, for he was at his best in this kind of careful shaping of proposals and defining of terms. Perhaps the contribution that will longest endure was his doggedness in pursuing, and his clarity in defining, three different categories of conditionality attached to the resolution. When international legal scholars disagreed in the face of his questioning as to whether or not the Soviet Union would be bound by reservations contained in the U.S. instrument of ratification, he helped shape three categories:

- provisions that do not require formal notice to or approval of the Soviets, but that bind the president;
- provisions that would formally be communicated to the Soviets but not require their agreement; and

• provisions that would require explicit Soviet agreement in order to come into force.

Using this framework, the committee eventually passed two reservations, two declarations, and sixteen understandings, designed to provide members of the committee and eventually of the Senate as a whole a diverse set of ways to demonstrate their relative inflexibility and toughness in dealing with the Soviets. Only the two reservations required affirmative Soviet approval. All of the potential "killer amendments" were defeated in committee. Provisions dealt with procedural issues such as the formal status of documents accompanying the treaty, assertion of U.S. rights to conduct certain tests and deployments, expectations of Soviet constraints on the use of Backfire bombers, testing encryption, and antisatellite systems, expectations for SALT III and a certification that would be required of the president with respect to Soviet military forces in Cuba.[25]

CONCLUSION

The experience of trying and failing to gain Senate approval of SALT II provides some valuable lessons about how to make our system work. That this treaty, which was observed in its essentials for six years under an informal pattern of national unanimous consent, was not approved by the Senate suggests that, in this case, the system did not work.

Lesson One. The Senate is not, and should not be expected to act like, a bureaucracy that can shape coherent arms control proposals. It can consider coherent proposals presented to it and then approve them, delay them, reject them, or change them incrementally. Its role, in short, is a safeguarding one: to assure that ill-conceived proposals are carefully reviewed and perhaps modified, given only conditional approval, or not approved at all.

Lesson Two. The president, as chief arms control negotiator, needs to develop a plan for arms control negotiations that is designed not only to assure a good bargain from the Soviets, but broad support in the Senate as well.

Lesson Three. The danger to the president is not from those who think he should have been more forthcoming with the Soviets (they are likely in the end to support his treaty) but from those who think he has been too flexible with the Soviets.

Lesson Four. Such a strategy will be especially difficult to implement for a president who has been elected on a platform of relative flexibility toward the Soviet Union. With a natural constituency of perhaps only about half of the Senate, he must obtain the support of all but the 34 most inflexible senators; he will be opposed by and have in some measure to accommodate additional senators who will want to 'link' their votes for the treaty to presidential support or commitment on other issues; and he will be open either to charges that he gave away too many of the provisions of his initial bargaining position or that he failed to extract sufficient compromise from his adversary.

Lesson Five. The president who has a reputation of relative flexibility in his dealings with the Soviet Union should pay early and regular attention to 'positioning' himself in the public and senatorial eye much farther toward the inflexible end of the senatorial opinion spectrum than he might naturally be inclined to do.

Lesson Six. Adopting some of the tactics of the negotiator in order to create uncertainty in the mind of the Soviets may increase the risk that the president's negotiation efforts would fail, but will also probably enhance the prospects of an eventual treaty before the Senate. Not only will it help to position the president more to the inflexible side of senatorial opinion, but it is likely also to improve the advantageousness of the agreement to the U.S.

Lesson Seven. Managing the timing of negotiations requires recognition that appearance of desire for quick agreement can convey a sense of vulnerability, but that negotiations will, in the absence of forcing mechanisms, tend to drag out. The presidential election cycle is the dominant forcing mechanism in arms control negotiations.

Lesson Eight. Strategic weapons procurement is the obverse of arms control. Vigor in plans to procure those weapons, and conscious integration of those plans in the president's arms control strategy, will better position the president to make accommodations in arms control without jeopardizing his support in the Senate. Weapons systems that are in relatively early stages of development make especially attractive bargaining chips.

Lesson Nine. Linkage policy sends its most important signal to the American public and the Senate. Efforts to delink arms control from other issues in the U.S.-Soviet relationship signal relative flexibility toward the Soviets.

Lesson Ten. When the reputation and credibility of the country are on the line, the Senate can act with striking skill and dedication to find politically plausible ways to avoid forcing defeat on the president.

120 STANLEY J. HEGINBOTHAM

NOTES

1. For a contemporary review of the Senate's procedural and substantive role in SALT II, see Leneice Wu, et. al., "Congress and National Security Policy: the SALT Agreement with the Soviet Union," in *Congress and Foreign Policy—1979*, prepared by the Congressional Research Service and edited by Ellen C. Collier (Washington, D.C.: U.S. House of Representatives, Committee on Foreign Affairs, 1980).

2. See, for example, I. M. Destler, "Congress," in *The Making of America's Soviet Policy*, edited by Joseph S. Nye, Jr. (New Haven: Yale University Press, 1984), 52; and Cyrus Vance, *Hard Choices: Critical Years in America's Foreign Policy* (New York: Simon and Schuster, 1983), 351. For key dates of SALT II, see *The SALT II Treaty*, Report of the Committee on Foreign Relations, United States Senate (Washington, D.C., 1979).

3. For an excellent introduction to bargaining theory, see Howard Raiffa, *The Art and Science of Negotiating* (Cambridge, Mass.: Belknap Press, 1982).

4. For a more extended treatment of this theme, see my "Congress and Defense Policy Making: Toward Realistic Expectations in a System of Countervailing Parochialisms," in *National Security Policy: The Decision-making Process*, edited by Robert L. Pfaltzgraff, Jr. and Uri Ra'anan (Hamden, Conn.: Archon Books, 1984).

5. Strobe Talbott, *Endgame: The Inside Story of SALT II* (New York: Harper and Row, 1979), 31–37.

6. Talbott, *Endgame*, 38–67; Vance, *Hard Choices*, 47–55; Zbigniew Brzezinski, *Power and Principle: Memoirs of the National Security Advisor, 1977–1981* (New York: Farrar, Straus, Giroux, 1983), 156–164.

7. Carter subsequently saw that the Soviets had misperceived his openness as a propaganda ploy. See his *Keeping Faith: Memoirs of a President* (New York: Bantam Books, 1982), 218.

8. Vance, *Hard Choices*, 63.

9. Talbott, *Endgame*, 214–15.

10. Defense outlay estimates provided by the Department of Defense.

11. In May, 1978, Senate Republicans "Issued a unanimous declaration which denounced the administration's softness on national security including the 'frightening pattern of giving up key U.S. weapons systems for nothing in return.' " Destler, "Congress," 51.

12. Carter, *Keeping Faith*, 214; Vance, *Hard Choices*, 28. For discussion of Shulman, see Stephen J. Flanagan, "The Domestic Politics of SALT II: Implications for the Foreign Policy Process," in *Congress, the Presidence, and American Foreign Policy*, edited by John Spanier and Joseph Nogee (New York: Pergamon Press, 1981), 64.

13. Brzezinski, *Power and Principle*, 185–186; Flanagan, "Domestic Politics of SALT II," 65.

14. Talbott, *Endgame*, 23–24.

15. See J. Philip Rogers, "The Senate and Arms Control: The SALT Experience," in *Legislating Foreign Policy*, edited by Hoyt Purvis and Steven J. Baker (Boulder, Colo.: Westview Press, 1977), 165–66.

16. Talbott, *Endgame*, 53–54 and 136–138; Rogers, "The Senate and Arms Control," 169.

17. Talbott, *Endgame*, 138.

18. Vance, *Hard Choices*, 55; Talbott, *Endgame*, 78.

19. Vance, *Hard Choices*, 63 and 350.

20. Talbott, *Endgame*, 153.

21. Wu, et. al., "Congress and National Security Policy," 40; Rogers, "The Senate and Arms Control," 182–84. Ironically, both Vance and Carter report in retrospect their belief in the need to increase defense spending. Neither seems to have been effective, however, in making the case for doing so at the time (see Vance, *Hard Choices*, 357; and Carter, *Keeping Faith*, 222–23).

22. Brzezinski, *Power and Principle*, 346–52; Vance, *Hard Choices*, 358–364; Carter, *Keeping Faith*, 262–64.

23. Vance, *Hard Choices*, 356.

24. Samuel P. Huntington, "Renewed Hostility," in *The Making of America's Soviet Policy*, edited by Joseph S. Nye, Jr. (New Haven: Yale University Press, 1984), 277–78. The fall of the Shah in Iran also contributed to the political weakening of the president, lessening his ability to provide persuasive leadership in the late stages of the SALT debate.

25. Committee on Foreign Relations, *The SALT II Treaty*, 111–13; Wu et. al., "Congress and National Security Policy," 28–32; and Vance, *Hard Choices*, 366.

PART THREE

Congress and the Executive: Oversight and Dissent

Introduction

Few debates between Congress and the Executive over foreign relations pass without some reference to what the Founding Fathers intended. Professor David Pletcher takes up this challenge with the apparently contradictory assertions that the framers of the constitution wanted a strong federal executive who could "present a single face to the outside world," yet wrote a document that seemed to deliberately blur the jurisdiction of Congress and the Executive in foreign affairs. It is Pletcher's contribution to delineate the forces that produced the result—and made it work.

Pletcher's story is one of increasing executive dominance over foreign-policy making, even to the extent of Congress' voting a substantial contingency fund with few strings attached to President Thomas Jefferson for acquiring territory. Rather more funds were available after World War II for protecting the territory of the Free World. One of the leading vehicles for those funds, as Professor Chester Pach, Jr. makes clear, was military assistance. During the early Cold War years, members of Congress actually wanted to devote more money—to Chiang Kai-shek's China—than the Truman administration thought wise. Sentiment for extending aid to nations resisting communism remained powerful, but it did not prevent Congress from vigorously resisting a global military aid bill that, in its view, granted the Executive sweeping discretionary powers.

Conscientious about reserving such power to itself, Congress has not been as effective in judging the success of the programs and agencies it funds. As Pach demonstrates, there never was any basic review of the military assistance program. Part of the problem, as Senator Mike Mansfield complained, was the Executive's failure to provide "specific objectives [and] specific yardsticks." Yet it seems equally clear that Congress fell into a mechanical process of foreign aid budget making with little attention to its impact worldwide.

This same pattern—of guarding congressional prerogatives vigilantly but utilizing them undeliberately—persisted through the 1960s after the Kennedy and Johnson administrations turned to promoting arms sales instead of grants, and through congressional supervision of covert actions undertaken by the Central Intelligence Agency. Professor Thomas Paterson draws a gloomy sketch of a Congress that sought "deliberate ignorance" of covert actions for decades, until the "dirty tricks" of the Nixon years—which also provoked sweeping change in Congress' power to regulate military assistance—resulted in an investigation of American covert action led by the Church Committee. One concrete result was Congress' blocking such action in Angola.

Still, Congress' execution of its supervisory role remained weak. Despite Senator Thomas Eagleton's wishes, the power to oversee covert actions was not written into the War Powers Act. Fundamental "charter legislation" for such oversight failed to pass. And the Reagan administration has viewed congressional attempts in this area with nearly open hostility. Some voters apparently agree: Church lost his Senate seat in 1980.

If Congress has largely failed to adequately supervise American covert operations, has it done better in overt ones? Professor George Herring maintains that it has not. Pointing to presidential ability as the prime factor, he argues that Lyndon Johnson achieved a "remarkable degree" of congressional support for his actions in Indochina. The key to Johnson's success was hewing closely to a middle-ground position—one vigorously assailed since the fall of Saigon, especially within the military. In fact, Herring suggests that Johnson set policy more to achieve agreement on Capitol Hill than progress in Vietnam.

In contrast, Richard Nixon defied Congress. The result was a rash of legislation, from restricting the use of funds in Southeast Asia to the sweeping War Powers Act. Nixon, whose personal promises formed a foundation for the 1973 agreement on Vietnam, was left with nothing after his personal disaster of Watergate.

Both approaches failed, with tragic results. No author in this volume has easy solutions to the difficulty of achieving successful congressional-executive cooperation in a successful foreign policy. But all make clear that, without such cooperation, there can be no successful policy.

8

What the Founding Fathers Intended: Congressional-Executive Relations in the Early American Republic

It is highly appropriate to open a historical review of congressional-executive cooperation and rivalry in the field of foreign relations by inquiring about the intentions of the Founding Fathers. However, it is much easier to raise the question than to answer it. The first problem is to determine who were the Founding Fathers. If one defines them simply as the framers of the Constitution, one must leave out John Adams, Thomas Jefferson, John Marshall, James Monroe, and others who made important contributions to our foreign relations but did not take part in the convention of 1787. A second difficulty is that however one defines them, the Founding Fathers were not a homogeneous group but differed greatly in their views of our political system—witness Alexander Hamilton and Jefferson. Also some of them changed their views several times during their active careers. For example, when we discuss James Madison, do we mean Madison the delegate to the constitutional convention, Madison the congressman, Madison the secretary of state, or Madison the president?

A third problem is that the Constitution deals with only a few of the many powers involved in foreign affairs, principally war, treaties, ambassadors, and commerce. It says nothing about recognizing other states or governments, breaking diplomatic relations, denouncing treaties, acquiring territory, regulating immigration, and many others. How are these to be divided between Congress and president? Even where the Constitution tries to apportion responsibility, it sometimes blurs rather than separates, so that, for example, John Quincy Adams could write near the end of his public service: "The respective powers of the President and Congress of the United States in the case of war with foreign powers are yet undetermined. Perhaps they can never be defined."[1]

In this brief survey of the subject I shall deal with the question of the Founding Fathers' identity by assuming that they include not only the framers of the Constitution but also any other leaders of that generation who contributed significantly to American political evolution during their active careers. I shall define the period to be covered as the first six presidencies under the new Constitution, when Founding Fathers were still active in public affairs. To be sure, the last of the six presidents, John Quincy Adams, was really too young to fit the definition, but he may be included by courtesy, since, as the son of one Founding Father and a prominent official under three others as well, he both represented their views and influenced their policies. I shall begin by describing the international problems that confronted the members of the 1787 convention and their response. Then I shall take up the principal areas of cooperation and rivalry between Congress and the president in the field of foreign affairs during the first forty years under the Constitution. Perhaps at the end it will be possible to determine something of what the Founding Fathers intended and to explain in a general way why congressional and presidential powers evolved as they did.

During the four years between the American peace treaty with England (1783) and the opening of the constitutional convention, the foreign affairs of the United States did not present any immediate life-threatening danger, but the country was weak and subjected to corrosive humiliations that might eventually eat through the cords loosely binding the states together. Stringent British restrictions on American trade with the British West Indies outraged the whole Atlantic coast. The country could not even protect its shipping in the Mediterranean from the Barbary raiders of North Africa. Good luck and skillful negotiation at the peace conference had given the United States an enormous hinterland across the mountains in the Ohio and eastern Mississippi valleys, but American control of the West was challenged by both Britain, which refused to surrender a chain of border forts, and Spain, which held New Orleans and could choke off access from the lower Mississippi to the Gulf of Mexico. The national government, the state governments, and private citizens owed foreign debts on whose payment the future national credit would depend. If European creditors were not satisfied, warned John Adams, "it will be but a few years, perhaps but a few months only, before we are involved in another war."[2]

The United States was quite unable to handle these problems effectively with the dwarfed and muscle-bound foreign policy establishment provided under the Articles of Confederation. The secretary of foreign affairs was responsible to a committee of Congress, which kept him in tight rein, even though John Jay, who held the office beginning in 1784, probably knew more about European affairs than any member of Congress at the time. Jay's department consisted of two ill-paid clerks, his offices of two rooms in a converted tavern.[3] Congress itself was almost impotent before the thirteen state governments, so it could neither retaliate effectively against foreign humiliations nor negotiate to lessen or remove them. When Congress asked the states to pass tonnage or tariff restrictions against British trade, most states complied in one way or another, except Connecticut, whose free trade policy nullified the laws of her neighbors. Elsewhere inconsistent regulations invited interstate smuggling. In 1785 Jay negotiated with Spain for the opening of the Mississippi River mouth to American trade, but the concessions he offered in return displeased all the southern states, which blocked the deal—in this case, probably wisely. In foreign affairs as in domestic matters the solution to problems under the Articles of Confederation seemed to many observers to lie in two changes: more power to the national government and the creation of a federal executive who could focus policies and actions and, in the case of foreign affairs, present a single face to the outside world.

The debates in the constitutional convention of 1787 suggest that its members were more urgently concerned with the division of powers between the federal government and the states than that between Executive and Congress. Nevertheless, the latter subject provoked many hot arguments, and the resulting Constitution represented a compromise on this subject in three areas of foreign relations: military affairs, treaties, and commerce. The compromise on military affairs reflected the victory of practical security needs over the traditional fear of centralized military power and a dictatorship. The states retained their militias, but these were to be correlated under federal direction, and a national army was not forbidden. The president was made commander in chief of this force, thereby preserving civilian control over the military, but he might not wage formal war without prior declaration by Congress. The possibility that the president might precipitate a war or create a tyranny with his command over a peacetime army disturbed some members, but no one could think of a good safeguard against this.[4]

In a monarchy, the power to make treaties was almost always vested in the Executive, but Congress had exercised it under the Articles of Confederation, and it seemed natural to divide the power, specifying that the president should act with the advice and consent of the Senate, since many deemed the House of Representatives both too flighty and too cumbersome for the requirements of diplomacy. The convention also followed the precedent of the Articles of Confederation in requiring a two-thirds majority in the Senate to approve a treaty, so as to safeguard the rights of a large regional minority, such as the bloc of Southern states which had prevented approval of Jay's Spanish treaty to open the Mississippi. More basic than these procedural matters was the problem of compelling the states to stop making their own treaties and carry out those of the federal government. This was done by forbidding state treaties and by making federal treaties the law of the land, to be enforced like any other law by executive order, backed by decisions of the Supreme Court and military strength if necessary.

The disposition of foreign commerce was scarcely a compromise at all, for Congress not only retained its former power but added to it at the expense of the states. The layman is apt to overlook the section of the commerce clause pertaining to foreign trade, since the part relating to interstate commerce has attracted so much attention, becoming in later years the basis for most federal control over the national economy. Actually the members of the 1787 convention were more interested in foreign commerce than in interstate commerce. Americans had rated their value to Europe as a trade partner very high since their successful boycott measures against the Sugar and Stamp Acts before the Revolution, and they had used this trade to help lure France into a wartime alliance. They now hoped that commercial retaliation would compel Britain to open the British West Indies, but this required that the federal government enforce conformity on the dissident states. The nature of congressional control over commerce was a major difference between the Virginia and New Jersey plans proposed to the convention, and the victory of the Virginia plan, with modifications, was a turning point in its deliberations. The noncommercial South distrusted such centralization and demanded several safeguards: outright prohibition of export taxes to protect their staple crops, a two-thirds majority to adopt import duties, and a guarantee of no interference with the slave trade. In an important compromise they obtained the first but only part of the other two.[5] Once the convention had won these broad commercial powers for Congress, it refused to share them with the president, except that it allowed him to veto commercial laws like any others, subject to an overriding vote.

In a few areas the Constitution specifies exclusive powers for the president or Congress. The president appoints and receives ambassadors (subject to Senate approval in the former case). He communicates with foreign governments and sees to the faithful execution of laws. Similarly, Congress has exclusive power to define offenses against the law of nations, punish piracy, regulate patents, copyrights, and the value of money, appropriate treasury funds, and enact necessary and proper laws. These powers, most of them general in nature, apply in one way or another to foreign relations.

In dividing powers between Congress and president, the 1787 convention was not always systematic, logical, or even clear. Under the Articles of Confederation the limited national powers were all vested in Congress. As the convention added to them at the expense of the states, it transferred some of them to the president—but reluctantly, often after much debate, and either limiting them as much as possible or obscuring them with vague language. Such vague language sometimes suggested to an assertive president that he could legitimately exercise any unspecified powers in the absence of congressional limitations or directives. This blurring of powers is sometimes attributed to imitation of the often overlapping powers in the British Constitution or to the experience of individual colonies before and during the Revolution. Perhaps also it was an expedient to secure agreement among the members on various hotly disputed clauses. Some members of the convention may even have welcomed an opportunity to encourage conflict between president and Congress as part of the elaborate system of checks and balances making up the Constitution.

During the first forty years of national history under the new Constitution—the period in which we are interested—one may notice a drift toward more executive power over foreign relations. Let us examine this process of drift in the three principal areas of power mentioned in the Constitution, military affairs, treaties, and commerce, and then in three other areas not mentioned there.

In the area of military affairs the United States waged declared war only once during the period. James Madison set the precedent of a war message against Britain in 1812, followed by a congressional declaration, but his message was no stirring call to arms and can hardly have influenced many votes. The Tripolitan War was declared by the bey of Tripoli. In both wars the president functioned as commander of the armed forces but took little part in detailed military decisions. It was rather in the handling of the peacetime army that the president expanded his functions. John Adams did not attempt to secure a declaration of war against France in 1797 after the XYZ affair, largely because he was afraid it would be voted down. Instead he recommended a number of defense measures to Congress, which passed them readily and offered no protest against the president for waging an undeclared war. This quasi-war was even terminated by a peace treaty, approved by the Senate in prescribed fashion. Madison and Monroe carried the peacetime use of the army one step further with extensive border raids against Spanish-held Florida concerning which they did not consult or fully inform Congress in advance. The House, resenting such secretive highhandedness, later tried to censure Andrew Jackson, the leader of the second raid, and argued over the affair at angry length. The full details of these episodes, especially Monroe's exact responsibility for the second raid, are still something of a mystery.[6]

In the case of treaties, the powers of both president and Congress have been expanded. The first time George Washington sought the advice of the Senate before concluding an Indian treaty, his presence on the floor proved so intimidating that the senators referred the whole matter to a committee, whereupon he left in disgust, and no president thereafter tried formal consultation. Instead Washington and his successors would talk informally to a few senatorial leaders, as, for example, before sending off the Jay mission to Britain in 1794. When the Jay treaty was submitted to the Senate the following year, its members set a precedent by deleting an objectionable provision. The House of Representatives insisted on debating the treaty too, since it alone had the power of initiating legislation to appropriate funds for the various commissions established by the treaty. The House debate proved even longer and more acrimonious than the one in the Senate and set a precedent for two-stage discussion of commercial treaties and others involving money. Jefferson set another kind of precedent in the case of the Monroe-Pinckney treaty of 1806 by declining to refer it to the Senate at all. In contrast to these cases the Pinckney treaty of 1795 with Spain, the treaty of Ghent following the War of 1812, and the Adams-Onís treaty of 1819 with Spain were unanimously approved by the Senate. Meanwhile presidents were beginning to bypass the treaty procedure with less binding executive agreements, such as Madison's unsuccessful Erskine agreement of 1809, repudiated by Britain, and Monroe's more fortunate Rush-Bagot agreement of 1817, which regulated naval armaments on the Great Lakes for the rest of the century. While the Senate had no part in these arrangements, it did not openly protest.

During the period under consideration Congress retained its control over foreign commerce but became increasingly subject to pressure from the president or his agents. Beginning with the First Congress in 1789, the House of Representatives tried more than once to coerce Britain into a more liberal trade policy by passing differential tonnage dues or tariffs, only to have these rejected by the more Anglophile Senate, influenced by Secretary of the Treasury Alexander Hamilton. During the crisis of 1794 preceding the Jay mission, both houses actually passed a temporary embargo, but Washington's envoy, John Jay, almost immediately clipped Congress' wings by agreeing to a ten-year moratorium on commercial restrictions, which the Senate reluctantly accepted by approving the Jay treaty.

From the expiration of this moratorium in 1805 to the outbreak of the War of 1812, Congress passed a series of acts restricting trade with Britain in one way or another, usually hoping to avoid war. All of these involved some cooperation with the president, but one, Jefferson's Embargo of 1807, was entirely his idea, maneuvered through both houses by skillful party organization and without much explanation to either Congress or country.[7] After the war was over, Congress used commercial coercion against France in a law of 1820, inspired by Secretary of State John Quincy Adams, that achieved its objective. In contrast, a series of restrictive measures against Britain, from 1817 to 1823, also inspired by Adams, provoked a disastrous British reaction virtually closing the West Indies to Americans. President Andrew Jackson later solved the problem by negotiation. Retaliatory trade laws had clearly outlived their usefulness, and both president and Congress resorted to them much less frequently thereafter. Instead in the 1820s the John Quincy Adams administration negotiated many commercial treaties, especially with Latin American nations. More relevant to our discussion, the president had gained much influence over foreign trade.

Among the functions of foreign relations not assigned or even mentioned in the Constitution, perhaps the most striking is the power to acquire territory. This soon became a major area of presidential initiative. When a lucky combination of circumstances in Europe and America made possible the Louisiana

Purchase of 1803, Jefferson's first impulse was to delay closing the deal until he could put through a constitutional amendment legalizing it. Practical considerations—the danger that it would fall through—soon changed his mind, and he was content with simple approval of the convention with France and appropriation of the purchase price. Having tasted success, he abandoned still more scruples and launched a campaign to obtain Florida that soon led him to maneuver Congress into granting him a contingent fund of two million dollars to buy it without clearly explaining the situation to Congress. Jefferson failed to persuade Spain to sell, but Madison secured a portion of the desired territory by what we would now call "covert actions"—encouraging a revolt by Americans living near the Spanish fort of Baton Rouge and then infiltrating troops into the Mobile area.[8] Monroe's final acquisition of the Florida peninsula by the Adams-Onís treaty of 1819 was more orthodox, but again the initiative lay solely with the president, and Congress merely approved his action. In 1828, near the end of our period, the Supreme Court affirmed the power to acquire and govern new territories, but it did not try to apportion this power between president and Congress.[9]

Another subject largely ignored in the Constitution was the transmission of information by the president. The convention debates show the members to have been well aware of the importance and delicacy of the issue, but the Constitution merely required the president to inform Congress "from time to time" concerning the state of the nation and did not indicate what information might be withheld on grounds of security. In general, presidents grew more secretive with the passage of time. Washington and John Adams usually sent to Congress all information requested, withholding only the minimum necessary to avoid difficulties with foreign nations. To be sure, during the bitter debates on the Jay treaty, Washington staunchly refused to transmit any of the demanded documents.

On coming to the presidency, Jefferson was much less cooperative than Adams, partly because he held a party majority in Congress. For much of his diplomatic correspondence he used a code and kept double sets of dispatches, one for public use, the other for his own eyes. He gave Congress incomplete information about the Two Million Bill, the Embargo, and the Burr conspiracy. Madison too withheld important information about the circumstances surrounding the Baton Rouge rebellion and later about fraudulent French concessions to American economic coercion that might have altered the public attitude toward the War of 1812.[10]

A final area of presidential influence unspecified by the Constitution is the determination and enunciation of general foreign policy. Here the leading precedent was set by Washington in the Neutrality Declaration of 1793, which stated, almost as an axiom, the wisdom of American noninvolvement in the Anglo-French war that had just begun in Europe. Long and thorough discussion of the subject by the cabinet preceded the declaration. Both Jefferson and Hamilton, though disagreeing on most other questions, approved the general principle and also Washington's decision not to consult Congress. Both houses of Congress later approved the declaration, and while Madison objected that it implied an infringement of the congressional power to declare war, it seems likely that he had in mind more the form than the content of the declaration.[11] At the end of Washington's presidency, his Farewell Address provided a more informal, retrospective view of this and other policies. Although more controversial at the time than the Neutrality Declaration, it caught and kept the public attention and remains one of the few official statements on foreign relations known to nearly everyone.

The only significant example of congressional participation in foreign policy statements during the period under consideration was the No-Transfer Resolution of 1811, disapproving the transfer of territory in the hemisphere from one colonial power to another. Even this statement, however, was requested by Madison as part of his aggressive Florida policy. The climax of presidential policy making during this period was the enunciation of the Monroe Doctrine in 1823, a combination of noninvolvement and European exclusion from the hemisphere. Like Washington's Neutrality Declaration, it was the product of many authors. Like all of the other policy statements I have mentioned, it had roots deep in American tradition and was therefore immediately accepted by the public. The House of Representatives, to be sure, considered a resolution to add a gesture in favor of the Greek revolution against Turkey, but thanks to Secretary Adams' influence it was abandoned.

Thus during the first forty years of national existence under the Constitution the division of powers between Congress and the president in the conduct of foreign relations drifted steadily toward the president, giving him authority that was perhaps not contemplated by the members of the 1787 convention. There were many good reasons why this should have happened. In the first place, the president had tradition on his side, for in nearly all other political systems the executive had directed foreign policy and diplomacy. Unlike Congress, he never went out of session and was always at hand or within easy reach to evaluate a suddenly developing international situation. He could react quickly or make decisions under stress of time since he could choose whom he would consult or, indeed, consult no one if he wished.

Beyond these inherent advantages in being one man rather than a body of men, the president enjoyed other advantages from the nature of our political system as it developed during this period under the Constitution. He held a virtual monopoly over communication with foreign governments and could thus present his own view of American policies, qualified only by what foreign governments might learn from their diplomats or from American newspapers. As commander in chief of the armed forces, he controlled an implied threat even in peacetime, as well as a means for dramatizing his policies—for example, through visits of warships. Even more important, the American party system, though unmentioned in the Constitution, enabled him to command the loyalty of a bloc of followers in Congress and among the public.

Nevertheless, the powers of these early presidents were still hedged in by the ever-recurring need to go to the people or to Congress for confirmation of their policies. The shortness of the presidential term and the two-term tradition strictly limited the duration of their power. As for Congress, its power to approve treaties, declare war, appropriate money, and confirm appointments directly affected what the president could or could not do in conducting foreign relations. Just as important, the power of Congress to influence his domestic program by similar restraints gave it indirect leverage in foreign affairs, especially as the president's popular following often rested largely on his domestic program.

In this manner early presidents, usually with the tacit consent of Congress, erected a carefully balanced edifice of foreign policy making on the meager foundations contained in the Constitution. Was this what the Founding Fathers intended? Since they included five of the first six presidents and many influential leaders in Congress until about 1815, we must conclude that on the whole it was. It is true that the party system insured a permanent, automatic opposition to almost any presidential action, but no one has ever demonstrated that the Founding Fathers envisioned or presented a united front on anything except the preservation of the country. Sustained, organized protest, such as that represented by the Kentucky and Virginia Resolutions or the Essex Junto, rarely developed and soon disappeared. The American system of conducting foreign relations, part planned and part improvised, usually worked. This, above all, was what the Founding Fathers intended.

NOTES

*The author thanks Maurice G. Baxter for his assistance in preparing this chapter.

1. John Quincy Adams, *An Eulogy on the Life and Character of James Madison* [etc.] (Boston, 1836), 47.

2. John Adams to Robert R. Livingston, July 8, 1783. Francis Wharton, ed., *The Revolutionary Diplomatic Correspondence of the United States*, 6 vols. (Washington, 1889), VI: 562.

3. Frank Monaghan, *John Jay, Defender of Liberty* [etc.] (1935; reprint, ed., New York, 1974), 244.

4. W. Taylor Reveley III, "Constitutional Allocations of the War Powers between the President and Congress, 1787–1788," *Virginia Journal of International Law*, XV (Fall 1974): 103–108, 126–33.

5. Import duties were made subject to majority vote like any other law, and the international slave trade was allowed for twenty years. Congress prohibited the trade beginning 1 January 1808.

6. Among the many works dealing with the raids, a convenient summary with special reference to congressional and presidential powers in Abraham D. Sofaer,

War, Foreign Affairs and Constitutional Power: The Origins (Cambridge, Mass., 1976), 303–65.

7. Bradford Perkins, *Prologue to War: England and the United States, 1805–1812* (Berkeley and Los Angeles, 1961), 153–56.

8. Sofaer, *War, Foreign Affairs and Constitutional Power*, 291–303.

9. American Insurance Co., et al. v. Canter (1828) (1 Peters), 524–25.

10. Sofaer, *War, Foreign Affairs and Constitutional Power*, 178–82.

11. Ibid., 114. For Madison's arguments, in his "Helvidius" letters on the Neutrality Declaration, see James Madison, *The Writings of James Madison* [etc.] ed. by Gaillard Hunt, 9 vols. (New York, 1900–1910), VI: 138–88.

9

Military Assistance and American Foreign Policy: The Role of Congress

CHESTER J. PACH, JR.

"This is a shot that will be heard around the world," declared Representative Jacob K. Javits on 28 September 1949, during the congressional debate on the Mutual Defense Assistance Act. The first in a long series of global, Cold War, military aid bills, the Mutual Defense Assistance Act, according to Javits, was a dramatic indication of American resolve to contain communist expansionism. Its principal purpose, Javits explained, was "to fortify the morale of the people of Europe"—the recipients of the bulk of American arms aid—"so that they felt the self-respect, dignity, and nationhood, which would give them the will to . . . [resist] any Communist tide."[1]

A generation later, on 28 April 1976, Senator Jacob Javits urged passage of the International Security Assistance and Arms Export Control Act, a sweeping overhaul of the military aid program. Stressing the legislation's historic nature, Javits argued that it restored a balance between president and Congress in decisions about furnishing arms to foreign nations. "What we [have] tried to do," he asserted, "was find a technique by which we [Congress] could, without embarrassment to the President, be a party to the process."[2]

On both occasions, Javits expressed the views of a majority of Congress. In both instances, the themes he emphasized—halting the spread of communism in 1949, executive-congressional cooperation in regulating arms transfers in 1976—reflected the principal concerns of his colleagues.

In the generation between those speeches, military assistance had grown into a major instrument of American foreign policy. In the thirty years after the end of World War II, the United States provided approximately seventy-five billion dollars in military equipment and training to some ninety countries. Despite frequent congressional criticism of this enormous effort, especially because of its cost, a consensus that arms aid was vital to American security insured the program's annual renewal. By the late 1960s, however, economic reservations combined with doubts about the program's effectiveness and concerns about unchecked presidential power in distributing armaments to bring about congressional reform of military assistance policy and procedures. Sales replaced grants as the principal means of transferring military equipment, and Congress gained new power to regulate the flow of arms to foreign nations. A different military assistance program emerged, but the United States remained the world's largest supplier of armaments and the difficulties of integrating security assistance into American foreign policy only grew more complex.[3]

Military assistance emerged as a major instrument of American foreign policy after World War II despite persistent congressional reservations about the cost and consequences of such aid. At the end of the war, congressional support for expensive subsidies to foreign armed forces quickly evaporated. Legislators of both parties also expressed fears that military assistance might stimulate arms races, undermine the peace-keeping efforts of the United Nations, or embroil the United States in war.[4] Such sentiments encouraged the Truman administration to rely heavily on existing authority, such as the Lend-Lease and Surplus Property Acts, to implement the first postwar programs of arms aid. During 1946, Congress consented only to limited additions to the president's powers to arm foreign nations. Both houses approved bills for military aid to the Philippines and naval assistance to China, neither of which required new appropriations.[5] The Congress balked, however, at enacting Inter-American Military Assistance legislation, which proposed an enormous transfer of arms to Latin America to solidify hemispheric defenses.[6] Congress also refused to grant the president power to dispatch military and naval missions to any country that requested such help.[7] Yet despite these defeats, the Truman administration developed during the first year of peace an extensive and heterogeneous military assistance program, one that provided equipment and training to armed forces in Europe, the Middle East, the Far East and the Western Hemisphere, and one that aimed at a variety of objectives, including cultivating good will overseas, gaining access to bases and strategic raw materials, halting the spread of communism, and securing customers for American defense industries.[8]

The development of the containment policy in late 1946 and early 1947 provided the Truman administration with a powerful weapon to shape congressional opinion on foreign aid. Containment transformed the military assistance program, giving it greater unity and new importance.[9] Yet extensive use of foreign aid to contain communism required congressional action. Accordingly, in the hope that common concern about Soviet expansionism would outweigh partisan differences, the White House and the State Department assiduously cultivated leaders of the Republican-controlled 80th Congress, especially Arthur H. Vandenberg of Michigan, Chairman of the Foreign Relations Committee. Stern public rhetoric neutralized many of those who could not be courted. The president, for example, justified his request for $400 million in aid to Greece and Turkey in March 1947 by delivering an "all-out" speech, in which he proclaimed the Truman Doctrine: "it must be the policy of the United States to support free peoples who are resisting attempted subjugation by armed minorities or by outside pressures." Vandenberg compared Truman's message to "a Presidential request for a declaration of war[;] . . . there is precious little we can do except say 'Yes.' "[10]

Yet Congress did not so easily accede to the administration's China policy. Instead, military aid to the Nationalist Government of Chiang Kai-shek became a heated and divisive issue, especially after the enunciation of the Truman Doctrine.[11] Repeatedly during 1947 and 1948, a vocal group of Republican legislators led by Walter H. Judd of Minnesota in the House and William F. Knowland of California in the Senate, attacked the administration for failing to implement containment as vigorously in Asia as in Europe. During the hearings on the Greek-Turkish Aid bill in 1947, for example, Judd rebuked the administration for withholding arms and encouraging the Nationalists to negotiate with their communist foes, while helping the Greeks to defeat a communist-led insurgency. "I do not think that we can have one kind of policy in Europe with respect to the danger of Communist-dominated governments and another in Asia," Judd insisted. Increasingly the thrust of this Republican criticism was that China was the victim of the administration's double standard in applying the Truman Doctrine.[12]

The Truman administration was vulnerable to such charges because of its reluctance to issue a frank, public explanation of its China policy. By the spring of 1947, Secretary of State George C. Marshall had decided that a major commitment to Chiang promised to imperil rather than advance American security interests. After a futile, year-long effort to mediate the Chinese Civil War, Marshall was convinced that Chiang was stubborn and intractable, unwilling to make the reforms necessary to alleviate his government's pervasive corruption and inefficiency and solidify popular support. Lavish American military aid immediately after World War II had not persuaded Chiang to negotiate an accord with his Communist opponents. Subsequent restrictions on the flow of arms had not dissuaded him from seeking a military victory that Marshall was sure lay beyond his grasp. Defeat of the Communists, Marshall ultimately concluded, would require the United States to take over the war efforts from the Nationalists. Such a heavy investment in China would jeopardize containment in Europe, an area of far greater political, economic, and strategic importance. Administration officials, however, scrupulously avoided public expressions of such views for fear of accusations that they were "pulling the rug" from under Chiang. Instead Marshall hoped that limited aid would prevent Chiang's collapse and moderate the fury of congressional critics.[13]

Such was the purpose of the China Aid bill. The State Department introduced this legislation in early 1948 in part to conciliate Republican members of Congress whose votes were needed to enact the Marshall Plan. The bill proposed only modest economic aid, little more than "three cheers for the Nationalist Government," according to Vandenberg. Prodded by Judd and others, the House demanded military aid as well and American operational advice to Nationalist army units in the field. The administration resisted this challenge, with bipartisan help from the Senate Foreign Relations Committee. Senator Tom Connally of Texas, the ranking Democrat, contemptuously compared aid to Chiang with a handout to a beggar. Alexander Wiley, Republican of Wisconsin, warned that "the military aid they [the Nationalists] need is American troops, and we don't want to be sucked into that." Vandenberg wanted to appease House members who were "hell bent" on military aid, but avoid any commitment to underwrite the Nationalists' military campaigns. The final legislation simply reserved one hundred twenty-five million dollars for the Chinese to spend as they wished on their own responsibility. The China Aid Act thus represented a major victory for the administration over the China bloc in Congress, which proved to be more vocal than powerful.[14]

By the middle of 1948, the Truman administration decided to consolidate its separate country and regional efforts into an expanded, global military assistance program. For more than a year, defense officials had urged passage of new legislation that broadened the president's power to meet foreign requests for armaments.[15] Truman and Marshall, however, had been reluctant to seek such authority for fear that their request might endanger congressional approval of the Marshall Plan, the principal instrument of containment in Europe.[16] This objection vanished, however, in the spring of 1948, when the administration decided to rearm Western Europe. Such help was not needed to resist Soviet military action, which American intelligence authorities dismissed as improbable, but to shore up European morale and stiffen the will to resist in the aftermath of the communist coup in Czechoslovakia and amid growing difficulties in Berlin. Accordingly, American representatives joined conversations that eventually produced the North Atlantic Treaty. At the same time, political and military planners formulated a "coordinated military assistance program," one in which Western Europe received highest priority. This new, global effort rested on an expansive and durable rationale for arms aid—as a means of providing political and psychological reassurance to friendly nations and demonstrating American resolve to resist communist expansion.[17]

Truman's submission in July 1949 of a global military assistance bill to Congress precipitated, according to Senator Connally, the greatest struggle over foreign policy legislation since the enactment of lend-lease. State Department officials had expected problems from congressional isolationists and economizers.[18] But they had not anticipated the objections of a bipartisan group of internationalists who favored an arms aid program, but condemned the administration bill. Led by Vandenberg, who had been Truman's most important congressional supporter of the North Atlantic Treaty, these members of Congress denounced the proposed legislation for conferring upon the president unduly broad powers to arm any nation on terms he deemed appropriate.

"It would virtually make him the number one war lord of the earth," Vandenberg fumed. Angered and embarrassed by such criticism, Secretary of State Dean Acheson, who had only glanced at the bill, vented his wrath on his subordinates. "Even a child," Acheson sarcastically told his staff, "would have picked up the weakness in the . . . legislation." The Truman administration promptly sent Congress a new bill, far more restrictive in its grant of executive power.[19] "They have totally surrendered," Vandenberg exulted, "on eighty per cent of my criticisms."[20]

Despite these concessions, the administration still faced an uphill fight. Fiscal conservatives in the House slashed by one-half the proposed assistance to the NATO allies. Hoping to reverse this defeat in the Senate, the State Department cultivated Republican leaders Vandenberg and John Foster Dulles of New York, but at the price of further changes in the bill. Fearful of encouraging the uncoordinated expansion of European armed forces, Vandenberg and Dulles introduced a series of amendments to insure that arms aid to the NATO countries would be "geared into the integrating processes of the North Atlantic Treaty at the earliest practical date." Following their lead, the Senate made only a small reduction in the administration request for the NATO countries, but prevented the president from allocating all but a small portion of the aid until he approved allied plans for "an integrated defense of the North Atlantic area." The House accepted these terms in the final version of the bill, but only after the Truman administration announced that the Soviets had exploded their first atomic device.[21]

A far more acrimonious dispute erupted over the administration's failure to request funds for military aid to China. The vehemence of congressional protests surprised State Department officials, who thought that further help to the nearly-defeated Nationalist armies was a dead issue. Only a few months earlier, Acheson had easily thwarted the efforts of Chiang's congressional backers, who proposed a new China Aid bill of $1.5 billion. Acheson had also counted on the China White Paper, which the State Department released in early August, to disarm the administration's critics. In his introduction to this lengthy, official explanation of American policy, Acheson argued that Nationalist woes did not arise from a lack of arms and that the United States could do nothing more "within reasonable limits of its capabilities" to save Chiang from defeat. Congressional supporters of the Nationalist Chinese, however, read the enormous documentary appendices of the White Paper and reached antithetical conclusions. Led by Judd in the House and Knowland in the Senate, they clamored for a last-ditch effort to sustain Nationalist resistance in the Chinese Civil War.[22]

Acheson suggested an alternative that preserved the administration's freedom of action. While opposing further aid specifically for the Nationalist Chinese, Acheson announced that he would not object to the establishment of a confidential fund for use in the Far East. Representative John M. Vorys, Republican of Ohio and ardent supporter of the Nationalist Chinese, condemned such an account as an "anything you please proposition" and urged restrictions on the president's discretion. But both houses ultimately approved an unvouchered fund of seventy-five million dollars, which the president could expend in the "general area" of China. Such flexibility appealed to many legislators because it would enable the president to furnish covert aid to a variety of anti-communist forces in China. Yet none of the money went for that purpose. Instead Truman used most of the confidential fund for the first direct military assistance to halt communism in Southeast Asia. Ironically and unwittingly, a Congress suspicious of broad executive power to arm foreign nations, granted the president exceptional authority to pursue military containment in Indochina.[23]

Truman had good reason to be pleased on 6 October 1949, when he signed the Mutual Defense Assistance Act. Congress had not rubber-stamped his military aid proposals, but neither had it forced major changes. Despite the rumblings of fiscal conservatives, Congress appropriated $1.314 billion, almost the entire sum Truman requested. Despite complaints about excessive executive power, Truman secured wide latitude to distribute arms in East Asia without any accounting to Congress. The Dulles-Vandenberg amendments required of the administration no more than it had originally intended: the arming of European forces that could contribute to any conceivable NATO defense plan.[24] What Congress did not demand of the administration was far more significant: specific standards for gauging the effectiveness of aid and a clear indication of how long it would be necessary to provide arms to sustain foreign morale and the will to resist communism.

The military aid program gathered even greater momentum during the early 1950s. The logic that justified the creation of the program in 1949 supported its continuation in 1950 at the same level of expenditures. The State Department and the Joint Chiefs of Staff warned that any major reduction in aid would endanger foreign morale and sow doubts about American leadership.[25] The outbreak of the Korean War brought an enormous increase in the size and scope of the military aid program. Alarm over the danger of Soviet military aggression in other parts of the world elevated arms aid from secondary to preeminent status in the foreign aid program. In 1951, the Truman administration combined its separate assistance efforts into a Mutual Security Program, in which the ratio between military and economic aid was three to one, just the reverse of prewar proportions.[26] The Mutual Security legislation also gave the president new authority to arm more nations and to allocate funds among recipients at his discretion.[27]

Like Truman, President Dwight D. Eisenhower stressed that the overriding purpose of the Mutual Security Program was to halt the spread of communism. Bent on economy in defense expenditures, Eisenhower argued that it was less costly to build up the armies of allies than to maintain large American forces overseas. Accordingly, most American military aid during Eisenhower's presidency went to so-called "forward defense areas," nations along the periphery of the Soviet Union and China. During the 1950s, the

NATO countries received the greatest share of American arms, but by the end of the decade deliveries to the Far East equalled those to Europe. A small, but in Eisenhower's view, significant amount of military aid went to Third World countries in order to counter communist influences.[28]

Eisenhower had great difficulty persuading Congress to approve his annual request for military assistance. Repeatedly the House and Senate slashed Eisenhower's proposed foreign aid budgets, with military assistance absorbing the largest cuts. Senator Mike Mansfield, Democrat of Montana, observed that the submission of the Mutual Security bill marked the beginning of an annual ritual in Congress: "We shall assume that the Administration has asked for too much money. . . . Therefore we shall cut the amount requested. . . . The administration will protest the size of the cut, however large or small it may be. . . . That is what has been done year after year." Mansfield warned of rising pressure in Congress to use "a meat ax instead of a scalpel in dealing with foreign aid appropriations." Such an attitude arose from the administration's failure to provide "specific objectives [and] specific yardsticks against which to measure cost in any rational fashion." Such omissions, Mansfield concluded, were indications that the foreign aid program had become aimless, driven more by habit and "sheer bureaucratic inertia" than by a systematic calibration of means against ends.[29]

More than a fear that the military aid program had lost direction accounted for the annual congressional reductions. After the Korean War, fiscal conservatives were unwilling to tolerate heavy spending on arms assistance. One such economizer, Representative Otto Passman, Democrat of Louisiana and chairman of an appropriations subcommittee, had a chance each year to act on his conviction that "giving away the wealth of this nation will [not] win us a single friend." Another group of legislators, led by Senator J. William Fulbright, Democrat of Arkansas, complained that the Eisenhower administration placed too much emphasis on military aid and not enough on economic help. Still other members of Congress protested that the United States was subsidizing nations—particularly those in Western Europe—whose economies could bear the burden of higher defense spending.[30] Eisenhower tried mightily to overcome such opposition, but with unimpressive results. During his presidency, Congress cut his annual requests for military aid by an average of twenty-six per cent. After one legislative reduction of a foreign aid request, Eisenhower exploded: "I am repeatedly astonished, even astounded, by the apparent ignorance of members of Congress in the general subject of our foreign affairs."[31]

Congressional discontent with the high cost of arming foreign nations hardened during the early 1960s. In 1962, Congress instructed the president to reduce and, as quickly as possible, terminate grants of military equipment to nations capable of maintaining their own defenses. The following year, Congress slashed John F. Kennedy's foreign aid request by one-third, the largest cut in the program's history. The sharp decline in military aid, according to Secretary of Defense Robert S. McNamara, produced "absolute chaos" in American national security policy. Yet McNamara dismissed as futile any effort to obtain from Congress assistance he considered adequate to protect American foreign interests. Instead he asked for arms aid appropriations in fiscal 1965 equal to those of the previous year because Congress had made "crystal clear" its unwillingness to provide more.[32]

Such pressure from Congress contributed to an important shift during the 1960s from grants to sales as the principal means of arming foreign nations. Sales rose from less than twenty per cent of Americans arms transfers during the Truman and Eisenhower years to almost sixty per cent during the Kennedy and Johnson administrations. In 1961, the Department of Defense established the Office of International Logistics Negotiations, which vigorously sought customers for American armaments industries. Most sales were for cash, but some depended upon government credit, which came from a special revolving fund financed through congressional appropriations and repayments of previous loans. During the 1960s, the developed nations, particularly those in NATO, were the largest foreign purchasers of American military equipment. These transactions, according to Secretary McNamara, yielded the same military and political benefits as did grants of arms. They even provided the United States with the added bonuses of easing balance-of-payment problems and lowering the cost of foreign aid. Although Congress did not regularly or closely monitor the export of arms during the early 1960s, it seemed to approve of the spectacular rise in sales. Indeed in 1964, Congress gave the Defense Department new authority to guarantee loans from financial institutions to foreign countries for the purchase of American military equipment.[33]

The Pentagon's use of this authority, however, soon raised a storm of controversy on Capitol Hill. At issue was the Defense Department's underwriting of loans from the Export-Import Bank to developing nations for the purchase of military equipment. The terms of these transactions were highly unusual: the bank's directors did not know which countries received the loans, only that the Pentagon distributed the money to borrowers that did not meet the Eximbank's regular credit requirements. To protect against default, the Defense Department kept in its revolving credit fund only one-fourth of the loan amount. Thus the Pentagon quadrupled the arms credits it could offer to developing nations without securing any new appropriations from Congress. After the staff of the Senate Foreign Relations Committee reported in early 1967 on these Country X loans, as they were known, defense officials explained that they were simply trying to get more mileage out of limited military aid funds. Congressional critics, however, maintained that the Country X loans smacked of deception and evasion. Senator Allen Ellender, Democrat of Louisiana, accused the Defense Department of trying to circumvent congressional ceilings established several years earlier on arms transfers to Latin America and Africa. After a lengthy battle, Congress enacted legislation that phased out the Country X loans and imposed new restrictions on the credit sales of armaments. The new law prevented the financing of sales of advanced weapons to developing nations and ordered the termination of assistance to countries that acquired excessive amounts of military equipment.[34]

The program of grant military aid also encountered strong opposition on Capitol Hill during the late 1960s, primarily because of congressional discontent with the Vietnam War. Senator Fulbright, the Chairman of the Foreign Relations Committee, insisted that it was "not possible to talk about foreign aid, or indeed any problem of this country's foreign relations, without discussing the war in Vietnam."[35] Accordingly, the annual hearings on the military aid program frequently became searching inquiries into the Southeast Asian policies of the administrations of Lyndon B. Johnson and Richard M. Nixon. Critics of the war, such as Fulbright, Mansfield, and Frank Church, Democrat of Idaho, blamed the promiscuous distribution of aid in support of a narrow anti-communism for helping to mire the United States in Vietnam. They seriously questioned, in short, for the first time the justification that had sustained the military aid program since the late 1940s. These opponents of the war joined with fiscal conservatives, who were worried about budget deficits and inflation, to mount an unprecedented challenge to grants of arms to countries outside Southeast Asia.[36] Three times between 1969 and 1973, for example, the Senate rejected legislation authorizing or appropriating funds for foreign aid.[37]

Reforms in the House and the Senate in the early 1970s enabled Congress to continue to challenge the military aid program. These reforms weakened the seniority system, expanded committee staffs, and reposed major authority in new subcommittees. Members of Congress increasingly had available to them the resources and expertise they needed to render independent judgments of presidential proposals, a capability, Representative Javits had complained as early as 1949, the Congress had lacked.[38] These changes also made Congress more difficult to control. No longer could a president woo a handful of party leaders, as Truman had Vandenberg, to insure the success of his legislative programs. "We used to have a bipartisan foreign policy," observed Speaker of the House Thomas P. O'Neill. "If a member didn't like a particular proposal, he would swallow hard and support the president. Today we no longer have a bipartisan foreign policy. Everyone is for himself. . . ."[39] Dissatisfaction with uncontrolled executive power during the Vietnam War and the Watergate scandal reinforced the resolve of many legislators to use these reforms to protect the constitutional prerogatives of Congress—especially in foreign policy. Wayne Morse, Democrat of Oregon, was one of the first to express an increasingly common view: "I think that there has developed in this country in recent years a growing public insistence that this Congress do a more effective job in its constitutional checking."[40]

During the early 1970s, congressional reformers aimed primarily at limiting government arms transfers. Fulbright noted in 1971 that the military aid program had become enormously large and complex. Indeed he confessed that the did not know its exact dimensions and doubted that any one else did. Senator William Proxmire, Democrat of Wisconsin and chairman of the Sub-committee on Economy in Government of the Joint Economic Committee, similarly complained about discretionary authority of the Executive that allowed the transfer to the military aid program of funds appropriated for Food for Peace. While grants specifically for military aid were declining, sales for cash and credit and economic subsidies to encourage expanded foreign defense efforts had reached new highs.[41] Secretary of State Henry A. Kissinger found arms aid a most important tool of foreign policy and liberally promised such assistance, particularly to nations in the Middle East. Sales to Israel and Saudi Arabia in fiscal 1974 amounted to more than $2 billion each, while those to Iran totalled more than four billion dollars. Owing in part to Kissinger's failure to consult in advance with Congress, these spiralling sales reinforced opposition to unchecked executive power. Members of Congress also worried that no clear and consistent vision of American security interests accounted for these transfers. Fulbright's solution to these problems was to get the government out of the armaments business. He advocated the phasing out of grant military aid and a shift of sales from government to commercial channels. Fulbright was unable, however, to win congressional approval of these pro-posals before he left the Senate in 1974.[42]

Congress, however, did make important, but less sweeping changes in military aid policy. In 1974, Congress secured the power to veto by concurrent resolution proposed government sales of military equipment amounting to at least $25 million. Legislators also insisted on the importance of human rights considerations in decisions to provide arms to foreign nations. Indeed in 1974, Congress halted military aid to Chile because of its repressive internal policies. Congress also stopped military aid to Turkey in 1975 because of its invasion of Cyprus.[43] Such actions indicated a renewed willingness to challenge on a case-by-case basis administration assessments of the relationship between American security interests and armaments assistance.

Congressional activism produced more comprehensive reform with the passage in 1976 of the International Security Assistance and Arms Export Control Act. The principal architects of this legislation were Senator Hubert H. Humphrey, the Chairman of the Foreign Assistance Subcommittee of the Foreign Relations Committee, and Senator Javits, its second ranking minority member. Despite extensive conversations between the congressional sponsors and the White House, President Gerald R. Ford vetoed an earlier version of the bill, protesting that it elevated Congress to a "virtual coadministrator" of American foreign policy. The revised legislation, which Ford signed into law, nonetheless considerably strengthened congressional controls over the transfer of arms to foreign nations. The new law allowed grants of arms and the stationing of American military advisory groups abroad only with the specific approval of Congress. It also strengthened government regulation of arms sales by requiring all transfers of armaments of at least twenty-five million dollars to occur through government channels. Congress, however, could block such sales by the use of the concurrent veto. Finally, the legislation also stipulated criteria that the president should consider to determine whether a sale would advance the national interest.[44] Together these provisions amounted to the most extensive changes in military assistance policy since the Truman years.

These reforms, however significant, did not elevate Congress to parity with the executive branch in formulating military aid policy. During the late 1970s, Congress used its legislative veto to modify, rather than block, arms sales it found objectionable. It curtailed, rather than eliminated, grants of military aid. Despite the controls Congress imposed, arms transfers continued to increase, reaching a level of seventeen billion dollars in 1980. Congressional reforms, in short, did not constitute a revolution in policy making that led to "Foreign Policy by Congress," as some observers prematurely concluded. Much of the congressional activism of the 1970s may have been the product of extraordinary and temporary circumstances: an unsuccessful and unpopular war, an executive mired in scandal and disarray. In recent years, for example, Congress has removed some of its restrictions on the military aid program by granting the president new discretionary power to furnish arms to countries he deems important to the nation's security.[45]

Yet Congress did indeed help reshape the military assistance program between 1945 and 1980. Congress played a major role in encouraging an emphasis on sales rather than grants and eventually in limiting the number of recipients of American arms. Congress also insisted—at least temporarily during the 1970s—that anti-communism not be the sole consideration in furnishing security assistance. Congress, however, can by no means insure a wise assessment of those factors that influence arms transfers.[46] Indeed with the containment of communism no longer necessarily the sole or even primary objective of arms aid, decisions on grants or sales of military equipment were undoubtedly more complex in 1980 than a generation earlier. With the shift from grants to sales, American influence over recipient nations may well have diminished. Congressional reform, however, has resulted in increased information and wider public discussion of arms transfers. Such debate perhaps is the best hope for effective integration of military assistance into American foreign policy.

NOTES

1. U.S. Congress, Senate, *Congressional Record* 95: 13472.

2. Ibid., 122: 11583–11584.

3. U.S. Department of State, International Development Agency, *U.S. Overseas Loan and Grants and Assistance from International Organizations, July 1, 1945–September 30, 1977*, 6.

4. Chester Joseph Pach, Jr., "Arming the Free World: The Origins of the United States Military Assistance Program, 1945–1949," (Ph.D. dissertation, Northwestern University, 1981), Chapter 1.

5. 60 Stat. 315; 60 Stat. 539.

6. On the demise of the Inter-American Military Cooperation Act, see Chester J. Pach, Jr., "The Containment of U.S. Military Aid to Latin America, 1944–49," *Diplomatic History* 6 (Summer 1982): 225–243.

7. U.S. Congress, Senate, Senator Robert A. Taft speaking on a bill for the "Detail of Military and Naval Missions to Foreign Governments, S. 1847, 79th Cong. 2d sess., 29 July 1946, *Congressional Record* 92: 10336; SWNCC 201, 2 October 1945; SWN 3387, 22 October 1945, both in folder SWNCC 201, Records of the State-Army-Navy-Air Force Coordinating Committee, Record Group 353, National Archives, Washington.

8. Pach, "Arming the Free World," 30–31.

9. For the effect of containment on the military assistance program see, ibid., 211–233; SWNCC 360, 21 April 1947, U.S. Department of State, *Foreign Relations of the United States, 1947,* 8 vols. (Washington, D.C.: Government Printing Office, 1971–1973), III: 204–219; SWNCC 360, 21 April 1947, *Foreign Relations of the United States, 1947,* I: 724–734.

10. *Public Papers of the President: Harry S. Truman, 1947* (Washington, D.C.: Government Printing Office, 1963), 178–179; Memorandum, Elsey to Clifford, folder Truman Doctrine Speech 12 March 1947, Papers of George M. Elsey, Harry S. Truman Library, Independence, Missouri; U.S. Congress, Senate, Committee on Foreign Relations, *Legislative Origins of the Truman Doctrine (Historical Series)* (Washington, D.C.: Government Printing Office, 1973), 128; Thomas G. Paterson, *On Every Front: The Making of the Cold War* (New York: W. W. Norton & Company, 1979), 129–137; Arthur H. Vandenberg, Jr., ed., *The Private Papers of Senator Vandenberg* (Boston: Houghton Mifflin Company, 1952), 342–343. The Senate approved the Greek-Turkish Aid bill on 22 April by a margin of 67 to 23; the House consented on 9 May by a tally of 287 to 107. One conservative Republican, Representative Francis H. Case of South Dakota, wrote to Truman that at least seventy-five members of Congress, himself included, voted for the bill only because they feared "pulling the rug out from under you or Secretary Marshall." Quoted in Susan M. Hartmann, *Truman and the 80th Congress* (Columbia: University of Missouri Press, 1971), 66. For discussions of the congressional and public debate on the Greek-Turkish Aid bill, see ibid., 60–66; and John C. Campbell, *The United States in World Affairs, 1947–1948* (New York: Harper & Brothers, 1948), 34–48.

11. Vandenberg, *Private Papers of Senator Vandenberg,* 519; Tang Tsou, *American's Failure in China, 1941–1950* (Chicago: The University of Chicago Press, 1963), 447–448; Richard M. Freeland, *The Truman Doctrine and the Origins of McCarthyism: Foreign Policy, Domestic Politics, and International Security* (New York: Alfred A. Knopf, 1972), 109–112; H. Bradford Westerfield, *Foreign Policy and Party Politics: Pearl Harbor to Korea* (New Haven: Yale University Press, 1955), 241–247. For Judd's background, see Barbara Stuhler, *Ten Men of Minnesota and*

American Foreign Policy, 1898–1968 (St. Paul: Minnesota Historical Society, 1973), 169–174. For a lengthy exposition of Judd's views on American security interests in Asia, see transcript, Walter H. Judd Oral History Interview, 13 April 1970, passim, Truman Library.

12. U.S. Congress, House, Committee on Foreign Affairs, Hearings, *Assistance to Greece and Turkey*, 80th Cong. 1st sess., 1947, 16–18, 47–50.

13. U.S. Congress, House, Committee on International Relations, *Selected Executive Session Hearings of the Committee, 1943–1950*, VII: *United States Policy in the Far East*, Part I (Washington, D.C.: Government Printing Office, 1976), 159–168; PPS 13, 6 November 1947, *Foreign Relations of the United States, 1947*, I: 770–777; Pach, "Arming the Free World," 261–278; Thomas G. Paterson, "If Europe, Why Not China? The Containment Doctrine, 1947–49," *Prologue* 13 (Spring 1981): 19–24.

14. U.S. Congress, Senate, Committee on Foreign Relations, *Foreign Relief Assistance Act of 1948 (Historical Series)* (Washington, D.C.: Government Printing Office, 1976), 422, 433, 439, 448, 469; House Report 1585, 20 March 1948, in U.S. Congress, Committee on International Relations, *Selected Executive Session Hearings of the Committee, 1943–1950* III: *Foreign Economic Assistance Programs* Part I (Washington, D.C.: Government Printing Office, 1976), 216–219; "Legislative History of the China Aid Program," encl. to memorandum, Butterworth to Moore, 20 April 1948, 893.50 Recovery/4–2048, General Records, Department of State, RG 59, National Archives.

15. Defense officials had advocated such legislation as a way of balancing commitments to provide military aid against resources. The Surplus Property Act was still the only general authority for the provision of arms to foreign nations. Yet by early 1947, surplus inventories were insufficient to sustain any major military assistance program. Defense officials feared that in the absence of new legislation and appropriations, the military services might have to use equipment from war reserves to arm foreign nations. For a more detailed examination of this issue, see Chester J. Pach, Jr., "The Truman Administration and the Decision for a Global Military Assistance Program," paper presented at the annual meeting of the Society for Historians of American Foreign Relations, August 1984.

16. SWNCC 382, 5 August 1947, folder SWNCC 382, Records of the State-Army-Navy-Air Force Coordinating Committee.

17. NSC 14/1, 1 July 1948, U.S. Department of State, *Foreign Relations of the United States, 1948*, 9 vols. (Washington, D.C.: Government Printing Office, 1972–1975), I, pt. 2: 585–588. On the possibility of Soviet military action, see CIA Special Evaluation No. 27, 16 March 1948, file 350.05 Top Secret (82), Records of the Plans and Operations Division, United States Army Staff, RG 319, National Archives; ORE 22–48, 2 April 1948, file CD 12–1–26, Records of the Office of the Secretary of Defense, RG 330, National Archives; and Chester J. Pach, Jr., "Launching the Military Assistance Program," paper presented at the Missouri Valley History Conference, March 1985. On the psychological effects of military aid, see especially, ORE 41–49, 24 February 1949, file N7–1(1)–E.8, Records of the Assistant to the

Secretary of Defense for Foreign Military Assistance, RG 330, National Archives; U.S. Congress, Senate, Committee on Foreign Relations, *The Vandenberg Resolution and the North Atlantic Treaty (Historical Series)* (Washington, D.C.: Government Printing Office, 1973), 213–216; and Chester J. Pach, Jr., "Arming the Free World: The Origins of the United States Military Assistance Program, 1945–1950," paper presented at the annual meeting of the Organization of American Historians, April 1985.

18. Consultations between Acheson, Secretary of Defense Louis Johnson, and Vice President Alben W. Barkley, on the one hand, and congressional leaders, on the other, had alerted the administration to the opposition to the military assistance bill and persuaded Truman to delay submission of the legislation until the Senate had consented to the North Atlantic Treaty, which it did on 25 July 1949. See: memorandum of conversation by Acheson, 13 April 1949, folder Memos of Conversations—April 1949, Papers of Dean G. Acheson, Truman Library; memorandum of meeting with the President, 27 June 1949, folder Memos of Conversation—May–June 1949, ibid.; memorandum of conversation by Berkner, 1 July 1949, folder Memos of Conversation, July 1949, ibid.; note by Lloyd, 30 June 1949, folder Military Assistance, July 25, 1949, Papers of David D. Lloyd, Truman Library; memorandum, Gross to Acheson, 3 May 1949, 840.20/5–349, General Records of the Department of State; memorandum, March to Gross, 27 May 1949, 840.20/5–2749, ibid.; telegram no. TELAC 56, Webb to Acheson, 3 June 1949, 840.20/6–349, ibid.; "Present Time Schedule . . .," 1 April 1949, folder 16, State Department Correspondence, 1948–1949, White House Central Files, Confidential Files, Papers of Harry S. Truman, Truman Library; memorandum, Acheson to Truman, 12 May 1949, U.S. Department of State, *Foreign Relations of the United States, 1949*, 9 vols. (Washington, D.C.: Government Printing Office, 1974–1978), IV: 298–299.

19. The revised legislation proposed the same amount of assistance, $1.4 billion, as the previous bill, but empowered the president to grant military assistance only to specific countries in specific amounts: $1,160.0 million to the NATO countries; $211.4 million to Greece and Turkey; and $27.6 million to Iran, Korea, and the Philippines. The revised bill also allowed the president to sell military equipment to any nation "which has joined the United States in a collective defense or regional arrangement."

20. Vandenberg, *Private Papers of Senator Vandenberg*, 503–504, 508; U.S. Congress, Senate, Committee on Foreign Relations, *Military Assistance Program: 1949 (Historical Series)* (Washington, D.C.: Government Printing Office, 1974), 5–46; memorandum of conversation by Acheson, 26 July 1949, *Foreign Relations of the United States, 1949*, I, 361–364; *New York Times*, 29 September 1949, 14; notes of telephone conversation by Battle, 3 August 1949, folder Memos of Conversation—August-September 1949, Acheson Papers; memorandum to Senator Smith, 1 August 1949, unmarked folder, Box 99, Papers of H. Alexander Smith, Seeley G. Mudd Library, Princeton, New Jersey; Summary of Daily Meeting with the Secretary, 3 August 1949, folder Minutes of Secretary's Daily Meetings—1949, Office of the Executive Secretariat, General Records of the Department of State; Lawrence S. Kaplan, *A Community of Interests: NATO and the Military Assistance Program, 1948–1951* (Washington, D.C.: Office of the Secretary of Defense, 1980), pp. 46–47.

21. "Explanation of Amendments . . . to the Military Assistance Bill," n.d., folder Military Assistance Programs, Papers of John Foster Dulles, Mudd Library;

memorandum of telephone conversation by Acheson, 22 August 1949, folder Memos of Conversation—August–September 1949, Acheson Papers; Vandenberg, *The Private Papers of Senator Vandenberg,* 508–518; House Committee on International Relations, *Military Assistance Programs,* Part I: 438–449.

22. U.S. Department of State, *United States Relations with China, with Special Reference to the Period 1944–1949* (Washington, D.C.: Government Printing Office, 1949), iii–xvii; Smith Diary, 8 August 1949, 256, Smith Papers; Gaddis Smith, *Dean Acheson* vol. XVI of the American Secretaries of State and Their Diplomacy (New York: Cooper Square Publishers, Inc., 1972), 112–121; U.S. Congress, House, Committee on International Relations, *Selected Executive Session Hearings of the Committee, 1943–1950* V: *Military Assistance Programs,* (Washington, D.C.: Government Printing Office, 1976) Part I, 186–207, 225–242; Senate Foreign Relations Committee, *Military Assistance Program: 1949,* 515–550.

23. Memorandum of conversation by Acheson, 18 August 1949, folder Memos of Conversation—August–September 1949, Acheson Papers; House Committee on International Relations, *Military Assistance Programs,* Part I: 452–460; Robert M. Blum, *Drawing the Line: The Origin of the American Containment Policy in East Asia* (New York: W. W. Norton & Company, 1982), 129–142.

24. Pach, "Arming the Free World," 414–415.

25. NSC 52/3, 29 September 1949; NSC 52, 5 July 1949, both in *Foreign Relations of the United States, 1949,* I: 349–357, 385–398; JCS 2032/3, 15 August 1949, file JCS Papers, Records of the Deputy Chief of Staff of the United States Army, G–3, Plans and Combat Operations, RG 319, National Archives; Kaplan, *A Community of Interests,* 68–95.

26. U.S. Department of Defense, *Military Assistance Facts,* 1 May 1966, 5.

27. Robert A. Pollard, "Economic Security and the Origins of the Cold War: Bretton Woods, the Marshall Plan, and American Rearmament, 1944–50," *Diplomatic History* 9 (Summer 1985): 284–289; Richard D. Byrne, "Origins of the Mutual Security Program," paper presented at the joint meeting of the Society for Historians of American Foreign Relations and the Pacific Coast Branch, American Historical Association, June 1985.

28. Stephen E. Ambrose, *Eisenhower;* vol. 2: *The President* (New York: Simon and Schuster, 1984), 118–119, 379–380; Harold A. Hovey, *United States Military Assistance: A Study of Policies and Practices* (New York: Frederick A. Praeger, Publishers, 1965), 12–15; U.S. Department of Defense, *Military Assistance Facts,* 1 May 1966, 14–15; John Lewis Gaddis, *Strategies of Containment: A Critical Appraisal of Postwar American National Security Policy* (New York: Oxford University Press, 1982), 152–154.

29. U.S. Congress, Senate, *Congressional Record* 105: 8240–8242; U.S. Congress, Senate, Committee on Foreign Relations, *Executive Sessions of the Senate Foreign Relations Committee (Historical Series): Volume XI* (Washington, D.C.: Government Printing Office, 1982), 653.

30. Burton I. Kaufman, *Trade and Aid: Eisenhower's Foreign Economic Policy, 1953–1961* (Baltimore: The Johns Hopkins University Press, 1982), 108–109,

168–175, 203–204. See also, U.S. Congress, Senate, Special Committee to Study the Foreign Aid Program, *Foreign Aid*, 85th Cong. 1st sess., 1957, S. Rept. 300).

31. Ambrose, *Eisenhower*, 376–381.

32. 76 Stat. 259; *Congressional Quarterly Almanac XX* (Washington, D.C.: Congressional Quarterly, Inc., 1964), 255–297; U.S. Congress, House, Committee on Foreign Affairs, Hearings, *Foreign Assistance Act of 1964*, 88th Cong. 2d sess., 83–97.

33. U.S. Congress, Senate, Committee on Foreign Relations, *Arms Sales and Foreign Policy*, Staff Study (Washington, D.C.: Government Printing Office, 1967), 1–13; David J. Louscher, "The Rise of Military Sales as a U.S. Foreign Policy Instrument," *Orbis* 20 (Winter 1977): 933–964; 78 Stat. 1011.

34. U.S. Congress, Senate, *Arms Sales and Foreign Policy*, 1–13; U.S. Congress, Senate, Committee on Banking and Currency, Hearings, *Export-Import Bank Participation and Financing in Credit Sales of Defense Articles*, 90th Cong. 1st sess., 1967, 3–26; Stockholm International Peace Research Institute, *The Arms Trade with the Third World* (Stockholm: Almqvist & Wiksell, 1971), 170–178.

35. *Congressional Quarterly Almanac* XXIV (Washington, D.C.: Congressional Quarterly Service, 1969), 427.

36. Beginning in fiscal 1966, the Johnson administration incorporated military aid for South Vietnam and for other countries contributing to the Vietnam War in the Defense Department budget.

37. See, for example, U.S. Congress, Senate, Committee on Foreign Relations, Hearings, *Foreign Assistance Act of 1968: Part I-Vietnam*, 90th Cong. 2d sess., 1968.

38. House Committee on International Relations, *Selected Executive Session Hearings of the Committee, 1943–1950* V: 138–139.

39. Charles W. Whalen, Jr., *The House and Foreign Policy: The Irony of Congressional Reform* (Chapel Hill: The University of North Carolina Press, 1982), 126.

40. U.S. Congress Senate, Committee on Foreign Relations, Hearings, *Foreign Assistance Act of 1967*, 90th Cong. 1st sess., 176; Whalen, *The House and Foreign Policy*, 3–25; Thomas M. Franck and Edward Weisband, *Foreign Policy by Congress* (New York: Oxford University Press, 1979), 210–257.

41. U.S. Congress, Subcommittee on Economy in Government of the Joint Economic Committee, Hearings, *Economic Issues in Military Assistance*, 92d Cong. 1st sess., 1971, 1–2.

42. Ibid., 2–31; Richard M. Moose, with Daniel L. Spiegel, "Congress and Arms Transfers" in *Arms Transfers and American Foreign Policy*, ed. by Andrew J. Pierre (New York: New York University Press, 1979), 228–236; Lewis Sorley, *Arms Transfers Under Nixon: A Policy Analysis* (Lexington: The University of Kentucky Press, 1983), 42–133.

43. Franck and Weisband, *Foreign Policy by Congress*, 34–45, 84–89; John Rourke, *Congress and the Presidency in U.S. Foreign Policymaking: A Study in Interaction and Influence, 1945–1982* (Boulder, Col.: Westview Press, 1983), 270–273.

44. Moose and Spiegel, "Congress and Arms Transfers," 236–260; Philip J. Farley, "The Control of United States Arms Sales" in *Congress and Arms Control*, ed. by Alan Platt and Lawrence D. Weiler (Boulder, Col.: Westview Press, 1978), 111–133.

45. Whalen, *The House and Foreign Policy*, 66–69; Andrew J. Pierre, *The Global Politics of Arms Sales* (Princeton: Princeton University Press, 1982), 45–72; Rourke, *Congress and the Presidency in U.S. Foreign Policymaking*, 294–310.

46. On the difficulties of assessing national interests in arms transfers, see Philip J. Farley, Stephen S. Kaplan, and William H. Lewis, *Arms Across the Sea* (Washington, D.C.: The Brookings Institution, 1978); and Stephanie G. Neuman and Robert E. Harkavy, *Arms Transfers in the Modern World* (New York: Praeger Publishers, 1979).

10

Oversight or Afterview?: Congress, the CIA, and Covert Actions Since 1947

Thomas G. Paterson

His temper flaring, Senator Daniel P. Moynihan resigned his vice chairmanship of the Select Committee on Intelligence, complaining that the Central Intelligence Agency (CIA) had not properly briefed the committee as required by law. "I am pissed off," Senator Barry Goldwater lectured the CIA director at the same time. "This is an act violating international law. It is an act of war. For the life of me, I don't see how we are going to explain it." In the spring of 1984 the CIA's mining of Nicaragua's harbors and the subsequent destruction of foreign merchant ships had stirred Congress. But Moynihan soon withdrew his resignation and Goldwater cooled down after CIA Director William Casey offered profound apologies for having neglected Capitol Hill.[1]

Yet clashes between intelligence officials and congressional overseers stormed again and again, as in May of 1985 when a car bombing in Beirut, Lebanon, killed more than eighty people. The massacre was carried out by agents working for a Lebanese group that was in turn working for the CIA. The new Vice Chairman of the Senate Intelligence Committee, Patrick J. Leahy, protested that the CIA's counterterrorism program in the Middle East had not been adequately explained to him; he had discovered the covert operation on his own. Senator Moynihan allowed that he had been officially notified some months before about the secret program, but that he had not pushed for details.[2] Many wondered not only if the CIA once again had lost control of foreigners whom the agency helped organize, fund, and supply with arms, but also once again had hoodwinked Congress.

Whether the question is the CIA's studied reluctance to inform Congress about covert actions or Congress' own laxity in pressing for information, congressional oversight of intelligence activities since the 1940s has been highly controversial, often flawed and ineffectual, seldom alert, frequently tardy, perhaps impossible, yet certainly necessary. One newspaper cartoonist depicted the problem graphically when he sketched a sign in front of CIA headquarters; the acronym "CIA" was spelled out as "Congress Isn't Aware."[3] Representative Wyche Fowler of the House Permanent Select Committee on Intelligence has aptly remarked that "it is not oversight if it comes as an afterview."[4] Since the founding of the CIA in 1947, in fact, "afterview" has been the more common characteristic.

When he was criticized for first aiding and then abruptly abandoning the Kurds in Iraq, contributing to the deaths of thousands of them, Secretary of State Henry A. Kissinger coldly replied that "one must not confuse the intelligence business with missionary work."[5] Indeed, we are not dealing here with "missionary work," monotonous legislative history, or abstract constitutional questions. Covert action is a murderous business. People of all ages and both sexes suffer and die as victims of CIA operations. Assassinations, bombings, torture, arson, paramilitary expeditions, and various "dirty tricks" maim, kill, and destroy—and they hurt the innocent. In 1971, for example, a covert operation introduced into Cuba, through a sealed vial, the African swine fever virus. The outbreak of swine fever a few weeks later decimated the hog population and caused severe pork shortages for the Cuban people— pork was a major component of the Cuban diet.[6]

Some veteran public servants and analysts like George W. Ball and George F. Kennan have argued that covert action—as distinct from the collection of intelligence data—can never be kept secret, seldom attains policy objectives, undermines diplomacy, and is fundamentally incompatible with democratic principles and ethical values. Covert operations have exposed the basic tension between open and closed government, between public accountability and secrecy. Public review, most would agree, is essential if citizens are to acquire the knowledge necessary to change policy and make leaders responsive. For all of these reasons, some critics have called for strict limits on or the outright abolition of covert actions.[7] To study the problem of congressional oversight, then, is to probe matters of life-and-death and of great national consequence and to demonstrate the extreme extent to which American leaders were willing to go to meet the Communist threat they thought omnipresent.

The story has evolved through three stages. First, from 1947 to the early 1970s, when a series of shocks exposed the delinquency of congressional oversight. Second, from the early 1970s to 1980, a period called by some the "oversight revolution," when Congress investigated past covert operations, found much wrongdoing, created new watchdog committees on intelligence, and required the executive branch to keep Congress better informed and more closely involved in deciding whether covert actions should be undertaken.[8] And, third, the 1980s, when the Reagan administration and the new oversight process coincided—and collided—to raise doubts about whether the reform of the 1970s amounted to anything more than a temporary respite from Congressional timidity and laxity on intelligence questions.

There are basically three kinds of intelligence activities: espionage, counterintelligence, and covert action.[9] The first is the gathering and analyzing of information, sometimes through spying. Neither this activity nor counterintelligence—the protection of information and the spy system—have been major points of contention, although members of Congress sometimes have complained that the CIA does not predict accurately from the information it has collected. No, covert action has aroused the most controversy. Covert action seeks through manipulation to influence governments, organizations, and individuals abroad so that they support United States foreign policy. Such secret activities have included not only propaganda, disinformation, bribery, and economic sabotage, but also paramilitary operations wherein weapons and force are used. In short, covert action has often constituted the waging of war. On this the Constitution is explicit: *Congress* must declare it. It does not matter, as Senator Thomas Eagleton once explained, whether Americans who go to war wear green uniforms or seersucker suits. War is war. And "from little involvements—little CIA wars, big wars grow," he warned in an unsuccessful attempt to persuade Congress to extend the provisions of the 1973 War Powers Resolution to cover covert action[10]

From the creation of the CIA in 1947 to the early 1970s, the first stage of this history, the agency expanded from its initially intended mission of information gathering to covert action.[11] Although Congress had (and still does have) an obligation to monitor executive activities and to control the budget—specifically to insure that the CIA meets acceptable legal standards and is accountable for its actions, Congress seemed content to leave oversight responsibilities to the executive branch. But executive oversight proved woefully inadequate, despite the fact that the president, Special Assistant for National Security Affairs, National Security Council (NSC), Forty Committee, Department of State, American ambassadors, and president's Foreign Intelligence Advisory Board were well-positioned to oversee CIA activities and to check abuses.[12] In some cases, presidents themselves may not have known what the CIA was doing—including its plots to kill Cuba's Fidel Castro and the Congo's Patrice Lumumba.[13] In the 1960s, Secretary of State Dean Rusk was sure that *he* knew; but when asked later if he had been given thorough information about covert actions, he answered: "I must confess at the time I thought the answer was yes, but it turned out not to be yes, and I feel very badly about that."[14] He recalled that the NSC, of which he was a member, did not even conduct an annual review of the CIA budget; indeed, he never saw a CIA budget.[15] "There are some things that you don't tell Congress; some things you don't even tell the President," admitted a CIA official.[16] Apparently CIA officials did not even tell the CIA director himself about some projects. For example, counterintelligence chief James Angleton built a miniempire within the CIA for twenty years until he was fired in 1974.

One of his more abusive activities in the early 1960s was the three-and-a-half year imprisonment of Soviet defector Yuri Nosenko. Angleton suspected Nosenko was a double agent sent to the United States to spy. For 1277 days Nosenko was tormented in an austere, solitary prison near Washington, D.C. Apparently he was not a Soviet spy at all. Not until 1976 did an internal CIA study reveal the travesty.[17] And when John McCone became director in 1961, William Harvey, the CIA officer who was plotting with crime bosses to kill Castro, deliberately withheld information on the murder plots from McCone.[18]

If the president and CIA director were not privy to all of the agency's covert operations, it is hardly surprising that Congress knew even less. But Congress did not want to know. Senator Leverett Saltonstall expressed a widely held view when he remarked that "it is not a question of reluctance on the part of CIA officials to speak to us. Instead it is a question of our reluctance, if you will, to seek information and knowledge on subjects which I personally . . . would rather not have."[19] Senator Goldwater added years later that "we would be better serving our country by not hearing it."[20]

Why did most members of Congress accept "deliberate ignorance?"[21] Why did they prefer not to know? In the heady days of the Cold War mentality and "imperial presidency," the CIA was admired as a presidential instrument for meeting the Communist threat—and it should not be fettered. Members of Congress did not want to appear to impede the agency's anti-Communist crusade by raising potentially embarrassing questions. In some cases, they shied away from moral issues raised by some of the CIA's dirtiest tricks. Ignorance may not always be bliss, but it can be escape. Representatives and senators also preferred ignorance because they worried about breaching a national security secret through an inadvertent public utterance. Under the lights and in front of the microphones, some legislators found it difficult to recall which information was classified and which was not. Others resisted secret information because they feared cooptation. If they received notice of a covert action and did nothing, this could be interpreted as acceptance. And if the covert action later became controversial, they would be hard pressed to explain why they had earlier failed to prevent it. This point is closely related to another: there was little political payback from activist congressional oversight. The information was confidential, hearings or briefings were held behind closed doors, and legislators were not supposed to go public.[22]

The Congress's hesitancy to delve into CIA operations was conspicuously evident in the system of congressional oversight. With no legal basis, this system was highly personalized and episodic, responsive to the whims of the CIA director and a handful of leaders in the two houses. Someone jokingly tagged the system with the acronym BOGSAT—"bunch of guys sitting around a table."[23] Information on the CIA and its budget, and hence oversight, was restricted largely to subcommittees of the Appropriations and Armed Services Committees of both houses.[24] Powerful senior senators like Richard Russell, John Stennis, and John McLellan dominated the structure.

One intelligence official noted in an internal CIA report that "they tend generally toward conservatism and hawkishness."[25] CIA Director William Colby appreciated them, for they "faithfully and patriotically" protected the CIA from "public prying."[26] In Russell's words, the CIA's methods had to be taken "on faith."[27]

This senior command with oversight responsibilities occasionally received CIA briefings, but usually only after covert action had been initiated. The subcommittees lacked adequate staff and seldom convened.[28] Attendance was poor and members asked few questions of intelligence officials. Nor did the subcommittees issue reports. "We met annually—one time a year, for a period of two hours in which we accomplished virtually nothing," observed Representative Walter Norblad, a House Armed Services intelligence subcommittee member for four years in the 1960s.[29] In some years the Senate Armed Services intelligence subcommittee did not meet at all.[30] One CIA official who attended sessions reported to his superiors that the members were "prone to intermittent dozing" and "failing faculties." With some mocking disdain, he told the story of the elderly chairman who, when shown a diagram of covert actions, demanded to know "what the hell are you doing in covert parliamentary operations." When reassured that the chart read "paramilitary operations," he shot back: "the more of these the better—just don't go fooling around with parliamentary stuff—you don't know enough about it."[31]

These subcommittees became cozy with the CIA, in part because they prided themselves on being its protectors but also because the CIA cleverly cultivated them. The problem, of course, is a perennial one: regulators often come to reflect the views of the institution they are supposed to be regulating. "The clandestine services give them a peak under the rug and their eyes pop," a CIA official remarked. "It doesn't take long before the congressional overseers acquire that old-school feeling."[32] Sometimes subcommittee chairmen became "insiders" when they visited CIA headquarters for special breakfasts. In the 1950s Director Allen Dulles fed tidbits of information about secret projects to the select few. "Allen used to find the congressmen were intrigued with little personality stories and quasi-clandestine details which would amuse [them]. But I think he found it an effective way of building a rapport with them," a former CIA officer commented.[33] But, as Representative Michael J. Harrington later complained, members of Congress became "accomplices," because "the more they know, the more they are responsible for hiding."[34]

If the Congress was both ill-informed and lax about oversight, the CIA was determined to keep it that way. Agency officials followed the practice of never volunteering information, and if asked about an operation, to provide a minimum of details. In some cases, the CIA ignored Congress altogether, flatly refused to answer questions, or told lies in briefings. CIA officer Ralph W. McGehee has written that in 1964 he helped prepare a briefing on operations in Laos that Far Eastern division chief William E. Colby presented in secret to Congress. According to McGehee, "it was a complete hoax contrived to deceive Congress, which naturally swallowed it hook, line, and sinker."[35] Allen Dulles once told a colleague: "I'll fudge the truth to the oversight committee, but I'll tell the chairman the truth—that is, if he wants to know."[36] CIA officials feared leaks, but more, they believed that Congress had no right to information. When Senator J. William Fulbright, chairman of the Foreign Relations Committee, asked the CIA if the Fulbright academic awards were ever used as covers for CIA activities, the agency would not tell him.[37]

An instance demonstrating well the combination of Congress's reluctance to know and the CIA's reluctance to tell occurred in 1971 in the Senate. The issue was the CIA's 1960s covert war in Laos—a five billion dollar program using over ten thousand Meo tribesmen as mercenary troops. Congress never directly voted the funds—money from the Defense Department and Agency for International Development had been secretly transferred to the CIA—but apparently some senators had been briefed. The heated exchange pitted Senators Fulbright and Alan Cranston against Allen Ellender:

FULBRIGHT: Would the Senator [Ellender] say that before the creation of the army in Laos they [CIA] came before the committee [intelligence subcommittee of Appropriations Committee] and the committee knew of it and approved it.

ELLENDER: Probably so.

FULBRIGHT: Did the Senator approve it?

ELLENDER: It was not—I did not say anything about it. . . . It never dawned on me to ask about it. I did see it publicized in the newspaper some time ago.

CRANSTON: The chairman stated that he never would have thought of even asking about CIA funds being used to conduct the war in Laos. . . . I would like to ask the Senator if, since then, he has inquired and now knows whether that is being done?

ELLENDER: I have not inquired.

CRANSTON: You do not know, in fact?

ELLENDER: No.

CRANSTON: As you are one of the five men privy to this information, in fact you are the number one man of the five men who would know what happened to this money. The fact is, not even the five men know the facts in the situation.

ELLENDER: Probably not.[38]

Another Senator, Stuart Symington, was outraged to learn about the Laos operation from the press: "The large majority of Congress was deceived by Laos. . . . We now get reports that Americans died in Laos and that we had been lied to, because we were told they died in Vietnam. We are getting pretty sick of being lied to. . . ."[39]

Unlike that for any other government agency, the budget for the CIA was kept secret from Congress—except from the few overseers. Although the Constitution prescribes that "a regular statement and account of the receipts and expenditures of all public money shall be published" (Article I, Section 9), the CIA enjoyed covert financing. The CIA budget was concealed in the figures for other departments—usually Defense—and then moneys were transferred to the agency. Congressman Ed Koch once asked Director Richard Helms about the size of the CIA budget. Helms said the CIA did not answer such questions, and members of Congress had no right to know. Helms then explained that the CIA budget was properly hidden. "Do you mean that it might be included under Social Security?" asked the irritated representative. Helms's and the CIA's arrogance then shone: "We have not used that one yet, but that is not a bad idea."[40] Moreover, the agency's "Reserve for Contingencies," created in 1952, permitted the CIA great flexibility in using its dollars for covert operations without congressional scrutiny. In short, there was almost no accountability. Lucien Nedzi, a House subcommittee member, told his colleagues: "I have to be candid and tell you I don't know whether we are getting our money's worth."[41] Congress has always voted down bills to disclose intelligence budget figures.[42]

This state of affairs—shallow congressional oversight and CIA secrecy and deceit—did not go unchallenged. Indeed, in the period 1947–1974, about one hundred and fifty proposals to improve oversight were introduced in Congress—many called for the creation of joint or select intelligence committees—but only two bills ever reached the floor of Congress.[43] In the mid-1950s Senator Mike Mansfield asked for closer scrutiny of an agency he considered uncontrolled. In 1956 his reform proposal earned the bipartisan support of thirty-four cosponsors, and the Rules Committee passed it by an eight to one tally. Besides setting up a joint congressional committee with a professional staff, the resolution required the CIA to keep the committee fully informed. The chief argument for the new structure was that a specialized committee would permit Congress to concentrate on intelligence with the same degree of professionalism and thoroughness it gave to other subjects and thus meet its obligations under the checks-and-balances system. From such congressional surveillance, it was believed, a better intelligence service would emerge. But freshman Senator Mansfield collided head-on with the "high brass" of the upper chamber.[44] They defended as workable the system they themselves dominated; they countered that intelligence should not be "watchdogged to death."[45] The CIA itself fought the legislation. As Mansfield later recalled, CIA officials were able to defeat reform bills because "they had the hierarchs in the Senate in their pockets. . . ."[46] Losing several of its cosponsors, the Mansfield resolution suffered defeat, fifty-nine to twenty-seven. Four years later, at a White House meeting with President Dwight D. Eisenhower, Mansfield again advocated a congressional oversight committee. The suggestion was quickly "knocked down" by other senators present. Russell complained that the committee's staff might leak secret information that would endanger the lives of intelligence officers.[47]

Not until 1966 did another oversight resolution reach the Senate floor, although many had been introduced. Then Senator Eugene McCarthy sought to end what he called the "invisible government" of the CIA that was responsible for the Bay of Pigs and the Vietnam War.[48] McCarthy proposed that some members of the Foreign Relations Committee be invited into the oversight process. The chairman of that committee, J. William Fulbright, backed the McCarthy initiative, but Senator Russell, chairman of Armed Services, once again blocked reform. In a testy debate with Fulbright, the Georgia Senator warned him against "muscling in on my committee."[49] Russell persuaded the Senate to refer the resolution to his committee, where he killed it. The intent of the motion was nonetheless satisfied in January, 1967, when Russell invited Fulbright and two other members of Foreign Relations to attend meetings of the Armed Services intelligence subcommittee. But this new system served oversight only minimally: still a mere handful of senior legislators held responsibility; still they heard largely what the CIA wanted them to hear; still covert actions went unquestioned and unknown; still the CIA budget remained secret.[50] In other words, Congress could not determine if the CIA was meeting its statutory mandate.

The feebleness of oversight continued until the early 1970s when the Vietnam War, Watergate scandals, and revelations of unsavory CIA covert actions at home and abroad weakened the executive branch's ability to resist a stronger congressional voice in foreign policy and intelligence. Congressional oversight is alert and active, it appears, only when a foreign policy consensus is shattered, when executive authority is vulnerable, or when investigatory journalism has stimulated uncommon public concern.

The origins of the so-called "oversight revolution" owed much to Watergate, the array of scandals that ultimately drove Richard M. Nixon from office in shame. First, Watergate induced a temporary shift of power from the executive to the legislative branch. The Vietnam War after the 1968 Tet Offensive, various reports published in the early 1970s on the CIA's role in the removal of the Diem government and the secret war in Laos, and the passage in 1973 of the War Powers Resolution—all had already begun this rearrangement of governmental power. Second, some of the burglars arrested for the 1972 break-in at Democratic National Committee headquarters were former CIA personnel, and the CIA had participated in the Watergate cover-up by issuing cover stories designed to impede the FBI investigation. Third, the CIA had helped Nixon politicos in various illegal activities at home.

Several committee reports in 1973–1974 chided the CIA for its transgressions, including the destruction of records related to Watergate.[51]

Events in Chile accelerated oversight reform.[52] In October, 1973, President Salvador Allende was overthrown in a military coup. Rumors quickly circulated that the CIA had helped undermine the elected Marxist leader. Under oath, American officials, including Secretary Kissinger, assured Congress that the allegations were false. But, then, in April, 1974, as suspicions were taking on more substance, CIA Director William Colby told a closed session of the intelligence subcommittee of the House Armed Services Committee the truth about the CIA's considerable covert program to topple Allende. Representative Harrington, who considered oversight a "sham," urged house leaders to conduct hearings on the Chilean affair.[53] Getting nowhere, in part because Congress was so absorbed with the process of impeaching President Nixon, but having obtained Colby's report from the subcommittee chairman, Harrington decided to break the rules and speak out. "I couldn't believe my eyes. . . . There it was, forty pages in black and white . . . telling in clinical detail how we were engaged up to our eyebrows [in Chile]."[54] At a 12 September 1972 press conference the congressman from Massachusetts revealed Colby's testimony. Embarrassed veteran overseers like Senator John Stennis admitted that they had not known much about the CIA's role in Chile. In fact, of the thirty-three CIA covert projects in Chile during 1963–1973, only eight had been reported to the appropriate congressional committees.[55] "I do not think there is a man in the legislative part of the Government who really knows what is going on in the intelligence community," Senator Howard Baker remarked. "I am afraid of this lack of knowledge. For the first time, I suppose, in my senatorial career I am frightened."[56]

Apprehensions like Baker's helped pass the Hughes-Ryan Amendment to the 1974 Foreign Assistance Act, the first significant congressional oversight reform.[57] Hughes-Ryan held that the CIA could engage in a covert action abroad only if "the President finds that each operation is important to the national security of the United States and reports, in a timely fashion, a description and scope of such operation to the appropriate committees of the Congress, including the Committee on Foreign Relations of the United States Senate and the Committee on Foreign Affairs of the House of Representatives."[58] The Hughes-Ryan reform thus required reports on covert action to Congress; and it expanded the number of overseers—now to include members of six committees. The measure did harbor shortcomings: the CIA did not have to report to oversight bodies *before* implementing an operation; the reports were not required to be thorough; and after receiving classified information in the vaguely mentioned "timely fashion," Congressional overseers had no veto power unless they were bold enough to violate the pledge of secrecy and halt CIA covert action by denying funds through a vote of the entire Congress. Nonetheless, this new reporting procedure apparently had a "chilling effect" on clandestine actions, which dropped dramatically in number.[59]

The Hughes-Ryan Amendment hardly quieted the intelligence tempest, for in late December, 1974, the *New York Times* revealed extensive CIA spying on Americans at home in violation of the agency's statutory charter.[60] Soon James Angleton and other CIA influentials were fired; and the president appointed a commission to investigate the charges.[61] What would Congress do this time? On January 27, 1975, by an eighty-two to four margin, the Senate created a new committee—the Select Committee to Study Governmental Operations with Respect to Intelligence Activities. Soon known as the Church Committee after its chairman Frank Church, this investigative body hired a professional staff, established careful guidelines to maintain the security of classified materials, held extensive hearings, and produced a shelf of publications detailing CIA activities.[62] In July, the House also created an investigative committee chaired by Otis Pike.

While the two committees probed and pressed, shocking public opinion leaders with information on assassination plots and illegal mail openings, the Hughes-Ryan Amendment encountered its first major test. The issue: CIA covert action in Angola, that African nation just about to be liberated from colonial bondage by Portugal and already wracked by civil war.[63] Before 1975, the United States had backed one faction and the Soviets another. In January of that year the Ford administration decided to increase the stakes through more covert political aid. The following month the leaders of the six congressional committees received notification; they apparently made no fuss. Then in July the administration opted for covert military assistance to two Angolan factions. Senior members of the congressional committees duly received CIA notices. This time, however, Senator Dick Clark of the African Affairs Subcommittee of the Foreign Relations Committee asked for more details, which were given to his group in a briefing. Controversy surrounds this briefing and others, for it appears that they were neither complete nor accurate.[64] Clark, especially after an August trip to Africa, grew worried that the United States was rejecting a viable diplomatic alternative and exaggerating the Soviet threat in Angola. About the same time, the Assistant Secretary of State for African Affairs quietly resigned with much the same reasoning after his futile attempt to stop covert military aid.[65]

Still the president wanted more; in September he notified the appropriate committees that military aid was being hoisted to the level of twenty-five million dollars. Clark began to lobby the Foreign Relations Committee, which was becoming wary of deeper American involvement in volatile Angola. When, in December, the administration informed the committees that an additional seven million dollars was being sent as covert military aid to Angola, the senator from Iowa decided to go public. He thereupon persuaded his Foreign Relations colleagues to report an amendment to the 1976 foreign assistance bill to prohibit any funds for covert action in Angola. Legislative jockeying and political opportunism converted the Clark Amendment into the Tunney Amendment to the Defense appropriations bill, where, it was assumed, the CIA budget for its Angolan operation rested.[65] On 19 December, the

Senate, by a count of fifty-four to twenty-two, barred covert action in Angola; the House agreed on 27 January 1976 (323–99); and the president reluctantly signed the act on 9 February. An obstinate Congress had halted a covert action and had as well exposed the weaknesses of Hughes-Ryan oversight. Some legislators began to ask for more reform—for notification before projects were launched and greater control over covert actions.

But the case for stronger congressional oversight sputtered in February, 1976, because of the way the final report of the Pike Committee was handled. Pike's committee completed its work in January, yet the full House refused to publish its report until the administration had a chance to give it a classification review.[67] Pike thereupon released a brief summary of the committee's recommendations only; but a draft of the final report came into the hands of CBS-TV reporter Daniel Schorr, who passed it on to the *Village Voice*. The publication of excerpts of the report in this weekly New York newspaper distracted attention from the committee's findings on CIA abuses and inadequacies and put it on the source of the leak (which was never determined) and Congress's leakiness. The Pike Committee urged, among other changes, the creation of a new committee on intelligence to which the CIA director would report fully on any covert action within forty-eight hours of the decision to initiate the action.[68]

The impressive final report of the Church Committee, published in April, 1976, encouraged oversight reformers. After detailing excessive presidential use of covert action, the Church Committee asked the Senate to increase the congressional role in intelligence through a legislative charter; publish an overall intelligence budget figure; and create a new Senate committee on intelligence.[69] The Senate soon voted, seventy-seven to twenty-two, to create the Select Committee on Intelligence. (The House waited until July of 1977 to launch a similar committee.) Because Hughes-Ryan was not repealed, the CIA now had to report to eight committees. But the new system faced an uncertain future: vocal opponents began a counterattack, the question of a charter remained unresolved, and the incoming Carter administration had its own ideas.[70]

The Carter administration moved quickly to reorganize the maligned CIA, reduce its bloated bureaucracy, improve its intelligence production, and restrict its activities. The administration was not adverse to covert action; Carter officials, CIA Director Stansfield Turner recalled, "turned easily and quickly to covert devices. . . .," especially in its last two years.[71] On the whole, congressional intelligence committees were properly notified, to the effect that some planned actions were scaled down and at least one stopped.[72] In a 263-page bill titled the National Intelligence Reorganization and Reform Act of 1978, oversight advocates offered an elaborate statutory charter for the intelligence community, including prohibitions on assassination. Critics pilloried the legislation as both too restrictive and too permissive; and the administration cooled toward it.[73] Then the taking of the American hostages in Iran and the Soviet bludgeoning of Afghanistan further undermined the oversight reform movement. "Why cripple an already weakened CIA when it was urgently needed as a weapon in the post-détente Cold War struggle with the Soviet Union?" critics asked.

New, but shortened charter legislation was introduced in early 1980. As the first administration witness, Director Turner singled out several provisions for complaint. The bill required the CIA to notify congressional intelligence committees before starting a covert action. Turner found this a detriment to presidential flexibility at times when speed and secrecy were paramount. In general, the Carter administration believed that a statutory reporting requirement was an "excessive intrusion by the Congress into the president's exercise of his powers under the Constitution."[74] The basic issue was joined once again: the president vs. the Congress in matters of foreign policy.

Several weeks after this testimony, the kind of problem Turner had identified arose in the covert expedition to rescue the hostages in Iran. President Carter worried about maintaining secrecy for the complicated mission, so he planned to notify congressional leaders only after "the rescue operation had reached the point of no return." But because the mission had to be aborted while in progress, the president "never got around to that."[75] Given the emergency nature of the problem, congressional overseers gave the president the benefit of the doubt, but continued to argue for prior notification.

With Iran as a backdrop and with critics such as Republican presidential candidate Ronald Reagan charging that the CIA was being hamstrung by burdensome restrictions, Congress jilted charter legislation in favor of a two-page document—the Intelligence Oversight Act of 1980. The new legislation required the CIA to report only to the House and Senate Intelligence Committees (thus revising Hughes-Ryan) and to give prior notification *except* when the president determined that "extraordinary circumstances affecting vital interests" existed, in which case only eight leaders of Congress would be notified.[76] And the president could actually *waive* prior notification altogether if later, "in a timely fashion," he explained his reasons. Finally, the act required the CIA to furnish any information—classified materials included—requested by the two committees, and to report "any illegal intelligence activity or significant intelligence failure. . . ."[77] This legislation hardly satisfied those who preferred a major statutory charter; it carried a certain ambiguity permitting the president to skirt prior notification; it placed no time limit on covert actions and did not provide for a congressional veto (in this regard it was different from the War Powers Resolution). In essence, then, Congress only had to be informed.

The new Reagan administration greatly expanded CIA covert actions. At the same time, it publicly undertook covert operations which in earlier periods probably would have been kept secret: aid to Nicaraguan *contras*, Cambodian rebels, and Afghan insurgents. In part this seemingly contradictory practice stemmed from Washington's eagerness to send an unmistakable signal to the Soviets that the United States would contest them wherever they were thought to be. But it also derived from an awareness that secret wars seldom remain secret. In this atmosphere, the Reagan administration showed minimal respect for congressional oversight and the briefing process. As well, it preferred executive orders to a statutory charter.[78] But, more, Congress in the 1980s retreated from the reform mood of the 1970s, coming to focus more "on enhancing effectiveness" than "on circumscribing [the CIA's] capabilities and activities."[79] In 1985, for example, Congress repealed the 1976 Clark (or Tunney) Amendment banning covert action in Angola; the following year, the Reagan administration informed Congress that it was extending $15 million to a rebel group led by Jonas Savimbi to help it overthrow the Angolan government. The result: talks between Angola and the United States to resolve the issue of Namibia broke down.[80]

Still, some legislators protested Reagan's approach to covert action and oversight. One Democratic member of Congress complained that, to the reinvigorated CIA, "we are like mushrooms," because "they keep us in the dark and feed us a lot of manure."[81] Another lamented that Congress had "little leverage" over the intelligence community. "You don't have a veto, so you have to satisfy yourself by hollering inside the tin can."[82] A critic described CIA briefings of intelligence committees as a "tooth-pulling process, and sometimes the dentist can't see all the teeth."[83] According to a Republican member of Congress, CIA Director William J. Casey "wouldn't tell you if your coat was on fire—unless you asked him."[84] Indeed, Casey frankly lectured congressional overseers: "I do not volunteer information. If you ask me the right question I will respond."[85] This familiar executive arrogance, combined with incomplete reportage to oversight committees, helped produce the bitter public confrontation over the CIA's not-so-secret war against Nicaragua.[86]

In the Reagan eighties, Congress found it difficult to halt a covert action it disliked. When notified by the president and CIA of an impending covert activity, the intelligence committee members could ask questions, press for changes, demand termination, or contact the president and register doubts with the White House.[87] If such pleading failed, a member could attempt to amend a money authorization bill to prevent the expenditure of funds for a particular clandestine project. In short, a member of Congress had to be willing to confront or embarrass a president with formidable rhetorical and patronage powers.[88] It was not a task many took on.

Perhaps congressional oversight can seldom be satisfactory or effective. Obstacles remain numerous. First, oversight seems to be most ardent only when the press and then the public opinion elite are stimulated to debate foreign adventurism. But the extreme secrecy that shrouds CIA activities, the intelligence budget, and the oversight process itself prevents this from occurring very often and stymies the public airing so vital a governmental accountability. In 1984, Congress actually succumbed to the CIA's preference for more secrecy when it passed the Central Intelligence Agency Information Act, which exempted operational files from the Freedom of Information Act.[89]

Second, presidential power dominates most foreign policy debates, and precedent favors presidential initiative and prerogative in times of crisis. To put it bluntly, the executive branch can get away with murder: it can quietly expand a program beyond what members of Congress originally intended, or it can redefine a problem to circumvent congressional oversight.[90] In 1981, for example, the CIA secretly sent a team into Laos in a vain effort to find missing-in-action soldiers from the Vietnam era. Director Casey did not give Congress prior notification because, he claimed, the mission was not a covert action but an operation to gather information.[91] Third, the great number of intelligence bodies makes it difficult for Congress to monitor the intelligence community and it permits the executive branch to utilize for projects those agencies that receive less congressional scrutiny. Fourth, Supreme Court decisions have shielded the CIA from public scrutiny.[92]

Fifth, the persistence of the Cold War and virulent anti-Communism, replete with exaggerated rhetoric, cascading crises, and impassioned appeals to patriotism, favor giving the CIA a wide range within which to roam. When détente is down and confrontation is up, Congress tends to retreat from careful oversight and to accept "dirty tricks" as a necessary evil. Sixth, vagueness is a characteristic of much legislation, including the 1980 act. It is not clear when prior notification must be given or when it can be waived. This ambiguity affords the executive branch considerable latitude. Seventh, some members of Congress prefer not to know about the CIA's covert business, for the reasons discussed earlier. Eighth, members of Congress are "busy generalists," too overwhelmed by a multitude of assignments fully to watch over the CIA.[93] Ninth, given the restraints imposed by secrecy, access to knowledge about the CIA budget is obstructed. The House Permanent Select Committee on Intelligence, for example, has made available for inspection to members of Congress a classified report on CIA activities at budget time. But very few representatives ever perused the looseleaf notebook. "Nobody reads the stuff, or almost nobody," observed one. "The hard thing is that this material is not accessible to your staff, so you don't have them review it," said another. Because they are so busy, members of Congress in essence cast blind votes.[94] And, finally, there is little political reward from controversial vigilance over intelligence when compared to farm, health, or other issues. "I have to go now," Senator Hubert H. Humphrey abruptly announced during a hearing on covert operations in Chile. "I am trying to get jobs for four hundred people in Minnesota today. That is a great deal more important to me right now than Chile."[95] The lesson from Senator Frank Church's experience is conspicuous; in 1980, just a short time after his highly publicized stewardship of the investigating committee, he was defeated in Idaho for reelection to a fifth term, in part because right-wing groups charged that his disclosures had seriously wounded the CIA.[96]

In the 1980s the congressional monitoring system created during oversight reform in the last decade did not follow the scenario reformers had written for it, and the CIA seemed quite "willing to go off on its own and risk getting caught by Congress."[97] The Reagan administration, of course, deliberately inhibited the process. But, also significant, the oversight system that reformers had hoped would restrain covert actions had actually helped to augment them. Put another way: the system largely worked. Legislators received earlier than ever before in the history of oversight more information about more covert operations from more agencies; legislators knew more about the CIA budget than ever before.[98] The CIA generally answered to the Congress. The Congress liked the answers. Indeed, members of Congress were using the information not so much to question or thwart secret missions but to support them. Like predecessors in the forties, fifties, and sixties, Congress in the eighties favored an aggressive CIA to wage counterinsurgency and to meet the Soviet threat in the revived Cold War. To the reformers' chagrin, then, oversight became an instrument for expanded covert action. Thus future debate may focus on whether military and paramilitary covert actions should be prohibited altogether. Perhaps new revelations of CIA abuses or failures under the Reagan administration will push some future Congress beyond oversight to abolition.

NOTES

For their assistance in the preparation of this article, I thank Nancy B. Tucker (Colgate University), Mark M. Lowenthal (Congressional Research Service), Richard Baker (Senate Historical Office), and Barney Rickman III and J. Garry Clifford (University of Connecticut). The staffs of the following were especially helpful in identifying and providing materials: Georgetown University Library (Bowen Collection on Intelligence); University of Connecticut Library; Senate Select Committee on Intelligence; House Permanent Select Committee on Intelligence; and Center for National Security Studies.

1. For the controversy over Nicaragua, see U.S. Congress, Senate, Select Committee on Intelligence, Report (Senate Report 98–665; Washington D.C., 1985); *Newsweek*, CII, 23 April 1984, 22; *Time*, CXIII, 23 April 1984, 16 (Goldwater quotation); *New York Times*, 6–10 April 1984.

2. *New York Times*, 13 May 1985; *Hartford Courant*, 13 May 1985.

3. Ohman cartoon for *The Portland Oregonian* in *Washington Post National Weekly Edition*, 14 January 1985.

4. U.S. Congress, House, Permanent Select Committee on Intelligence, *Congressional Oversight of Covert Activities* (hearings, September 20, 21, 22, 1983; Washington, 1984), 24.

5. Quoted in John Stockwell, *In Search of Enemies: A CIA Story* (New York, 1978), 235.

6. *Washington Post*, 9 January 1977.

7. George W. Ball in "Should the U.S. Fight Secret Wars?" *Harper's*, CCLXIX, September, 1984, 37; George F. Kennan, "Morality and Foreign Policy," *Foreign Affairs*, LXIV (Winter 1985/86): 214; Herbert Scoville, Jr., "Is Espionage Necessary for Our Security?" ibid. LIV (April, 1976), 482–495; Morton Halperin in House, *Congressional Oversight*, 57–69; Richard J. Barnet, "The 'Dirty-Tricks' Gap," in Robert L. Borosage and John Marks, eds., *The CIA File* (New York, 1976), 214–217; Tom Wicker in *New York Times*, 13 January 1976; Dean D. Welch, "Secrecy, Democracy and Responsibility: The Central Intelligence Agency and Congress" (Ph.D. dissertation, Vanderbilt University, 1976), ch. I; Jeffrey T. Richelson, *The U.S. Intelligence Community* (Cambridge, Mass., 1985), 343–344.

8. Stansfield Turner, *Secrecy and Democracy: The CIA in Transition* (Boston, 1985), 188.

9. For definitions, I have largely followed U.S. Congress, Senate, Select Committee to Study Governmental Operations with Respect to Intelligence Activities (hereafter Church Committee), *Final Report: Book I, Foreign and Military Intelligence* (Senate Report 94–755; Washington, D.C., 1976), 131, and Kent A. Jordan, "The Extent of Independent Presidential Authority to Conduct Foreign Intelligence Activities," *Georgetown Law Journal*, LXXII (August, 1985): 1865.

10. Quoted in Arthur M. Schlesinger, Jr., *The Imperial Presidency* (Boston, 1973), 318. See also Newell L. Highsmith, "Policing Executive Adventurism: Congressional Oversight of Military and Paramilitary Operations," *Harvard Journal of Legislation*, XIX (Summer, 1982): 353.

11. Although there are about forty-five components of the "intelligence community," including the State Department's Bureau of Intelligence and Research, Defense Intelligence Agency, Federal Bureau of Investigation, intelligence services of the various armed forces, and National Security Agency, this article emphasizes the Central Intelligence Agency as the major vehicle of covert action.

12. Norman D. Sandler, *28 Years of Looking the Other Way: Congressional Oversight of the Central Intelligence Agency 1947–1975* (Cambridge, Mass., 1975), 69–84. In 1976 the Foreign Intelligence Oversight Board was added to this list; the Foreign Intelligence Advisory Board functioned 1956–1977 and 1981–present.

13. See Church Committee, *Alleged Assassination Plots Involving Foreign Leaders: An Interim Report* (Senate Report 94–465; Washington, D.C., 1975) and Church Committee, *Final Report: Book IV, Supplementary Detailed Staff Reports on Foreign and Military Intelligence* (Senate Report 94–755; Washington, 1976), 121–142.

14. Quoted in U.S. Congress, Senate, Committee on Government Operations, *Oversight of U.S. Government Intelligence Functions* (hearings, January–February, 1976; Washington, D.C., 1976), 81. See also Jerrold L. Walden, "The C.I.A.: A Study in the Arrogation of Administrative Powers," *George Washington Law Review*, XXXIX (October, 1970): 93n.

15. Loch K. Johnson, "Congress and the Control of Covert Operations: Paramilitary Operations," *Frist Principles*, IX (March–April, 1984): 2.

16. Quoted in David Wise, "Covert Operations Abroad: An Overview," in Borosage and Marks, *CIA File*, 18.

17. Turner, *Secrecy*, 43–45.

18. Loch K. Johnson, *A Season of Inquiry: The Senate Intelligence Investigation* (Lexington, KY., 1985), 61.

19. Quoted in Harry H. Ransom, *The Intelligence Establishment* (Cambridge, Mass., 1970), 169. See also Sandler, *28 Years*, 158.

20. Senate, *Oversight*, 334.

21. Representative Robert N. Giaimo et al., to colleagues, 9 July 1975, Box 125, Series IV, Giaimo Papers, University of Connecticut Library, Storrs, Connecticut.

22. For the points of this paragraph, see Mark M. Lowenthal, *U.S. Intelligence: Evolution and Anatomy* (New York, 1984), 109; Senate, *Oversight*, 334; Sandler, *28 Years,* passim; Ransom, *Intelligence Establishment*, 166; Francis O. Wilcox (Chief of Staff, Senate Foreign Relations Committee, 1947–1955) Oral History Interview, Senate Historical Office, Washington, D.C., 172 (from the notes of Professor Nancy B. Tucker).

23. House, *Congressional Ovesight*, 30.

24. Senate Foreign Relations Committee Chairman J. William Fulbright was informally consulted before the 1961 Bay of Pigs operation and in 1967 three members of that committee, on an informal basis, began to sit with the Armed Services intelligence subcommittee.

25. John Maury, "CIA and the Congress," n.d., but probably 1973 or 1974, Files of Central Intelligence Agency, Washington, D.C.

26. William Colby and Peter Forbath, *Honorable Men: My Life in the CIA* (New York, 1978), 401.

27. Quoted in Ransom, *Intelligence Establishment*, 167.

28. The subcommittees which had overlapping membership had only one part-time staff member. Francis O. Wilcox, *Congress, The Executive,* and *Foreign Policy* (New York, 1971), 87.

29. Quoted in John V. Lindsay, "An Inquiry into the Darkness of the Cloak, the Sharpness of the Dagger," *Esquire*, LXI, March, 1964, 109.

30. The record is sketchy, but it appears that the subcommittee met only once in 1969 and twice in 1970, but not at all in 1967, 1971, 1972, or 1974. Other subcommittees had similar dismal records. See Harry H. Ransom, "Can the Intelligence Establishment Be Controlled in a Democracy?" in Richard H. Blum, ed., *Surveillance and Espionage in a Free Society* (New York, 1972), 214; Welch, "Secrecy," 205–206.

31. Maury, "CIA and the Congress," 12.

32. Quoted in Sandler, *28 Years*, 118.

33. Quoted in ibid., 184–185.

34. Michael J. Harrington to Carl Albert, 8 July 1975, Box 126, Series IV, Giaimo Papers.

35. Ralph W. McGehee, *Deadly Deceits: My 25 Years in the CIA* (New York, 1983), 82–84.

36. Quoted in Johnson, *A Season*, 6.

37. Ransom, *Intelligence Establishment*, 175.

38. Quoted in Sandler, *28 Years*, 94–95. See also Welch, "Secrecy," 194, 201–202.

39. Symington was a member of the Armed Services intelligence subcommittee. Quoted in Fred Branfman, "The President's Secret Army: A Case Study—The CIA in Laos, 1962–1972," in Borosage and Marks, *CIA File*, 73.

40. Quoted in Church Committee, *Final Report: Book I*, 367n.

41. Quoted in Louis Fisher, *Presidential Spending Power* (Princeton, N.J., 1975), 218.

42. One citizen who insisted on knowing was William Richardson of Greensburg, Pennsylvania. In the late 1960s and early 1970s he pressed his case, based upon Article I, Section 9, that the CIA had to publish details on its funding. In 1974, in a 6 to 3 vote, the Supreme Court ruled that Richardson had no standing to sue, on the narrow ground that Congress had not granted individuals the right to sue for disclosure of government funds. U.S. Congress, Senate, Select Committee on Intelligence, *Whether Disclosure of Funds for the Intelligence Activities of the United States is in the Public Interest* (Senate Report 95–274; Washington, D.C., 1977), 1–2; Louis Fisher, *Constitutional Conflicts between Congress and the President* (Princeton, N.J., 1985), 247–251.

43. For the legislative history of the next several paragraphs, I have drawn upon Mark M. Lowenthal for Congressional Research Service, Library of Congress, "Intelligence Community: Congressional Oversight" (Issue Brief IB77079; Washington, D.C., 1980); William N. Raiford for Congressional Research Service, Library of Congress, "Legislation Introduced Relative to the Activities of U.S. Intelligence Agencies: 1973–1974" (Washington, D.C., 1975); Lyman B. Kirkpatrick, *The U.S. Intelligence Community: Foreign Policy and Domestic Activities* (New York, 1973), 60–65; Ransom, *Intelligence Establishment*, 163–179; Sandler, *28 Years*, 88–90.

44. Quoted in Gary Sperling, "Central Intelligence and Its Control: Curbing Secret Power in a Democratic Society," in *Congressional Record*, Vol. 112, Pt. 12, 14 July 1966, 15764.

45. Senator Carl Hayden quoted in Ransom, *Intelligence Establishment*, 166. The opponents argued also that intelligence was an executive prerogative and that America's allies would be less willing to cooperate if they knew that the information they shared with the CIA found its way into Congress and then into public view.

46. Senate, *Oversight*, 25.

47. Memorandum of Conversation, Bipartisan Leaders Breakfast with the President, 26 May 1960, Box 25, Alphabetical Subseries, Subject Series, Office of the Staff Secretary, White House Office Records, Dwight D. Eisenhower Library, Abilene, Kansas.

48. Quoted in Ransom, *Intelligence Establishment*, 172.

49. *Congressional Record*, Vol. 112, Pt. 12, 14 July 1966, 15677.

50. In 1967 intelligence subcommittees of the House and Senate Appropriations Committees began to receive notices within forty-eight hours of the CIA's use of contingency funds, although they had no veto power over such transactions.

51. Sandler, *28 Years*, 98–112.

52. Church Committee, *Covert Action in Chile, 1963–1973* (Staff Report; Washington, D.C., 1975); Welch, "Secrecy," 181–198; Sandler, *28 Years*, 112–121.

53. Michael J. Harrington, et al., *The CIA: Past Transgressions and Future Controls: A Symposium* (Providence, R.I., 1975), 5.

54. Quoted in Welch, "Secrecy," 193.

55. Church Committee, *Final Report: Book I*, 150.

56. *Congressional Record*, Vol. 120, Pt. 25, 2 October 1974, 33479.

57. The amendment was introduced 1 October 1974, and the president signed it 30 December.

58. Church Committee, *Final Report: Book I*, 151.

59. Thomas K. Latimer, "U.S. Intelligence and the Congress," *Strategic Review*, VII (Summer, 1979): 49. Latimer was serving as Staff Director of the House Permanent Select Committee on Intelligence when he wrote this article. See also Colby and Forbath, *Honorable Men*, 382.

60. Article by Seymour Hersh, 22 December 1974.

61. The Rockefeller Commission reported in June, 1975, that the CIA had in fact conducted domestic surveillance of critics of the Vietnam War. *Report to the President by the Commission on CIA Activities within the United States* (Washington, D.C., 1975); Sandler, *28 Years*, 130–134; Lowenthal, *U.S. Intelligence*, 39–40.

62. For the workings of the Church Committee, see Johnson, *A Season*. Johnson was a member of the committee's staff.

63. Besides the works cited below, see Stephen R. Weissman, "CIA Covert Action in Zaire and Angola: Patterns and Consequences," *Political Science Quarterly*, XCIV (Summer, 1979): 263–286, and John A. Marcum, "Lessons of Angola," *Foreign Affairs*, LIV (April, 1976): 407–425.

64. John Stockwell, the CIA task force chief in Angola, contends that the CIA lied to Congress by reporting that the aid was indirect (going through Zaire) and that

there were no American personnel in Angola working with the factions. (Stockwell, *In Search of Enemies*, 173, 179, 229–230.) Ralph W. McGehee, another CIA veteran, reports that he helped prepare briefing material for Director William Colby: "The briefings were designed to present a certain picture that would allow the CIA to sell covert programs to Congress. Very few of the facts in these briefings were true. They were complete whitewash jobs." ("Should the U.S. Fight Secret Wars," 43.) See also Thomas M. Franck and Edward Weisband, *Foreign Policy by Congress* (New York, 1979), 50 for administration rebuttals.

65. Nathaniel Davis, "The Angola Decision of 1975: A Personal Memoir," *Foreign Affairs*, LVII (Fall, 1978): 109–124.

66. Senator John Tunney, suffering from a mediocre record and "jet set" image and locked in a close primary contest in California, needed an issue to establish his own antiwar credentials against his rival, antiwar activist Tom Hayden. Fellow Democrat Clark bowed to Tunney's problem and need and let Tunney take the lead on the Angolan question. Neil C. Livingstone and Manfred Von Nordheim, "The United States Congress and the Angola Crisis," *Strategic Review*, V (No. 2, 1977): 38–40.

67. President Ford tried to preempt the congressional report on 8 February by issuing his own plan for CIA reorganization and oversight. But because he placed augmented oversight largely in the executive branch, which had already demonstrted its laxity, few gave his reform support. Welch, "Secrecy," 111–115.

68. Church Committee, *Final Report: Book I*, 533.

69. Ibid., 423–474.

70. For critics of reform and defenders of the CIA, see Harry Rositzke, *The CIA's Secret Operations* (New York, 1977) and Colby and Forbath, *Honorable Men*. In 1975 the Association of Former Intelligence Officers was organized as a lobbying group. The counterattack is discussed in Johnson, *A Season*, 70, 228.

71. Turner, *Secrecy*, 87.

72. For Carter's record on oversight and covert action, including Executive Order 12036 (24 January 1978), see Mark M. Lowenthal for Congressional Research Service, Library of Congress, "Intelligence Community: Congressional Oversight" (Issue Brief IB77079; Washington, D.C., 1980); Mark M. Lowenthal for Congressional Research Service, Library of Congress, "Intelligence Operations: Covert Action" (Issue Brief IB80020; Washington, D.C., 1980); John M. Oseth, *Regulating U.S. Intelligence Operations: A Study in Definition of the National Interest* (Lexington, KY., 1985), 105–148, 169–170.

73. See U.S. Congress, Senate, Select Committee on Intelligence, *National Intelligence Reorganization and Reform Act of 1978* (hearings, April–August, 1978; Washington, D.C., 1978).

74. U.S. Congress, Senate, Select Committee on Intelligence, *National Intelligence Act of 1980* (hearings, February–April, 1980; Washington, D.C., 1980), 170.

75. Jimmy Carter, *Keeping Faith: Memoirs of a President* (New York, 1982), 511, 518.

76. The eight were the chairpersons and ranking minority members of the two intelligence committees, Speaker and Minority Leader of the House, and Majority and Minority Leaders of the Seante.

77. For the act and a section by section analysis, see U.S. Congress, Select Committee on Intelligence, *Intelligence Oversight Act of 1980* (Washington, D.C., 1980). See also the discussion of the legislative history in Highsmith, "Policing," 355–362.

78. See Executive Order 12333 of 4 December 1981. President Reagan also reestablished the President's Foreign Intelligence Advisory Board. For the uncommon view that congressional oversight during the first Reagan administration worked effectively, see Oseth, *Regulating*, 184, and Mathew D. McCubbins and Thomas Schwartz, "Congressional Oversight Overlooked: Police Patrols versus Fire Alarms," *American Journal of Political Science*, XXVIII (February, 1984): 165–179.

79. Oseth, *Regulating*, 170. See also 149–150, 171.

80. *New York Times*, 16 June, 11 July, 14 July 1985, and 13 February 1986.

81. Norman Y. Mineta quoted in Johnson, *A Season*, 263.

82. Unidentified. Quoted in Jay Peterzell, "Can Congress Really Check the CIA?" *Washington Post*, 24 April 1983, C4.

83. Ibid.

84. Unidentified. Quoted in *Newsweek*, CIII, 23 April 1984, 24.

85. Quoted in ibid. See also this testy exchange: William J. Casey, "Oversight Gone Away," and Senator Dave Durenberger, "The Public Must Know That It Works," *Washington Post National Weekly Edition*, 2 December 1985.

86. In September, 1982, the Boland Amendment banned covert military aid to the *contras* "for the purpose of overthrowing the Government of Nicaragua." The administration partially side-stepped the restriction by stating that the aid was intended to interdict arms sent by Nicaragua to antigovernment insurgents in El Salvador. Moreover, the *contra* program was constantly enlarged, including the mining of Nicaraguan harbors. The Senate passed a nonbinding resolution on 10 April 1984 (84–12 vote) asking that no funds be expended for the mining of the ports; the House did the same 12 April (281–111). In Public Law 98–618, effective 8 November 1984, Congress forbade any intelligence agency from conducting military or paramilitary operations against Nicaragua. (See Senate, *Report* [98–665], with quotation on p. 5.) But in the summer of 1985 Congress acceded to presidential pressure and approved "humanitarian" aid to the *contras*. Much of this aid, it was reported, would be spent on uniforms, boots, backpacks, food, and medicine. In the summer of 1985, moreover, the administration admitted that an official of the National Security Council was giving or had given direct military advice to the *contras*. "We're not violating any laws," claimed President Reagan. (*New York Times*, 9 August 1985.) But Representative George E. Brown, Jr., a member of the House Intelligence Committee, complained that the CIA has "been giving lip service to the Boland Amendment. The [administration's] legal eagles are interpreting all of the laws in a way to favor the policies of

the President." *Hartford Courant*, 28 August 1985. See also Charles Mohr, "Frustration, Resignation and the C.I.A." *New York Times*, 1 October 1985; Stansfield Turner, "A Call for Congressional Oversight of CIA," *Hartford Courant*, 3 October 1985.

87. In 1983, after hearing congressional objectives, the administration apparently shelved a plan for the overthrow of the government of Suriname in South America. *New York Times*, 4 November 1985.

88. See House, *Congressional Oversight*, 22–23, 79.

89. Senate, *Report* (98–665), 18–22. See also Thomas G. Paterson, "The Present Danger of Thought Control," *Perspectives: American Historical Association Newsletter*, XXII (April, 1984): 14–16.

90. See note 86 above and U.S. Congress, House, Committee on Foreign Affairs, *The Mining of Nicaraguan Ports and Harbors* (hearing, April, 1984; Washington, D.C., 1984).

91. Peterzell, "Can Congress," 64.

92. See note 42 and *Washington Post National Weekly Edition*, 10 March 1986.

93. Comment by Stanley Heginbotham, Jacob K. Javits Collection Inaugural Conference on Congress and United States Foreign Policy, State University of New York at Stony Brook, 25 October 1985.

94. Quoted in David Shribman, "Few Go to Study Intelligence Reports," *New York Times*, 18 October 1983.

95. Quoted in Johnson, *A Season*, 8.

96. Of course, other factors, such as the impressive Reagan victory, help explain Church's defeat. Ibid., 276–277.

97. Comment by Senator John Kerry at Javits Conference, 26 October 1985.

98. George Picket, "Congress, the Budget, and Intelligence," in Alfred C. Maurer et al., *Intelligence: Policy and Process* (Boulder, Col., 1985), 157–175.

11

The Executive, Congress, and the Vietnam War, 1965–1975

GEORGE C. HERRING

The role of Congress in the Vietnam conflict has been a subject of persisting and sometimes bitter debate. Some legislators have claimed that they were duped by clever and conspiring presidents into supporting a war they did not approve. More recently, conservative critics including Richard M. Nixon have blamed Congress for America's failure in Vietnam, arguing that a spiteful and irresponsible legislature prevented the White House from taking the actions necessary to end the war and then in 1975 callously pulled the plug on a faithful South Vietnamese ally.[1] Such charges and countercharges badly distort the historical record. In the early years, Congress was a willing, if usually silent, accomplice in the formulation of Vietnam policies. Dissent developed slowly and assumed significant proportions only at the very end of the war. To a degree that has not been adequately recognized, moreover, the emergence of congressional dissent and its influence on policy reflected the distinctive approaches to executive-congressional relations taken by the presidents themselves.

In dealing with Vietnam, Lyndon Baines Johnson sought consensus and congressional support above all else, and to a remarkable degree he obtained it. Dissent in the Congress was no more than sporadic and isolated in the first years of the war. To be sure, Senators Wayne Morse and Ernest Gruening were vocal critics in the Tonkin Gulf crisis; Senators Frank Church and George McGovern vigorously opposed the bombing of North Vietnam; and dissent grew slowly and steadily thereafter. To the end of the Johnson presidency, however, congressional dissent influenced policy only slightly and such influence as was exerted was indirect. The Senate in particular and Congress in general were partners in the Johnson administration's policies.

The reasons why this was the case are clear. In the first two years of his full term, Johnson had lopsided majorities, and although he lost ground in 1966 he still had workable majorities. He inherited traditions of biparti-sanship and congressional deference in foreign policy that dated back to the Truman era, and when challenged he did not hesitate to remind his critics of them. In the first years of the war, he was able to capitalize on the rally-around-the-flag phenomenon. Richard Russell had opposed American involve-ment in Vietnam as early as 1954, but after July 1965 he fell into line. "We are there now," he wrote a constituent, "and the time for debate has passed. Our flag is committed and,—more important,—American boys are under fire. . . ."[2]

To attribute Johnson's support exclusively or even primarily to such factors is misleading, however. The image of LBJ ignoring and defying Congress to pursue an unpopular war simply does not hold up under close scrutiny. Johnson was a creature of Congress. His formative years had been spent there and his outlook toward the political system was shaped there. "Once in the oval office," John Rourke has written, "his fascination with Congress continued as did his beliefs that the techniques he had applied in the capitol corridors could be used with equal success as president."[3] Learning from Truman's experience with Korea and observing firsthand Eisenhower's close consultation with Congress, moreover, LBJ cared deeply about main-taining congressional support for his policies and worked assiduously to cul-tivate it.

Indeed, it is not exaggeration to suggest that Johnson's Vietnam policies were designed less on the basis of whether they would achieve results in Southeast Asia than whether they would sustain support at home and especially in the Congress. In 1964, 1965 and after, Johnson clung precariously to the middle ground where as majority leader in the Senate in the 1950s he had found the votes on controversial issues. He held the moderate conservatives by promising to defend the nation's honor and interests. At the same time, he sought to hold the moderate liberals by insisting that peace was his ultimate purpose and by persuading them that he would pursue that goal with sufficient caution to avoid World War III. "I'm going up old Ho Chi Minh's leg an inch at a time," he reassured McGovern in 1965.[4]

For the short run, at least, Johnson's strategy succeeded brilliantly. He amassed staggering majorities for the Tonkin Gulf Resolution. Although Majority Leader Mike Mansfield and others affirmed that there was little enthusiasm in the Congress for involvement in Vietnam, Johnson took the nation to war in July 1965 with only a few scattered whimpers of dissent.[5] The records make clear that congressional leaders knew what Johnson was up to and provided firm and willing support. The great majority probably agreed with what he was doing and the way he was doing it. Those who had doubts were quite content to let him take full responsibility for such momen-tous decisions.[6]

During the first years of the war, Johnson continued to keep a weather eye on the Congress and cultivated support with the utmost care. His aides studied and marked up the *Congressional Record* and had it ready for him to read by the time he ate breakfast.[7] Members of Congress who had good things to say about the administration would be singled out for special favors and attention. Critics might be called to the White House for the infamous Johnson treatment. This might involve friendly reminders of favors "going back to childhood," as Thruston Morton recalled it, or, as in the case of Church, pointed warnings that there once was another senator from Idaho who thought he knew "more about war and peace than the president." If they refused to come around, as with Church, they might be ostracized from the White House.[8] In any event, their charges were studied and carefully answered, either by the White House or senators and representatives put up to it by the White House. Presidential aides spent hours digging up material to supply to friends in the Senate and House to be used to discredit or embarrass opponents.

In what had become the traditional fashion of the Cold War, Johnson consulted closely with Congress, at least through the end of 1966. Administration officials spent long hours testifying before congressional committees (eighty-four hours in 1965, fifty hours in the first half of 1966).[9] Johnson himself from January 1965 to June 1966 on twenty different occasions held briefings for and discussions with congressional leaders. As in the Tonkin Gulf affair and the 28 July 1965 troop decision, his mind was usually made up before he sought congressional "advice." He appears to have listened carefully to the legislators, however, and at least some of them got the impression he was seeking their assistance in coming up with solutions to pressing problems.[10]

Having been himself a key instrument of bipartisan foreign policy under Eisenhower, Johnson cultivated Republican support as president and used his special relationship with Minority Leader Everett Dirksen to advantage. Indeed, he sought to establish with Dirksen the sort of working relationship he had with Eisenhower. To promote at least the appearance of bipartisan support and to embarrass his Democratic critics, he supplied information to Dirksen to counter Democrats who opposed his policies.[11] When McGovern and Church criticized administration policy in early 1965, it was Dirksen who viciously answered by saying that he never thought he would see the white flag of surrender raised in the United States Senate.[12] When Republican Gerald Ford criticized the administration for not using air power to full advantage, Dirksen reprimanded him.

Johnson's task was made easier by the nature of the opposition. At least until late in his term, his opponents in Congress were few in number. They did caucus on occasion and several times got together on round-robin letters opposing administrative policies. As McGovern later conceded, however, "The dissent was erratic, disorganized—or maybe I should say unorganized."[13]

Moreover, those who opposed the administration did so cautiously, refusing to challenge the president directly or offer drastic alternatives. Hawks like John Stennis of Mississippi and Mendell Rivers of South Carolina fussed and fumed that the United States should either win or get out. Doves like

Majority Leader Mike Mansfield and Republican George Aiken of Vermont did not question the purpose of the war either on grounds of morality or national interest and they did not propose withdrawal. Mansfield, potentially one of the most dangerous critics, placed his position as majority leader above his conscience, publicly soft-pedalling his opposition while privately imploring Johnson to negotiate. Aiken did not advocate a pullout, as is often alleged, merely a shift to a population security strategy.[14] Indeed, Harold Stassen was sufficiently frustrated with Republican 'me-tooism' to warn Senator Hugh Scott in late 1967 that if the party was to get anywhere in 1968 it would have to abandon its support for the president and press for an early and honorable end to the war.[15]

Congressional backing for the war remained steady until late in Johnson's presidency. To be sure, hawks probably restrained the president from any inclination toward a negotiated settlement and doves from a drastic escalation of the bombing. This merely left the president the middle ground he had sought. Votes were never taken on the war itself, only on appropriations which, because they were linked to support for troops were nearly impossible to vote against. In any event support for the president declined very slowly. A *Congressional Quarterly* poll taken in October 1966 indicated that 48.5 percent supported the president's policies, 26.4 percent favored escalation to win, and only 15.1 percent favored deescalation and greater efforts at negotiation.[16] Even in August 1967, when dissent had grown measurably in the country, a poll of the Senate showed forty-four still supported the president, forty opposed.[17] Johnson with good reason could argue that he had solid Congressional support and dismiss his critics as few in number, personally motivated, and lacking in viable alternatives. When the polls began to go against him in 1967, he could still retort that "the best poll is a roll call vote in Congress."[18]

Inasmuch as congressional opposition exerted an influence, it did so outside the Congress, an important and ironic result of Johnson's skill at molding support. J. William Fulbright took his opposition to the country in the form of public speeches, televised hearings on Vietnam and China, and later an investigation of the Gulf of Tonkin incident. This was a method well suited to Fulbright's personality and his background as an educator. It had the ironic effect, as Frank Church has pointed out, of taking Senate questioning of policy out of executive session, where the administration retained control, to the public forum, where the president had no control.[19] Dissent emanating from the Senate and especially from a conservative southern senator contributed significantly to the respectability of the antiwar movement. In the Tonkin Gulf hearings, Fulbright raised questions about the administration's veracity that widened an already large credibility gap. Thus by keeping a close rein on dissent Johnson may unwittingly have made it more dangerous.

Ultimately, the failure of Johnson's policies in Vietnam undercut his consensus at home, and the emergence of dissent in the Congress in turn began to exert an indirect influence on the shaping of his policies. As long as the administration's policy seemed to be working, congressmen were inclined to support it, but the growing cost of the war and the lack of perceivable gain produced by mid-1967 growing public anxiety and protest and led increasing numbers of legislators to break with the president. Such defections concerned Johnson's political advisors greatly, portending a massive erosion of support which could cost the Democrats the White House and control of Congress in 1968.[20] To head off further defections, the administration in late 1967 launched an intensive public relations campaign to show that the United States was in fact winning in Vietnam. Johnson also began to consider a shift from the strategy of gradual escalation to a strategy that would reduce American casualties and thus preserve public and congressional support.[21] The 31 March 1968 decisions merely confirmed a pattern of change already underway.

In contrast to Johnson, Nixon on grounds of expediency of principle gave priority to the formulation of foreign policy over the obtaining of domestic support. In part at least because of this approach, dissent in Congress and especially in the Senate increased dramatically in the Nixon years. Whether Nixon's policies would have worked in the absence of domestic opposition can never be known. In fact, his defiance of Congress produced a backlash which severely limited his freedom of action and ultimately destroyed his policies.

In fairness to Nixon, the problems he faced were enormous. He was elected by the barest margin, and he was the first president in 120 years to face a Congress in which both houses were controlled by the opposition party. Many Democrats who had reluctantly supported Johnson could for partisan reasons oppose Nixon more easily. Persuaded that they had been misled by Johnson, some congressmen treated every Nixon pronouncement with skepticism and bristled at the slightest sign of executive infringement on congressional prerogatives. In the country, opposition to the war was on the rise, and among liberals and conservatives alike there was growing frustration with a conflict that seemed to have no end. "The war is the most frustrating and complex situation ever to confront the American people," Russell wrote a constituent. "We are there, but don't want to be. We want to get out but we can't. It is one of the great tragedies of our history and has given me more sense of personal frustration than anything else I have ever attempted to deal with. I would do almost anything to get out of there. . . ."[22]

Nixon perceived that he must find a way to end the war and he recognized that his Vietnam policies would require congressional backing. Despite his fierce partisan temper, he saw the urgency of bipartisan support and sought to work at least with conservative Southern Democrats. Following long-established precedent, he went through the motions of consulting with Congress and maintaining liaison. When faced, as in the Cooper-Church Amendment, with a congressional challenge to his office, he made strenuous and generally successful efforts to head off restrictions on his power. On several occasions, moreover, the administration cleverly applied to domestic politics a variation of Senator George Aiken's proposal for getting out of Vietnam.

When repeal of the Tonkin Gulf Resolution seemed likely in 1970, for example, the White House made clear that such action would in no way affect its policies, declared itself in support of repeal, and left Senator Fulbright in the awkward position of opposing his own handiwork.[23]

Nixon and his National Security Adviser Henry Kissinger did not share Johnson's basic respect for Congress as an institution, however. They regarded it as an obstruction and nuisance as much as anything else. Ignoring the extent to which the war and Johnson's policies had undermined the Cold War consensus on executive-legislative relationships, they took the position that only the executive branch could responsibly develop foreign policies. By concentrating policy management in Kissinger's office, the administration removed it from congressional scrutiny. On the really important issues, the White House ignored Congress or consulted only a handful of congressmen whose support was certain. Where Johnson had carefully cultivated Dirksen, Nixon did not even keep his own minority leader, Hugh Scott, informed. Forced belatedly to shift from opposition to involvement in Cambodia to support for the president's policies, Scott complained bitterly to Kissinger that he must have "substantive evidence of support for my leadership," not simply "letters or statements" but "close consultation."[24] Nixon's preferred approach was to frame his policies and present Congress with an accomplished fact. When opposed, as was increasingly the case, he became defiant, deliberately seeking confrontation or accusing his foes of aiding and abetting the enemy.

Whether Nixon could have put together a workable majority in the very difficult circumstances he faced remains in doubt. The point is, however, that he did not really try. Hubert Humphrey in characteristically colorful language compared Nixon's approach to that of Johnson: "Now Johnson used to rob the Senate, but when he wanted to take something from you, he'd invite you to lunch. He'd put his arms around you and talk to you while he picked your pocket. . . . But Nixon stuck you up in the night. You didn't even see him. It was like rape without any personal contact. I mean, the Senators are used to being had, but not being ignored. That drives them mad. . . ."[25]

The result was predictable. The opposition that had developed in Johnson's last year assumed formidable proportion in Nixon's first term and relations between the White House and Capitol Hill became increasingly stormy. After a brief honeymoon in early 1969, congressional dissidents began to submit various end-the-war resolutions. Following the Cambodian incursion of April 1970 and each subsequent administration initiative, these resolutions gained support and several actually passed the Senate.

Senatorial dissidents failed to legislate an end to the war. In most cases, they remained divided on the best way to achieve their goals, thereby undercutting their own effectiveness.[26] As long as U.S. troops remained in Vietnam and North Vietnam held American POWs, many congressmen remained reluctant to challenge the president. A majority of senators also remained unwilling to assume responsibility for the consequences of ending the war. Even when the Senate acted, moreover, the more conservative House usually forced compromise in favor of the administration.

Congress did exert an increasingly significant indirect influence on policy in Nixon's first term. The threat posed by the Cooper-Church Amendment forced the administration to limit its involvement in Cambodia.[27] The growing fear that Congress at some point might agree on an end-the-war resolution, combined with electoral pressures, forced the administration in 1972 to make the concessions necessary to secure a settlement.[28] When that settlement broke down and the administration responded by launching the infamous Christmas bombing, outrage in Congress made clear the urgency of getting back to the negotiating table and achieving a quick settlement. "We took the threats from Congress seriously," one White House aide later recalled, "we knew we were racing the clock" and faced possibly "stern action."[29]

In large part as a result of Nixon's flawed approach, Congress began to exert direct influence on U.S. policy in Vietnam in 1973. The removal of U.S. troops in March 1973 and the return of the POWs eliminated what since 1965 had served as the major constraints on antiwar action. In the United States by this time, moreover, there was a general and pervasive war-weariness and a powerful determination to get the United States out of Vietnam as completely and quickly as possible without too much concern for the consequences. This was not confined to liberals and the mood was plainly reflected in Congress. Finally, of course, Watergate and the resignation of Richard Nixon brought the power and prestige of the presidency to the lowest point in at least one hundred years. Submissive on foreign policy matters since 1947, Congress in the aftermath of Vietnam and Watergate responded with angry defiance.

It was in this context that Congress for the first time took decisive steps to end the war. In June 1973, the legislature passed a law prohibiting the use of funds for any form of military action in Indochina. In November, it passed over Nixon's veto the War Powers Act. In 1974, it drastically slashed military and economic aid to South Vietnam. When the fall of Cambodia and South Vietnam appeared likely if not imminent in the spring of 1975 Congress rejected President Gerald Ford's request for additional military aid, approving only limited funds to get U.S. personnel out of Vietnam and for "humanitarian" reasons.

These measures significantly affected the outcome of the war. The clear indications from congressional action that the United States would not reintervene with military power in Vietnam could not but have demoralized South Vietnam. It seems equally clear that these actions encouraged North Vietnam to launch and then step up the timetable for its end-the-war offensive. The aid cuts had devastating economic consequences in inflation-ridden South Vietnam, and further demoralized the people, government, and armed forces. The turndown of aid in 1975 may have contributed to the panic that gripped that unfortunate nation in its death throes.

To conclude that Congress was primarily responsible for the debacle of 1975 overlooks several crucial factors, however. It ignores, first, the extent to which the Nixon administration had shot itself in the head through Watergate. More important, as P. Edward Haley has pointed out, the 1973 settlement was based on a deliberate deception of the Congress by the executive.[30] Nixon seems to have been determined to maintain the division of Vietnam—this was what he meant by peace with honor. He sought to do this primarily by keeping alive the threat of U.S. reintervention in the war, at least with air and naval power. This threat would impose restraints on North Vietnam. It would also encourage the Thieu government to hang on. To get Thieu to accept the agreement, Nixon promised to respond with full force if North Vietnam violated the agreement.

In making this commitment, Nixon did not take Congress into his confidence. He most likely feared, given the state of his administration's relations with Congress in January 1973, that he could not get approval of this sort of commitment. Nor did he anticipate the extent to which Watergate would cripple him. He may therefore have assumed that if he had to send air and naval power back to Vietnam he could force Congress to acquiesce by confrontation diplomacy.

This turned out not to be the case, of course, with disastrous and tragic results. Nixon's promises most likely encouraged Thieu to resist whatever chance may have existed of a political settlement in Vietnam. In the meantime, Congress, ignorant of the president's intentions and weary of the war, moved decisively in the summer of 1973 to liquidate American involvement. Congressional action in turn prevented Nixon and Ford from implementing the promises that had been made to Thieu. As Haley has put it, "The executive, acting in secret, had concluded an important international agreement that depended on the very thing—American military force—that Congress had denied a few months after the signatories had completed the agreement."[31]

In the final act of the drama, all the Vietnam chickens came home to roost, and the executive and legislature were mutually suspicious partners in what turned out to be an unmitigated disaster. With the fall of Cambodia and South Vietnam near, Kissinger and Ford tried to intimidate Congress into approving last-minute aid packages by warning that the blood of those two unfortunate countries would be on its hands if it failed to act. In reality, the administration had written off its two client states, but it did not take Congress into its confidence, perhaps for fear that leaks might be the last straw for South Vietnamese morale, perhaps in an effort to shift the political blame to Congress. Congress was so sensitive by this time to having been taken in by the executive that it viewed even proposals for evacuating Americans with suspicion and put tight limits on them. "It is a very sorry comment upon this period in our history that such precise precautions must be written into law," Church conceded. "But it is necessary because Congress had learned the hard way not to write blank checks."[32]

The debacle of April 1975 marked a sorry end to a stormy period in executive-congressional relations. "The two branches never joined in productive accomplishment," Haley has concluded. "Fearing and distrusting one another to the end, they made one last show of the disunity in American society and government that grew out of the Vietnam War."[33] Of the two branches, the executive was more to blame than Congress. Congress cannot be blamed for not supporting measures it had never been asked to approve or in some important cases not even informed about. In addition, both the Nixon and Ford administrations repeatedly poisoned the well of executive-congressional relations with predictable results. "Scolding and condemning Congress as cowardly, immoral, even decadent," Haley concludes, "they then marched up the Hill to ask for more money, more authority to use force, more cooperation."[34]

The actual pattern of executive-congressional interaction during the Vietnam War bears little resemblance to the myths that have been perpetrated on both sides. The Congress willingly, if unenthusiastically, followed Johnson's lead on Vietnam, and support for the war persisted in Congress late into the Johnson presidency. When the war began to go bad in late 1967, dissent assumed significant proportions, and it grew steadily thereafter, helped along by feelings on the part of many congressmen that they had been misled by Johnson and by Nixon's tendency to ignore or bypass Congress. Even in the Nixon years, however, Congress exerted no more than an indirect influence on policy. It was only at the very end, when the executive-legislative relationship broke down completely, that Congress took direct action to end the war. And that action to a considerable degree was made possible by Watergate and Nixon's mishandling of the January 1973 peace agreement.

This experience offers no easy lessons. Perhaps, a more active role on the part of Congress in the decisions for war might have averted disaster, and the War Powers Act was designed with that in mind, but there is little evidence here to support such a view. This account certainly does not sustain the argument that a return to the "imperial presidency" is essential for the national security. The only clear-cut lesson is the obvious one. To construct a foreign policy primarily on the basis of what will be acceptable to Congress, as Johnson discovered, may not be enough. On the other hand, to frame policies, however, intelligent, without regard to what would be acceptable to Congress, is an invitation to disaster. In the American system, a foreign policy, to be successful, must have support in the legislature, and presidents and their advisers ignore this at their own peril.

NOTES

1. Richard M. Nixon, *No More Vietnams* (New York, 1985).

2. Russell to Thomas Masterson, 14 August 1965, Richard B. Russell Papers, Richard B. Russell Library, University of Georgia.

3. John Rourke, *Congress and the Presidency in U.S. Foreign Policy* (Boulder, 1983), 109.

4. George McGovern, *Grassroots* (New York, 1977), 104–105.

5. Mansfield to Johnson, 27 July 1965, Lyndon B. Johnson Papers, Lyndon B. Johnson Library, National Security File, National Security Council Histories: Deployment of Major U.S. Forces to Vietnam, July 1965, Box 40. For the way in which Johnson built the consensus inside his administration, see Larry Berman, *Planning a Tragedy* (Norton, 1983).

6. See for example the memorandum of meeting with the congressional leadership, 27 July 1965, Johnson Papers, Meeting Notes File, Box 1.

7. Rourke, *Congress and the Presidency*, 109.

8. Author interview with Thruston B. Morton, Louisville, Kentucky, 10 September 1979. Frank Church Oral History Interview, Lyndon B. Johnson Library.

9. Benjamin Read memorandum to Walt Rostow, June 10, 1966, Johnson Papers, National Security File, Name File, Box 3.

10. James Eastland Oral History Interview, Lyndon B. Johnson Library.

11. See Johnson Papers, Marvin Watson Files, Box 32.

12. Church Oral History Interview, Johnson Library.

13. George McGovern Oral History Interview, Lyndon B. Johnson Library.

14. David Turner, "Mike Mansfield and the Vietnam War," (Ph.D. dissertation, University of Kentucky, 1984); Mark Stoler, "What Did He *Really* Say? The 'Aiken Formula' for Vietnam Revisited," *Vermont History*, 46 (Spring 1978): 11–108.

15. Stassen to Hugh Scott, 28 August 1967, Hugh Scott Papers, University of Virginia Library, Box 155.

16. *New York Times*, 29 October 1966.

17. John Lehman, *The Executive, Congress and Foreign Policy: Studies in the Nixon Administration* (New York, 1974), 42.

18. LBJ Diary Memorandum, 2 October 1967, Johnson Papers, Diary Backup File, Box 78.

19. Church Oral History Interview, Johnson Papers.

20. For indications of the administration's concern, see Harry McPherson to Johnson, 25 August 1967, Johnson Papers, McPherson Files, Box 29, and Jack Valenti to Marvin Watson, 14 December 1967, Johnson Papers, Watson Files, Box 32.

21. George C. Herring, *America's Longest War*, rev. ed. (New York, 1985).

22. Russell to Fred Wright, 3 February 1969, Russell Papers.

23. Lehman, *Executive, Congress and Foreign Policy*, 37–73.

24. Scott to Kissinger, 21 May 1970, Scott Papers, Box 70.

25. Quoted in Rourke, *Congress and the Presidency*, 115.

26. Lehman, *Executive, Congress, and Foreign Policy*, 45.

27. Ibid., 72–73.

28. See, for example, Vernon A. Walters, *Silent Missions* (New York, 1978), 516.

29. Charles Colson, *Born Again* (Old Tappan, N.J., 1976), 77–79.

30. P. Edward Haley, *Congress and the Fall of South Vietnam and Cambodia* (Rutherford, N.J., 1982), 44.

31. Ibid., 43.

32. Ibid., 130.

33. Ibid., 154.

34. Ibid.

Contributors

Wayne S. Cole has been Professor of History at the University of Maryland since 1965. His latest book, *Roosevelt and the Isolationists, 1932–45*, was published by the University of Nebraska Press. He is presently writing a book on United States diplomatic relations with Norway from 1905 to 1955.

William Conrad Gibbons, Ph.D. Princeton University, is Visiting Research Professor at George Mason University and Specialist in United States Foreign Policy, Congressional Research Service, Library of Congress. He has authored *The U.S. Government and the Vietnam War,* a five-volume study for the Senate Foreign Relations Committee, published by the Government Printing Office and Princeton University Press.

Stanley J. Heginbotham, Ph.D. Massachusetts Institute of Technology, is Chief of the Foreign Affairs and National Defense Division of the Congressional Research Service at the Library of Congress. He has taught political science at Columbia University and has published widely, including studies in organizational behavior and the congressional role in foreign and defense policy.

George C. Herring, Ph.D. University of Virginia, is Professor of History at the University of Kentucky. His most recent publications include *America's Longest War: The United States and Vietnam, 1950–1975* and *The Secret Diplomacy of the Vietnam War: The Negotiating Volumes of the Pentagon Papers.* His articles have appeared in *Journal of American History, Political Science Quarterly, Diplomatic History, Military Affairs,* and *Virginia Quarterly Review.* He served as editor of *Diplomatic History* from 1982 to 1986.

Jacob K. Javits, who died in March 1986 while this volume was in preparation, was Republican Senator from New York from 1957 to 1981 and Representative in Congress from New York from 1947 to 1955. He was a member of the Senate Foreign Relations Committee for twelve years and principal Senate author of the War Powers Resolution of 1973.

Chester J. Pach, Jr., Ph.D., Northwestern University, is a Visiting Assistant Professor at the University of Kansas while on leave from Texas Tech University. His research has focused on the history of United States military assistance programs. His article, "The Containment of U.S. Military Aid to Latin America, 1944–47," won the Stuart L. Bernath Prize of the Society for Historians of American Foreign Relations.

Thomas G. Paterson, Ph.D., University of California, Berkeley, is Professor of History at the University of Connecticut and President of the Society for Historians of American Foreign Relations. His books include *Soviet-American Confrontation* (1973), *On Every Front: The Making of the Cold War* (1979) and the forthcoming *Meeting the Communist Threat.* He is co-author of *American Foreign Policy: A History* (1983) and *A People and a Nation* (1986). His articles have appeared in the *Journal of American History, Diplomatic History, The Nation,* and *American Historical Review.* He has served on the editorial boards of *Diplomatic History* and the *Journal of American History* and has directed National Endowment for the Humanities Summer Seminars for College Teachers.

David M. Pletcher, Ph.D., University of Chicago, is Professor of History at Indiana University. He has specialized in the history of U.S. foreign relations during the nineteenth century and U.S.-Latin American relations. Among his books is *The Diplomacy of Annexation: Texas, Oregon, and the Mexican War* (1973).

Robert D. Schulzinger, Ph.D., Yale University, is Professor of History at the University of Colorado at Boulder. He is the author of several books, the most recent including *American Diplomacy in the Twentieth Century* (1984) and *The Wise Men of Foreign Affairs: The History of the Council of Foreign Relations* (1984). He is currently completing a book on the foreign policy of Henry Kissinger.

John H. Sullivan, Ph.D., American University, is the author of *The War Powers Resolution,* a book-length document published in 1982 by the House Committee on Foreign Affairs that describes the passage and application of the Resolution. He currently is working on a revised, updated version. Dr. Sullivan played a role in the Resolution's development and enactment as staff consultant to the House Committee from 1969 to 1976. At present he is Vice President for International Activities of Development Associates, Inc., an Arlington, Virginia consulting firm. He has taught political science at The George Washington University and Boston University.

Duane A. Tananbaum, Ph.D., Columbia University, is Assistant Professor of History at Lehman College, The City University of New York. His research focuses on Presidential-Congressional relations and his book on the Bricker Amendment will be forthcoming from Cornell University Press. His article on the amendment, which appeared in *Diplomatic History,* won the Stuart L. Bernath Prize awarded by the Society for Historians of American Foreign Relations.

Michael A. Barnhart, Ph.D., Harvard University, is Associate Professor of History at the State University of New York-Stony Brook. His *Japan Prepares for Total War: The Search for Economic Security, 1919–1941* was recently published by Cornell University Press.

Index